Studio Photography and Lighting

Art and Techniques

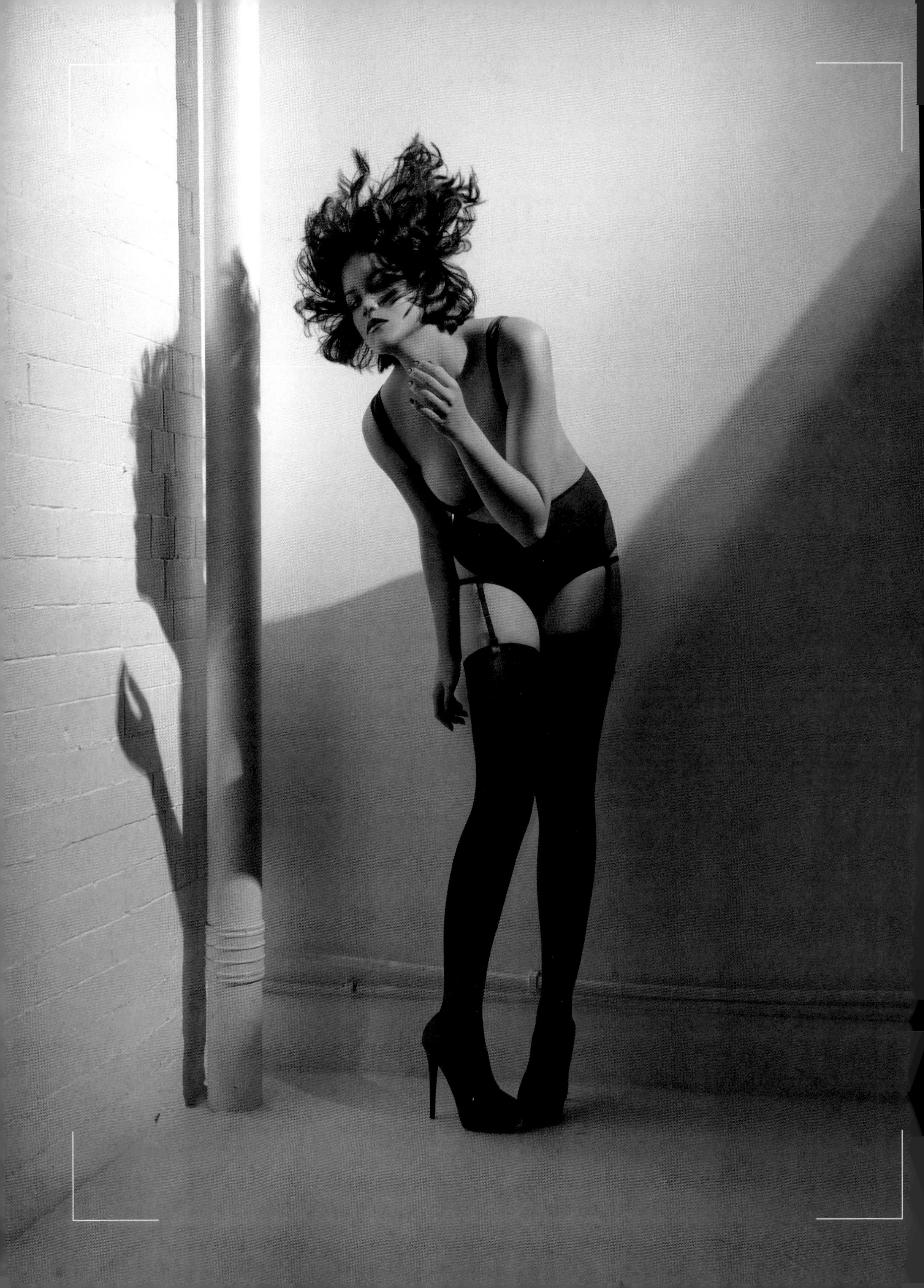

Studio Photography and Lighting

Art and Techniques

Christian Hough

CROWOOD

First published in 2013 by
The Crowood Press Ltd
Ramsbury, Marlborough
Wiltshire SN8 2HR

www.crowood.com

British Library Cataloguing-in-Publication Data
A catalogue record for this book is available from the British Library.

ISBN 978 1 84797 4860

Acknowledgements

I would like to thank all of the models and creatives involved in making this book possible, and I am grateful to my fans and followers for their continued support, ideas and feedback.

In addition, I would particularly like to thank the following people and organizations for their on going assistance, support or contributions towards this book:
David Hollingsworth and Robert Cook at Bowens International Ltd: www.bowens.co.uk.
Charles Woods at Cambo UK: www.cambo.co.uk.
Mark Witney and Paul Waterworth at Hasselblad UK: www.hasselblad.co.uk.
Hardy Haase at Flaghead Photographic Ltd: www.flaghead.co.uk.
Steven Davies and Joe Asai at Sony UK: www.sony.co.uk.
Beth Botterill at Lastolite UK: www.lastolite.com.
Jane Nicholson at Intro2020: www.intro2020.co.uk.
Paul Pell-Johnson at Linhof Studio: www.linhofstudio.com.
Siobhan Daly at Arri GB Limited: www.arri.de.
Jonathan Beer: www.jonathanbeer.co.uk.

Graphic design and layout by www.peggyandco.ca
Printed and bound in India by Replika Press Pvt Ltd

CONTENTS

Preface 7

1 Equipment Advice 9

2 Basic Skills 39

3 Expanding Your Skills 73

4 Artistic Nude 103

5 Still Life Photography 121

6 Basic RAW Processing 153

Glossary 165

Index 174

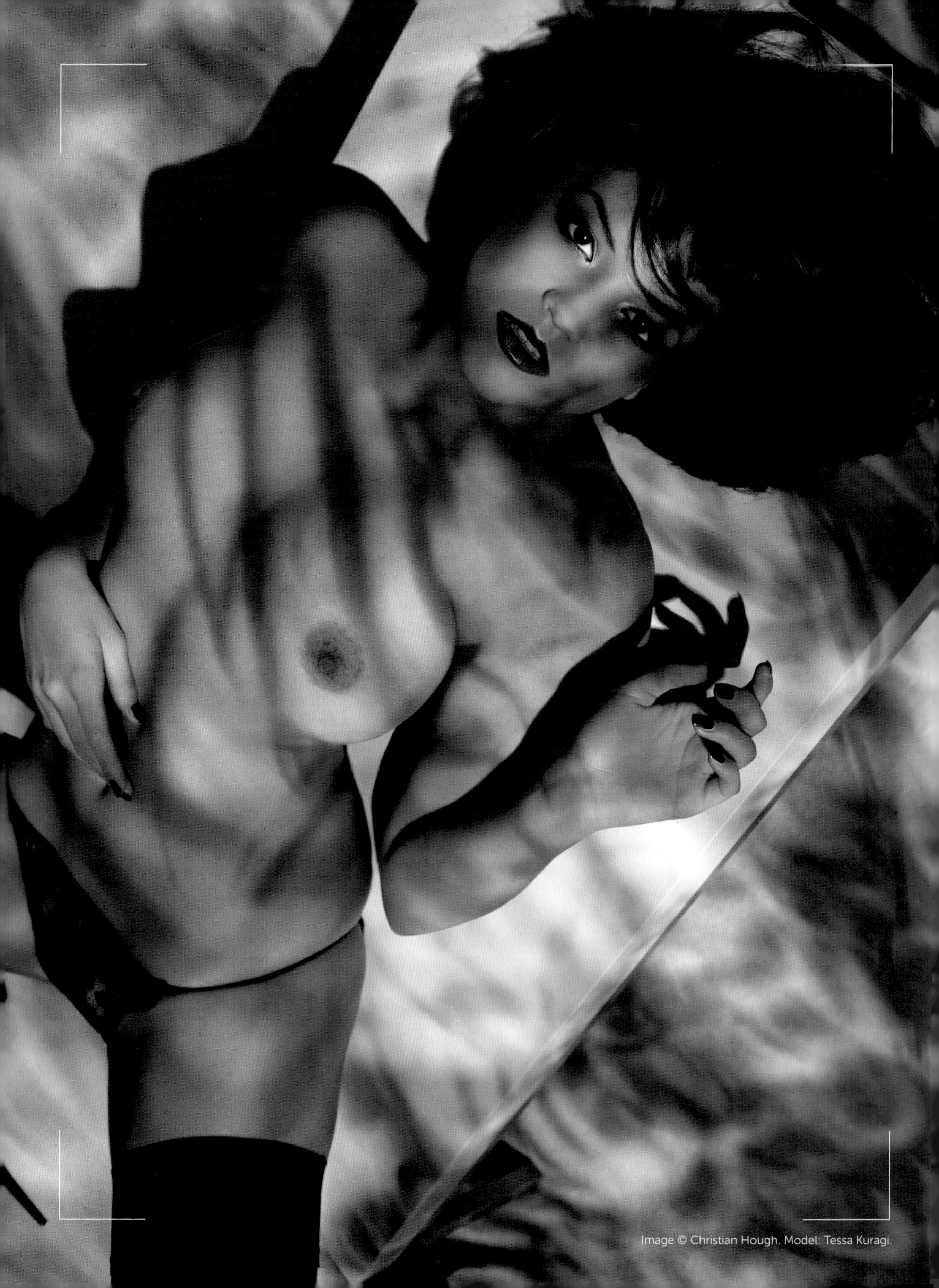

Image © Christian Hough. Model: Tessa Kuragi.

Preface

If you want to get into studio photography and learn how to take great studio photographs this book will help you. The book is designed to assist those just starting out as well as established photographers who wish to develop their lighting skills and photographic repertoire. Within these pages, you will find the relevant technical and practical information needed to get you started and further develop your understanding of studio photography.

There are many different genres of photography, yet they all have one thing in common, which is to capture light. Understanding how to make the most of light is a prerequisite for any photographer at any level in the business, the studio being no exception. As you would expect, there are some advantages to working within the studio, in that you are working within a contained environment and have full control over the light. However, without the props and the natural background environment found on location, the studio can at times seem quite sterile, and you will inevitably need to work harder and more creatively to make the most of the shoot. This is why your understanding and application of studio lighting and photography is important.

If there is one thing that I have learned from my experience of tuition, demonstrations and writing magazine features it is that photographers want clear practical advice. Having spoken to photographers at all levels, I am convinced that the majority are hungry for a combination of fresh lighting ideas, the concepts behind those ideas and a greater understanding of studio terminology. Many have searched the internet and books at length without being able to find all of the necessary information in a single cohesive format, which is why I decided to write this book. No remonstrations or internet forum arguing over the smallest points; just clear and open advice that combines the lighting and photographic techniques delivered in many of my demonstrations. Rest assured, this is a pixel-peeper free zone!

The advice is intended to help *you* understand how to get the best from *your* equipment and studio lighting, regardless of brand. Specific lighting examples have been set out in such a way as to enable you to understand how to light a subject, showing why it has been lit in a particular way and what type of equipment has been used. The techniques will also touch on common lighting mishaps and ways in which you can overcome them. You should find that they gradually increase in complexity as you progress your way through the book, yet remain sufficiently varied to enable you to steadily develop different ideas and apply the new skills you have mastered. Although the primary focus is on lighting techniques, other aspects of studio photography – such as equipment right through to the basics of RAW processing – are also covered. Understanding these areas helps raise both awareness and expectations.

Everybody enjoys a good photograph, and I truly believe that photography is accessible and that everybody can do it. It is one of the few skills that can be studied at leisure. Although there are rules for good lighting, rules are also there to be broken, so it remains important to strike a balance between technique and creativity. Eventually, as your confidence and technical ability increase, you will begin to stamp your own personality onto your photographs. Master the techniques within these pages, build and experiment with them to create something new and different. This is what will make you a confident and well-versed photographer.

Time to get shooting!

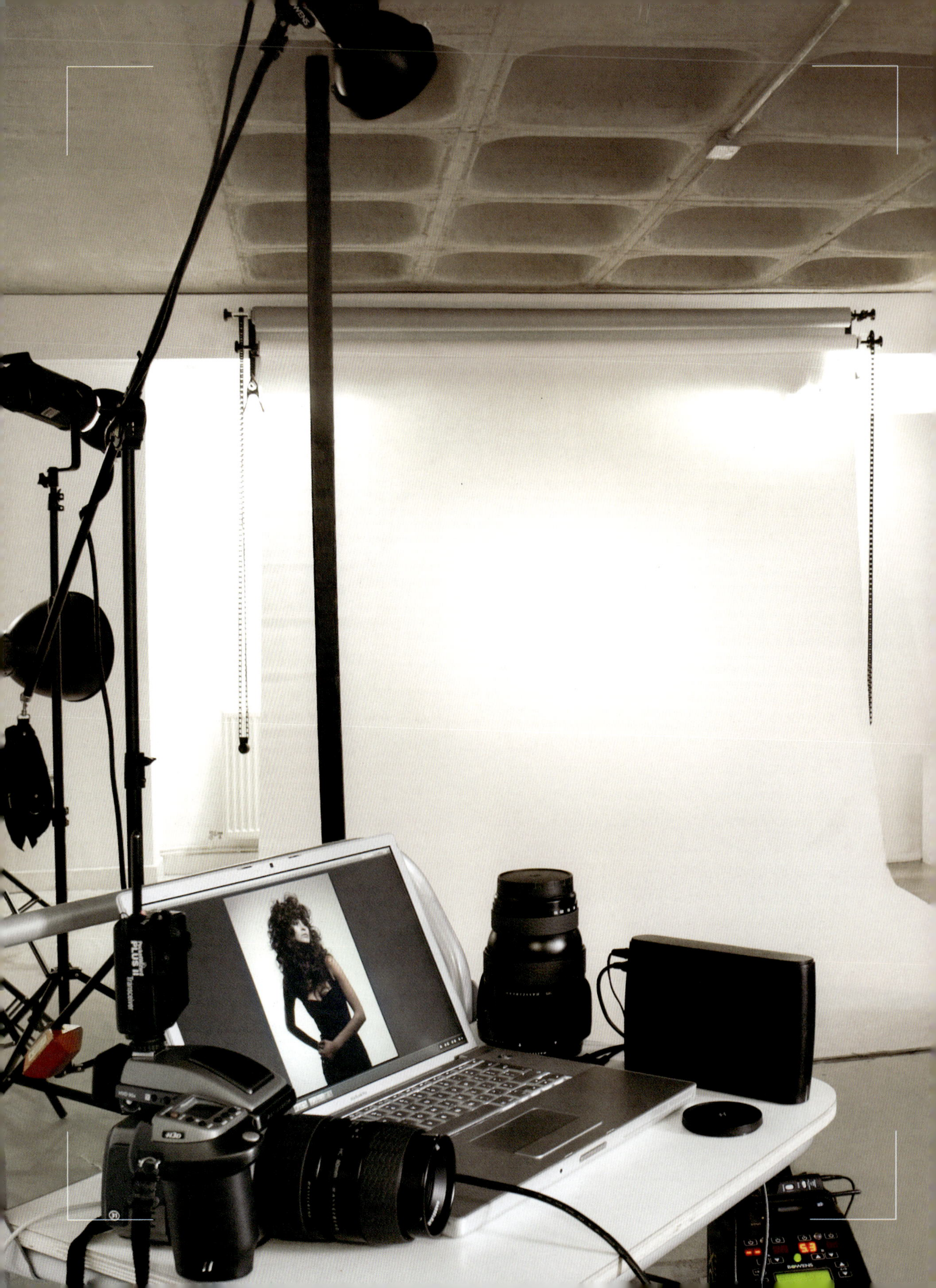
PLUS II
Transceiver
BOWENS

Chapter 1

Equipment Advice

LIGHTING

For many years, studio photography was for a large part controlled by the professional elite. However, with the introduction of digital photography, it has slowly filtered down to the semi-professional and enthusiast markets, seeing with it an increase in affordable equipment. What once was an extremely expensive investment is now available to suit every budget, from cheaper imports to high-end established brands. So what do you purchase?

As with everything, you get what you pay for, and your decision will depend on the intended use. So, if you're planning a busy high-end studio to shoot commercial campaigns on a daily basis, then budget lighting equipment won't be for you; however, if you shoot the occasional portrait or run a small business selling products online, then budget equipment might just suit your needs. Of course, it isn't always as simple as how often you shoot, but it also depends on what you are shooting; whether you need to freeze action, cover a wide area or need consistency with exposure and colour. As the demands of your photography increase, so will the demands for your equipment budget.

To this end, your first major decision will be regarding the type of light you will use – namely, continuous light or flashlight. Both have their pros and cons.

Continuous Light

Continuous light is 'continuous', in that it doesn't flash – the largest and best-known continuous light source we know is the sun! However, depending on your geographic location, sunlight isn't particularly reliable, and shaping and controlling both daylight and sunlight can prove to be difficult. This is where studio lighting comes in. There is a broad range of different continuous lighting systems on the market aimed at both photographers and filmmakers.

Continuous lighting systems are intuitive to use and are utilized by both amateur and professional photographers. They offer the benefit of visualizing the lighting levels and shadows with the naked eye, as opposed to metering each flash head with a light meter – so what you see is what you get. It has been this ease of use that has led to a growth and development by manufacturers for the enthusiast markets, meeting the demands for home portraits and small business e-commerce. Typically the continuous lights that are aimed at the amateur and beginner markets tend to be considerably cheaper than flash lighting targeted at the same level.

There are other benefits of course, such as the ease of balancing your lighting with ambient lighting levels, metering using your camera's inbuilt TTL (Through The Lens) meter instead of a handheld flash/light meter, and depending on which continuous lighting system you're using, it may also prove easier to balance the ambient colour temperature, such as daylight. However, continuous light does have its limitations and although it can be used for any subject it typically finds its niche in stills/product photography.

As you would expect, there are a number of different continuous lighting systems available; the prices can vary greatly, and each type has its strengths and weaknesses. Perhaps the most common type of continuous lighting is incandescent light, produced by the standard light bulbs found in many household lamps. As a main light source, incandescent light is particularly undesirable as it lacks power and is best described as the orange hue found on many amateur interior photographs. For this reason, many continuous lighting alternatives have been developed, including the following:

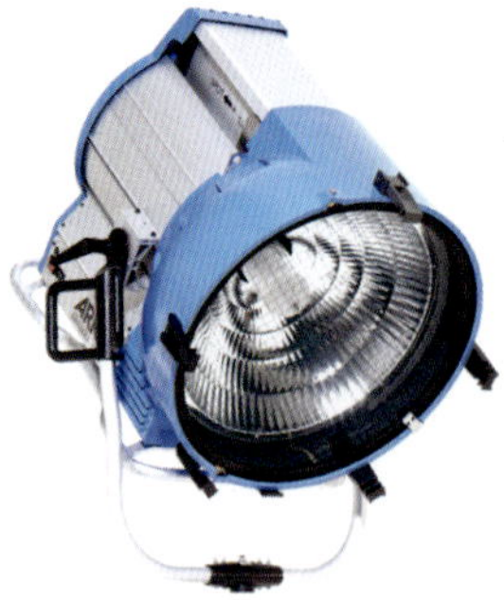

Fig. 1.1
HMI Lighting by Arri (also known as continuous/hot lighting).

HID Lights (High Intensity Discharge)

HIDs are basically arc lamps that rely on a combination of gas and metal salts and an electric arc between two electrodes to produce light when ignited by current. There are various types of HID lights available to photographers, each producing a different type of light, each with a slightly different colour temperature and, as you would expect, varying costs.

HMI Lights (Hydrargyrum Medium-arc Iodide)

Continuous lighting systems originally found their roots in the theatre with the use of incandescent hot lights, until the 1950s when a more efficient lighting system was designed by Osram-Sylvania, known as HMI lights. Instead of using incandescent light, HMI lights use arc lamps (light produced by an electrical arc inside the lamp) and are approximately four times more efficient than incandescent lights, whilst emitting less heat. HMI lights are typically expensive and can be found most frequently in theatres, broadcasting and film studios. They run at a colour temperature around 5600–6000 Kelvin (standard daylight colour temperature). HMI lights are used by many photographers, especially for lighting larger subjects such as cars and interiors, and are available in wattages that are sufficient to overpower the sun. HMI lights can be 'hot restarted', which means they can be restarted immediately after being switched off. HMI lights are traditionally known as 'Blonde' and 'Redhead' – Blonde with a power output of 1000–2000 watts and Redheads with a power output of 650–1000 watts.

CDM/CMH Lighting (Ceramic Discharge Metal/Halide)

CDM lights are commonly used for architectural lighting as they produce high power, yet less heat than HMI lighting, so may be run for prolonged periods. Typically, CDM lighting produces a bluish light that is close to daylight, although the exact colour temperature depends on the specific mixture of metal halide salts within the lamp. There are also warm-white CDM lamps, with somewhat warmer colour temperatures, that produce a more clear and natural-looking light. There are a range of CDM bulbs available that produce colour temperatures between 3000 and 8000 Kelvin. The benefits of these for photographers is that bulbs can be easily swapped to match a given colour temperature. CDM lamps are said to use one fifth of the power of comparable tungsten incandescent light bulbs for the same light output and retain colour stability better than most other gas discharge lamps. CDM lights tend to be cheaper the HMI lights; however, they are 'cold restarted', meaning they will take several minutes to warm up and will need similar downtime before they are restarted.

Tungsten Halogen Lights

Tungsten Halogen is incandescent lighting, utilizing a bulb with a filament of metal tungsten. Tungsten Halogen light was for many years the choice of studios for shooting stills and was used within film production, but has to some degree been superseded by flash and HMI lighting. Tungsten tends to vary on colour temperature depending on manufacturer, and the bulbs produce a lot of heat, so they can prove unsuitable for work in confined spaces, close-quarter portraits and culinary photography. Tungsten lighting is very cheap and readily available; however, there have been recent reports of their public use becoming more restricted due to the health and safety requirements of many venues.

Cool Lights and Fluorescent Lighting

Cool lights are fluorescent lights and are typically the entry-level of continuous lighting systems. They are available in a range of colour temperatures, although they are usually daylight balanced between 5600 and 6000 Kelvin for photographic use. The cool lights are available as low-voltage bulbs, which are used in single lighting heads, and in the traditional fluorescent tube format, normally installed in light banks and panels. Colour stability is reasonably good at around +/- 300 Kelvin. The bulbs have a very long life cycle, between 7000 and 10000 hours, and are flicker free. Florescent cool lights produce very little heat, so are ideal for portraits and stills, especially food and culinary photography. Some manufacturers are producing tubes that can be mixed with HMI units and coloured tubes specifically for lighting blue and green screens.

LED Lighting (Light Emitting Diode)

LED lights and panels have a similar application to that of the fluorescent cool lighting. The principle is to use high performance LED technology for improved power output, unit size and power consumption. Similar to the fluorescent tubes, they are daylight balanced, fully dimmable and flicker free. They are available in single head form, similar in appearance to the HMI lights or light panels.

It is possible to mix continuous lighting sources. However, if the sources are all balanced to different colour temperatures, you will encounter strange and somewhat distracting colour shifts in your images. The only realistic way to counteract this problem would be to utilize coloured gels in an attempt to equalize some of the colour shifts from the differing light sources. The degree of accuracy to which you will be able to correct the colour temperature

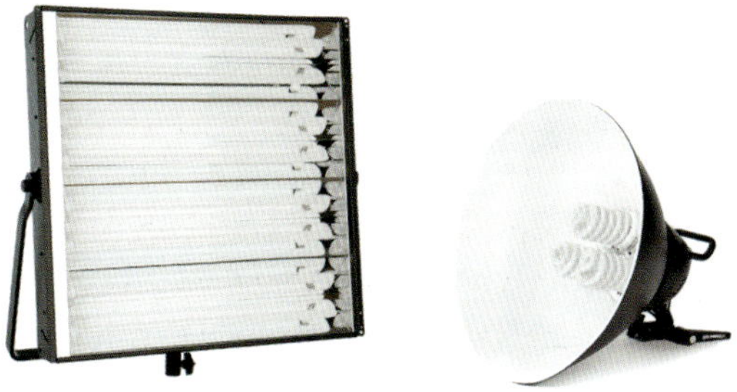

▲ Fig. 1.2
Cool lighting powered by fluorescent bulbs and tubes.

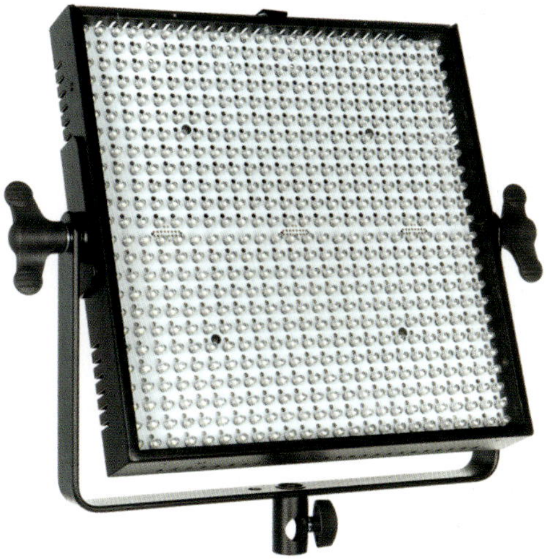

▲ Fig. 1.3
LED light panel, with low power consumption and low heat.

will ultimately depend on the colour temperature of the light source you are using and the availability of coloured gels. It is worth remembering that using a coloured gel will also reduce the power output of the light.

Continuous lighting has many benefits, but whilst it remains a realistic option for modern photographers, especially with the video capabilities of camera systems, allowing the photographer to engage in the worlds of both moving and still images, the quality and power output of the system depend greatly on your available budget. The entry-level cool lights and light panels may prove to be more financially attractive, yet they may also be the most limiting, with the more costly and robust and higher-powered HMI units remaining beyond the reach of all but the established professional. At the budget end of the market you will find that the availability of reflectors, shapers and modifiers for continuous lighting will be limited, especially for cool lighting and light panels. These offers may prove more restrictive as your skills and needs grow.

Power is a major influencing factor when looking at continuous light sources. Light panels and cool lights produce a relatively low power output compared to flash units of the same cost, which although acceptable for smaller portraits and products, will have limitations when shooting larger subjects and a reduced ability to freeze motion because of the lack of power output. This will ultimately result in a trade-off between shutter speed, aperture and ISO/ASA. If you need to shoot a fast moving subject with a large depth of field, then you may find yourself increasing the ISO to the point that it begins to affect the quality of your images.

HMI lighting has a much greater power output than other continuous lighting; however, it also consumes a lot of energy and as a result produces a great deal of heat. Heat can be a major health and safety concern to all photographers, especially when on location, and may prove unsuitable for certain applications such as culinary photography or anything where the heat may affect the product being photographed. Heat output can also affect portraits and model-based shoots within confined, non-air-conditioned spaces or over prolonged periods, rendering them very uncomfortable, with the added issue of bright continuous light causing the subject's iris to close down and pinpoint.

Finally, most continuous light sources, such as HMI and tungsten, have a finite lifespan and after time the colour temperature will begin to vary. Cheaper CDM units have the added issue of warming up and cooling down before they achieve the correct colour temperature. It is the combination of power output, heat, size and flexibility that leads to continuous lighting being most frequently and commonly used for products, automotive, video, theatre and broadcasting. Many of these systems may also require high-powered, three-phase power supplies, which are not generally available in your average home.

Flash Lighting

Flash lighting is by far the most popular choice for studio photographers. It is available in three different formats – on-camera/pop-up flash, flash guns (or speedlites) and studio flash (normally monobloc or generator based) – which normally have three very different uses. Every system is different in terms of design, use, flexibility and power output.

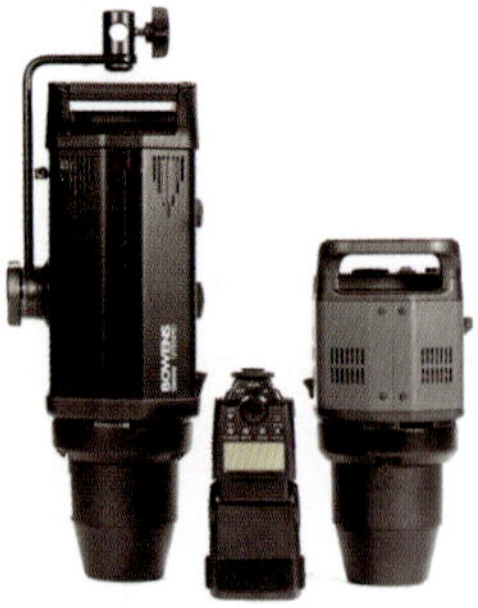

▲ Fig. 1.4
Different types of flash: (*left*) monobloc, (*middle*) speedlite, (*right*) generator head.

On-camera/Pop-up Flash

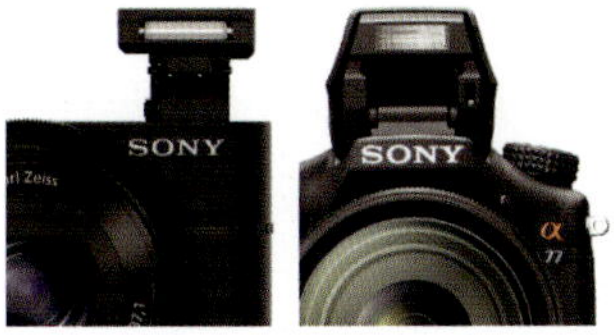

▲ Fig. 1.5
Inbuilt pop-up flash.

On-camera/pop-up flash is without a doubt the most instantly recognizable and widely available type of flash on the market. It is exactly what it says it is, and that is flash that is built into the camera or flash that pops up out of the camera when needed. Generally it is very small and highly portable, but has a very low power output and is fixed to the camera. It is most often found on compact cameras, entry-level DSLRs and occasionally some high-end DSLRs and is usually automatically controlled by the camera by way of program settings and in-camera metering. It produces a very flat, bright and unflattering light when used as the main light source, although it can be useful as fill-flash in bright sunlight or high-contrast scenes. As it is fixed, it lacks the flexibility of either hot shoe/flash guns or studio flash. Overall, it has limited professional use.

Flash Guns/ Speedlites

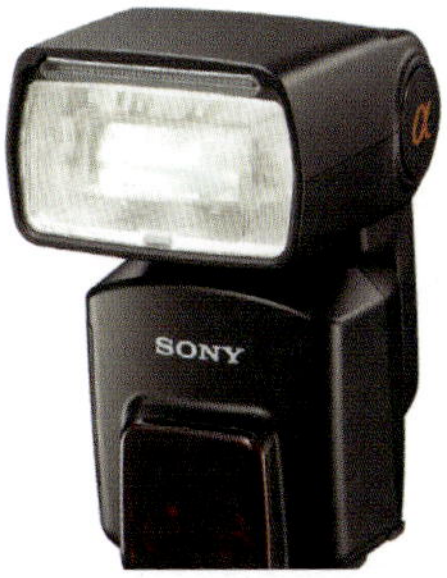

▲ Fig 1.6
Inbuilt pop-up flash.

Flashguns (also known as hot shoe flash or speedlites) are separate flash units that can be placed directly onto the hot shoe of the camera or off-camera by way of a cable between the camera and the flash, or infrared. Flashguns vary in size from manufacturer to manufacturer, produce considerably more power than on-camera flash and are generally battery operated. The more expensive models can be tilted and rotated, so that the light may be bounced off ceilings, walls and through diffusers, making the light more flattering than direct flash. Press, wedding, event and social photographers frequently use flash guns as they are highly portable and can be easily controlled by way of the camera's bespoke metering system, or with standard TTL (Through The Lens) metering.

Flash guns tend to be produced by individual camera manufacturers and are usually tailored to work with their own cameras and metering systems, although there are several third-party flash gun manufacturers that will produce systems designed to make the most of individual features offered by particular camera brands and models, such as Metz. Some bespoke flash systems will allow photographers to achieve extremely high sync/shutter speeds, that are not always available with studio-based flash systems. It is also possible to use several flash guns together to create different lighting effects; although the caveat is that new models are introduced by manufacturers every couple of years, and backwards compatibility may at times be an issue – generally not a problem with studio flash.

Although flash guns are cheaper to purchase than studio flash units and are extremely portable, they can prove to be somewhat limited when it comes to power output, colour accuracy and flexibility when shaping and controlling light.

Studio Lights/Studio Flash (also known as strobe lighting)

Studio lights offer more power and creative flexibility than flash guns and on-camera flash. There are many different brands, but three general types of studio light are available and their names specifically relate to their design and the way in which they are powered and operated, namely monobloc, generator operated or battery-powered. With the exception of battery power, studio heads are generally mains operated or can be connected to three-phase systems in larger commercial studios.

Monoblocs/ Monolights

Monoblocs are the most common and most popular studio light available as not only are they usually the cheapest to purchase, but they also offer a great deal of expandability and flexibility for the photographer. Monoblocs are an all-in-one design, meaning that the power supply, controls and flash are built into a single head unit. Because of this, they are generally larger in size than the heads controlled by a generator and vary hugely in power output depending on brand, anywhere from 150W to 1500W. The greater the power output, the larger the size (and heavier the weight) of the monobloc.

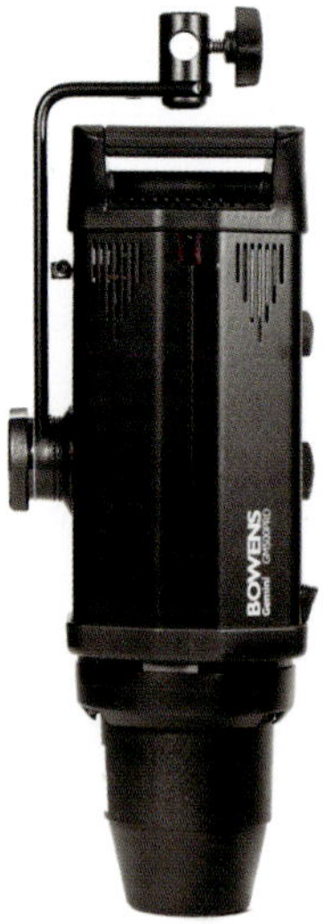

▲ Fig. 1.7
Monobloc studio head, with controls and power supply all integrated with a single light.

Monoblocs have the flexibility of being able to be plugged directly into the mains electricity supply, placed independently of other monobloc heads providing there is a suitable power outlet nearby. When you need to adjust the power of the monobloc, it is simply a case of adjusting the controls on the head itself, which is very convenient, unless the monobloc is placed somewhere that is not so accessible.

Studio Generators

Generators (also known as packs or studio packs) can usually power up to four studio heads (depending on model). The studio heads (or pack heads) are different in design to the monoblocs, as all the power and the controls for the head are found within the generator. The generator head will usually consist of just the flash bulb and a modelling light and on/off switch. A thick cable will connect the head directly to the generator that controls all the functions. Generators can offer many advantages over monobloc heads, such as power, recycling time, shorter flash durations and greater colour consistency, but they also demand a much greater price.

As with monoblocs, generators usually plug directly into the mains power supply; however, the positioning of the heads can be limited to the length of the cable between the head and the generator (extender cables are generally available from the main lighting manufacturers). Apart from performance advantages, generators allow photographers to adjust the power of their heads on the generator itself, reducing the need to climb on chairs and ladders to access controls on the heads as with monobloc heads. There is an obvious convenience benefit to this design, especially when heads are placed so that they may not be as accessible.

As a rule, generators will afford the photographer greater control over the distribution of power between the heads connected to it, either symmetrically or asymmetrically. So for example, if a generator has two channels, symmetrical power delivery will split the power distribution 50/50 across both channels, whereas asymmetrical power distribution would allow the user to, say, direct two-thirds of the power to one channel and the remaining third to the other. As generators can offer anywhere between 1500W and 5000W of power, it helps if you can divide the power output between the heads (or channels), to allow greater control over the power delivery, as there are many occasions when minimum power is more important than maximum power.

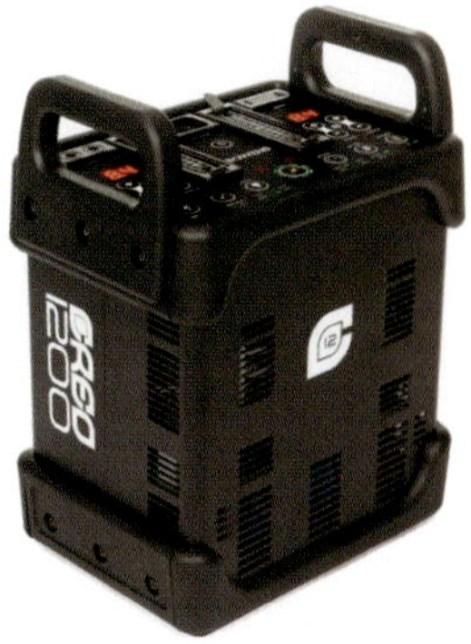

▲ Fig. 1.8
Generator-based flash: usually offers more power, with all controls located on the generator as opposed to the head.

Battery Generators

The battery generator is essentially a generator that runs from a battery power source. Some battery generators will also run from the mains and can be used in the same way as a normal AC-powered generator. As it is a generator, all of the controls to regulate the power output and modelling facility and so on will be operated from a control panel located on the pack itself and not on the heads. You will usually find that the studio-based generators and battery generators made by the same manufacturers will use the same heads and remain fully compatible. Some battery generators also offer a DC power source to operate battery-controlled monobloc heads. Battery generators are normally fairly expensive, but they offer more power and faster recycle times between flashes, plus the added flexibility of their use on location.

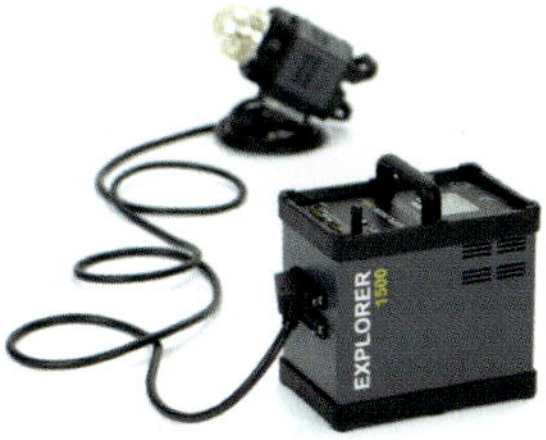

▲ Fig. 1.9
Battery generator: portable generator-based system for location shooting. Some battery generators are capable of powering generator-style heads as well as monobloc heads.

Battery Packs

Battery packs differ from battery generators as they offer only a power supply and basic interface, usually to a monobloc style head. As they are designed to provide DC power to monoblocs, all of the lighting functions are operated using the existing controls built into the monoblocs. On the whole, battery packs are smaller and cheaper than generators, and may also offer hot swappable battery systems to facilitate your shooting time whilst on location. The caveat is that they do not always offer a modelling light facility, they recycle slower than a battery generator and will require you to carry around larger monobloc heads.

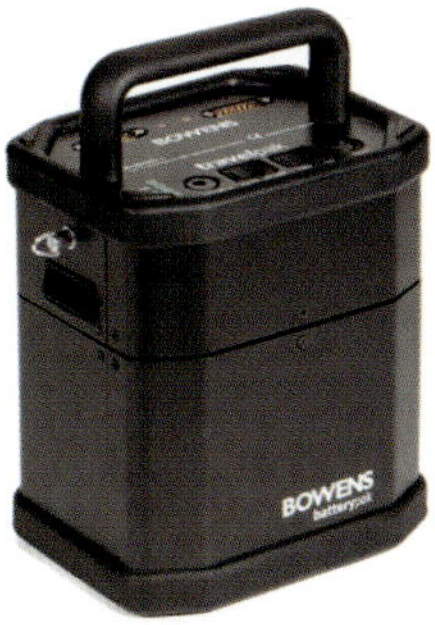

▲ Fig. 1.10
Portable batteries, used to power monobloc heads when shooting on location – the larger the battery, the more flashes are achievable.

Ringflash

Classic ringflash is typically an expensive generator-based flash that is shaped into a ring. The camera's lens is then pushed through the centre of the ring. It produces a very flat light as it is located directly on the camera axis. Ringflash was originally designed many years ago for dental photography, but became popular with fashion photographers, producing a continuous shadow/halo around the edge of the subject, yet it is equally useful as a fill light, evenly filling the shadows or even off-axis. The recent surge in popularity has seen more affordable products arrive on the market, such as battery-powered ringflash systems for macrophotography and even adapters to convert standard studio heads into a temporary ringflash.

Generally, photographers that are just starting out will make their first investment in monoblocs/monolights, simply because they offer extremely good value for money and a lot of flexibility. It is normally possible to purchase several monoblocs for the same price as a single generator, meaning that it is possible to quickly add heads and peripherals as your lighting develops. The difficulty is choosing the most suitable lighting manufacturer to invest your hard-earned cash in, as switching brands later on can prove expensive.

Most lighting manufacturers aim to produce a complete and compatible lighting system that can be expanded as the photographer's skills and business grow. They normally produce an extensive range of quality peripherals, softboxes, shapers and modifiers compatible with their system. The more established the manufacturer, the more shaping tools and peripherals they will offer and the more available and widely distributed they will be. For this

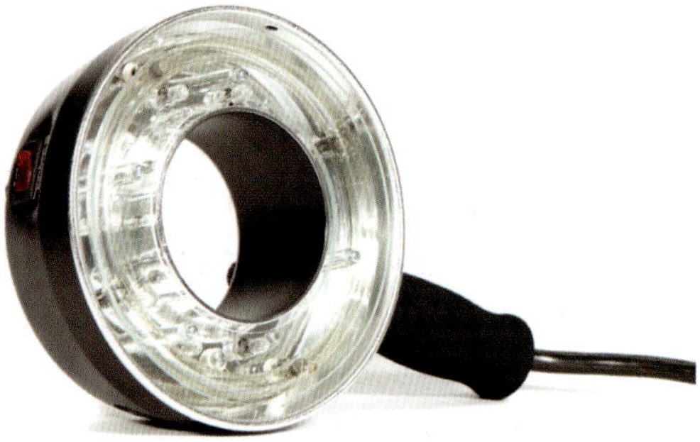

▲ Fig. 1.11
Generator-based ringflash, with 3kw of achievable power output.

reason, it is important to think ahead when purchasing your first system as cheaper equipment can often prove to be more expensive in the long run. It is worth considering that established brands are established for a reason, usually because they offer good service, continuous product development and a reliable product. To this aim, it is recommended that you think long term and purchase a quality marque, one that offers service in your country and the flexibility to expand the system, as opposed to purchasing the cheapest product available.

The basic prerequisites of all studio lights are very similar and have been for many years, in that they all have modelling lights, slave cells and dials to control the power output. To this extent, they will usually all work together, regardless of brand.

There are many professionals that use more than one brand of lighting, depending on the type of work they are doing, whether it be location or studio, continuous lighting or flash. Some photographers may use more than one brand, but tend to use them within different areas of their work; whereas other photographers that have invested heavily in a particular marque may purchase one or two lights from a different manufacturer to make the most of a unique quality or a particular modifier.

You will find that each lighting manufacturer's specifications will be different, and for the most part it should not be an issue with standard product shoots or portrait sessions. However, depending on how far you push the boundaries of your equipment, issues may begin to appear, such flash duration, colour temperature consistency and flash recycle time. Specifications aside, the main issue will undoubtedly come with the use and exchangeability of modifiers, shapers and softboxes. All of the established lighting manufacturers use their own mounting system – that is, the system used to attach modifiers and softboxes to the flash heads. Using lights from several different manufacturers will mean that you may not have the freedom to exchange modifiers and softboxes freely between your lights, limiting the flexibility of your equipment. Currently, the most common mounting system available for flash lighting is the S-type Bayonet mount that was originally designed by the UK manufacturer Bowens. A patent loophole has seen this mounting system adopted by several lighting manufacturers, resulting in a large number of available reflectors and modifiers.

Hiring equipment is not cheap by any means; however, it is a more cost-effective way in which you can try particular brands and pieces of equipment in your own time, without the added pressure of a salesman standing over you. If you are genuinely at a crossroads in making a decision, then hiring will be the best way to make an informed choice. It is also ideal for that one-off project where you may need a speciality or expensive item, allowing you to make use of the equipment at a fraction of the cost of the original purchase (and storage). Most hire charges are tax deductible and you will be required to register your details with the hire company prior to hiring. Remember to factor in insurance/damage waiver charges, plus delivery and return days into the total number of days hire.

Flash Duration

Flash duration – the time it takes for a flash to peak and trough – is important to many professional photographers. To the human eye, flash duration is indistinguishable from one system to another; however, it is vitally important to understand how and when you can use it. It may even influence your choice of lighting system.

For many photographers, especially those photographing static products or subdued portraits, flash duration is not an issue. This all changes from the point at which you wish to freeze motion such as splashing water or moving hair. In this scenario, the shorter the flash duration, the less motion blur you will get. It is a difficult concept for many newer studio photographers to grasp at first as most assume that any flash head will freeze everything, because they are still in the mind set of photographing in ambient light where they were wholly reliant on shutter speed to freeze subjects. However, in the studio, where most cameras are limited to a sync speed of 1/125–1/200sec it is flash duration that is king.

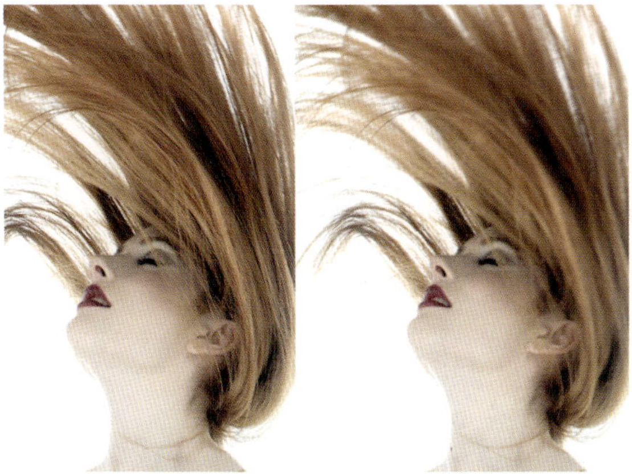

▲ Fig. 1.12
Illustration of long flash duration – the shorter the flash duration, the less blur.

CAMERAS AND CAMERA FORMATS

Many of you reading this will already have invested in a camera or be considering purchasing one. As you know, there are many different camera systems available, some of which are more suited to studio work. There are also some less commonly known, yet extremely useful, pieces of equipment that could prove to be extremely beneficial in your work.

This is not meant to be a guide on which brand of camera you should purchase, but instead will offer some guidance as to what type of camera is more suitable for different types of studio photography, plus some advice as to what is available and some of the differences between the varying camera formats.

The Film or Digital Debate

There is always a debate about film versus digital. Both systems are not without their advocates and critics; yet both have their place in the market. Film for many years has been the accepted method of capturing images, gradually becoming less popular with the continuing development of the digital camera. Film has for the large part become a niche market and as a result acquired a certain artistic and nostalgic merit, revered and loved by many established photographers who have toiled over single images for many hours in the darkroom. It is true to say that many of the world's iconic advertising, portrait and fashion images have all been captured on film, and it is still capable of producing the same quality of image today.

For the large part, film, paper and developing technology have been left behind in favour of development of digital technology. Digital photography is accessible, quick and intuitive to use, offering instant appraisal and feedback to the photographer and as such has opened up the photographic industry to many more people. The imaging quality on offer by some of the digital systems has surpassed all quality boundaries, offering photographers huge flexibility and opportunities that would have been thought of as impossible many years ago. Whilst digital photography has never had the prestige and illusiveness of film, the sheer competitiveness of the market has raised imaging standards everywhere, pushing all boundaries of the finished photograph, from lighting to post processing.

So which do I choose? There is no answer to this – it is purely down to personal choice. As far as this book is concerned, the lighting techniques used will be applicable regardless of whether you use a film or digital camera system. However, your rate of development and user experience may be enhanced more by using a digital system, as the instant feedback offered by the camera will enable you to immediately ascertain if what you are shooting looks as it should.

There are also certain market pressures that you need to consider when investing in a system. Not just the cost of equipment, consumables and time, but also expectations from your potential client base. For example if you are planning on shooting family portraits, press photography, fashion editorial or advertising, there may well be an expectation from family, editors, producers and clients to view images both immediately and remotely. These pressures have to some degree rendered film obsolete within these markets, as this type of instant image appraisal is not possible. If you don't offer this service and somebody else does, you will undoubtedly lose business. This is why so many photographers have chosen to invest in the digital market, and film to some extent has become a more specialized medium that is used within fine-art markets.

Camera Formats

Traditionally there were four common camera formats, some deriving their names from the size of the negatives they produced. The names and the uses of the systems remained virtually unchanged even with the advent of digital capture in the late 1990s. However, manufacturers have continued to provide models to fulfil demand and gaps in the market, introducing new models that bridge the gaps between the traditional formats, appealing to both professional and amateur photographers alike.

Compact Cameras

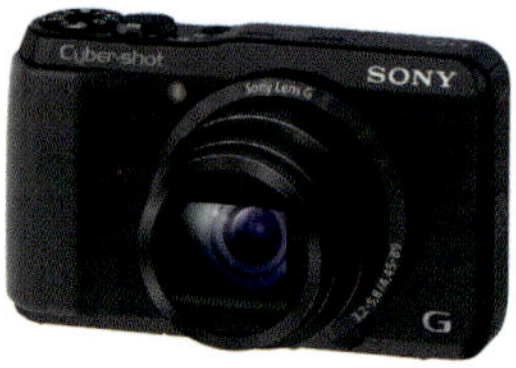

▲ Fig. 1.13
Compact camera: small, affordable and widely available.

Compact cameras are small and highly portable cameras aimed at the mass consumer market. They are almost fully automated with built-in flash and fixed or non-interchangeable tele-zoom lenses. Film-based compacts tend to be 35mm, whereas digital systems utilize a small CCD sensor that has seen a trend of increasing pixel count with limited picture quality. Most of the digital systems offer JPEG format only images. Quality and expandability are limited, making the compact camera unsuitable for studio photography.

Bridge Cameras

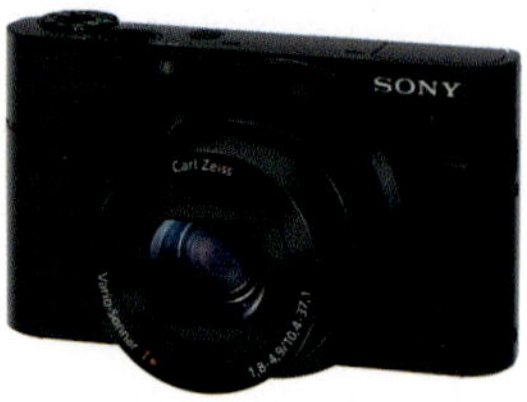

▲ Fig. 1.14
Bridge camera: offers more control than a compact for the more adventurous amateur.

Bridge cameras are a purely digital market. They are small and portable cameras offering the photographer more manual controls and longer zoom lenses than the traditional compact. Camera capabilities differ greatly from manufacturer to manufacturer. Some systems offer RAW, TIFF and JPEG image formats and higher

ISO capability, whereas others may be more limited. The quality of these cameras is usually average, although they do on the whole offer quality gains over the compact cameras. Bridge cameras offer an all-in-one solution, with greater flexibility than the compact range. Depending on model, bridge cameras are either not ideal or unsuitable for studio photography.

Interchangeable Lens Compact Cameras

Interchangeable lens compact cameras offer the photographer a small portable camera system with a small choice of lenses for improved quality. They are available in both film and digital formats. The most instantly recognizable film-based system is the rangefinder system produced by Leica, which utilizes 35mm film, and there are several digital systems to choose from. The cameras tend to employ a larger sensor than the compact and bridge markets, offering significant image quality advantages over compact and bridge camera systems. The cameras are fairly small in size (depending on lens) and are ideal for travel and street photography. Specifications differ from manufacturer to manufacturer, but most offer the photographer full manual control for creativity. Depending on specification they are suitable for studio photography, but not ideal.

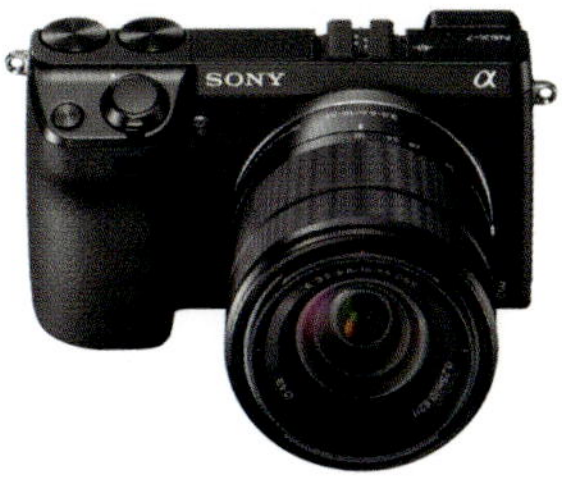

▲ Fig. 1.15
Interchangeable lens compact camera: massively improved image quality in a compact body, with a selection of lenses available.

35mm Based SLR/ DSLR Cameras

SLR is an abbreviation for Single Lens Reflex, and DSLR is simply the digital equivalent. Most of the old film-based SLR cameras utilized 35mm film and have become less common since the introduction of the Digital SLR. There are several SLR/DSLR systems available and most have a large number of lenses available, some of which are compatible between digital and film models. The larger body of the DSLR allows some camera models to employ a larger sensor than the compact, bridge and interchangeable lens cameras, offering significant image quality advantages. DSLR systems have been designed with flexibility in mind and offer the photographer full manual and creative control of the camera. The large number of lenses and peripherals available, plus the flexibility over controlling the camera, make SLR and DSLR systems ideal for professional studio photography.

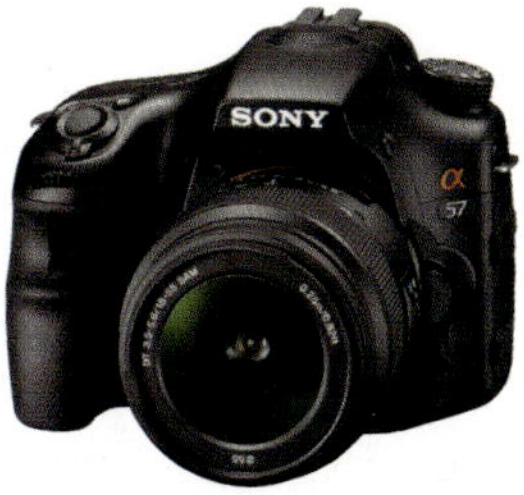

▲ Fig. 1.16
SLR/DSLR camera: the most recognizable type of camera, offering good portability, excellent image quality and a huge variety of lenses and peripherals.

Medium Format Cameras

Medium format has its traditional roots in the TLR (Twin Lens Reflex) cameras, such as the instantly recognizable Rolleiflex manufactured by Franke & Heidecke, which utilized the 120/220 roll film. As time progressed, many of these cameras developed into Single Lens Reflex systems manufactured by companies such as Hasselblad, Rollei, Mamiya and Pentax, yet retained the use of 120/220 roll film as the larger negative of 6x6cm or 6x7cm and produced better image quality than 35mm based systems. Modern digital medium format cameras are effectively DSLR cameras that utilize a much larger sensor for significant image quality gains than those offered by the 24x35mm DSLR equivalents. As with 35mm DSLR systems, there is

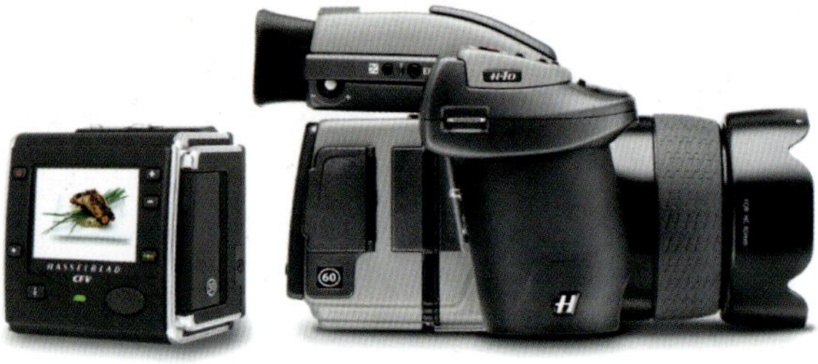

▲ Fig. 1.17
The modern medium format DSLR, offering outstanding image quality and flexibility.

a broad range of lenses and peripherals available for medium format digital systems, with some that may be compatible between film and digital. Medium format cameras come with detachable sensors, known as digital backs, similar to the film backs that housed the 120/220 roll film allowing the back to be utilized on large format systems too. Medium format cameras are renowned for extreme image quality and tonality, producing true 16-bit images, making them ideal for all genres of studio photography.

Large Format

Large format has become less common in modern photography. It was the original photographic format, long before medium format and 35mm. Originally it utilized very large negatives, more commonly 5x4in (102x127mm) but also 8x10in (200x250mm) or Ultra Large Format (ULF), offering negative size and image quality far in excess of medium format. The most recognizable large format systems are the monorail studio cameras, produced by manufacturers such as Linhof. These high-quality and precision-based cameras are ideal for product and architectural photography, utilizing an inherent tilt and shift system to facilitate the control of perspective and parallax issues. These cameras are still very much in use today by high-end professional architecture, interior and product photographers, although the film has largely been replaced by the medium format digital back, allowing the photographer to maximize the best elements of both the large format and digital systems – ideal for specific applications of studio photography.

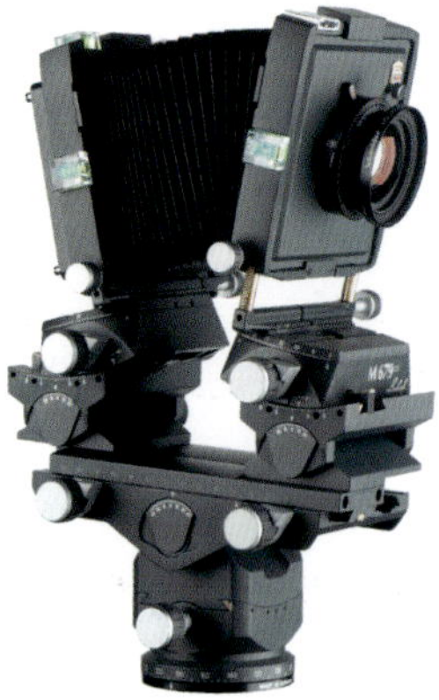

▲ Fig. 1.18
Large format technical camera with bellows: perfect for controlling parallax issues.

35mm and Medium Format Technical Cameras

Recent developments have seen innovative products arrive on the market, allowing 35mm and medium format DSLRs to be mounted directly onto a technical camera based system. Products such as the X2-Pro allow technical camera front standard movements such as rise, fall, swing, tilt and shift, affording control over perspective and focal plane issues. This type of system is a cost-effective way for all DSLR owners to obtain technical camera flexibility.

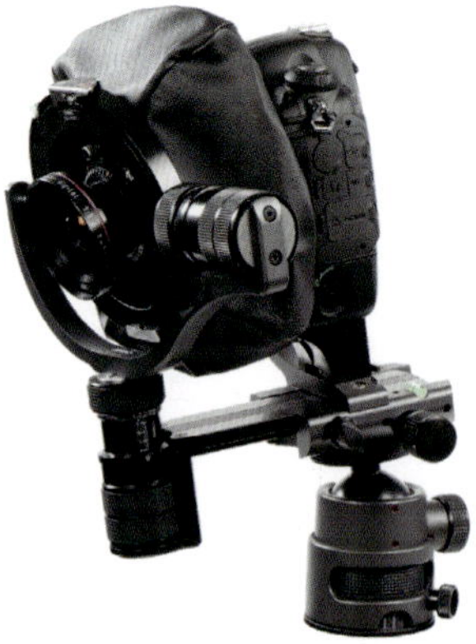

▲ Fig. 1.19
Cambo X2-Pro: technical based camera system for DSLR camera systems. (Photograph ©Andy Haslam 2012)

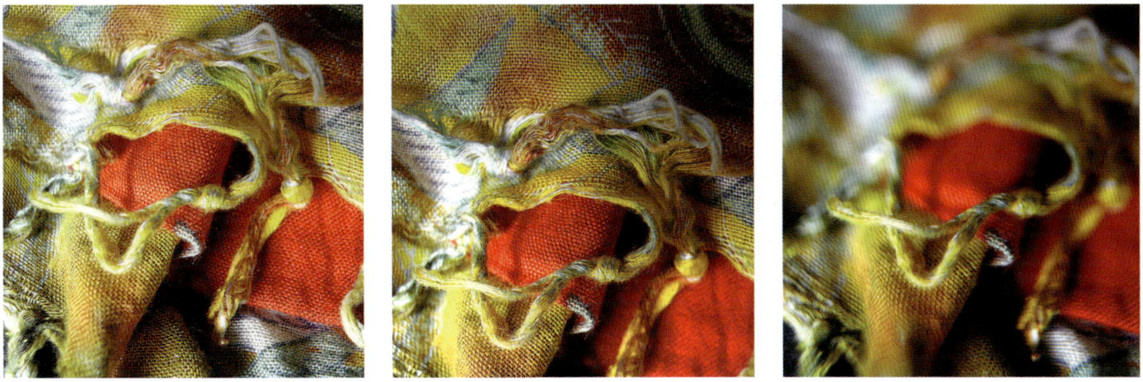

▲ Fig. 1.20
The effects of using a technical camera as shot on the Cambo X2-Pro.
(right) No movements of the lens plane;
(middle) Scheimpflug movement, where the object and lens planes intersect;
(left) Using the tilting lens plane to create a selective focus effect.

Prerequisites for Shooting with Studio Lights

Regardless of what type of camera system you intend to purchase, there are some absolute prerequisites for shooting with studio lights.

Most cameras will offer a variety of shooting modes, such as fully automatic, semi-automatic and fully manual. These will vary from manufacturer to manufacturer and depend entirely on each model, but are often known as **P** (program mode), **Av** (aperture priority), **Tv** (shutter priority) and **M** (manual).

The shooting modes you are able to use depend entirely on the type of lighting system you are employing. If you are using continuous lighting, then any of the camera's shooting modes can be used (although manual mode is preferential), as you will be able to meter the light through the camera's inbuilt TTL metering system. However, when shooting with studio flash, it becomes necessary to use the camera in fully manual mode (**M**) as the camera's inbuilt metering becomes redundant and is unable to meter the very short burst of flash. Studio 'flash' lighting operates completely independently to the camera's inbuilt system, so the flash needs to be metered independently and the correct ASA/ISO, shutter speed and aperture dialled into the camera system manually. Fully automatic and semi-automatic camera modes will not work with flash-based studio lighting. If your camera does not have the option of a manual mode or manual override, then it will only be suitable for continuous lighting and not studio flash.

One other prerequisite of studio flash is that it needs to be 'triggered'. This can be done in two ways, namely via a lead that connects to the PC Sync socket normally located on the front or side of the camera, or via a radio or infrared trigger fitted to the camera's hot shoe. The most popular method is by radio trigger, as unlike the PC Sync connector, it doesn't require a lead and offers freedom of movement up to 100 metres from the lighting equipment. PC Sync cables are the much cheaper option, but also become a hazard and are frequently tripped over or occasionally pull over the lights when the photographer attempts to stray too far! Regardless of your preferred method of triggering, it is essential that your camera has either a hot shoe or a PC Sync connector.

USING THE PC SYNC

Film cameras were originally designed to utilize the PC Sync for flash photography and may require you to set the shutter speed to a pre-defined sync mode. The most common of these settings can be found on the shutter control dial and is marked X. This is commonly known as the X-Sync and times the shutter to be completely open when the flash is at its peak illumination, thus correctly exposing the image. Depending on your camera system, you may find other settings, such as **F**, **FP**, **M** and **ME**, which were designed to be used with different types of flash bulbs, although the X setting is generally considered to be the most suitable with modern studio flash systems.

Care does need to be taken when using the PC Sync via sync cable with DSLR camera systems. Most modern studio flash systems will operate a sync voltage of less than 6 volts, whereas older flash systems may have a sync voltage well in excess of this. The specification differs depending on your camera; however, some manufacturers suggest that a PC Sync voltage in excess of 6 volts via the camera's hot shoe can cause irreparable damage.

As modern DSLRs are highly sensitive electrical devices, it is recommended that you refrain from connecting the camera via cable to the flash via the PC Sync or hot shoe without having some form of surge protection to protect your camera. There are several reports of DSLR cameras being damaged as a result of higher sync voltages of older studio flash systems, so please ensure you check with both the studio lighting and camera manufacturer to ascertain compatibility when contacting your DSLR in this way. If in doubt, always use a reputable radio trigger.

LENSES AND FILTERS

A lens is basically an optical device that transmits and refracts light. As to how well it does this depends entirely on the lens, the accuracy of the engineering and the quality of the optics inside. Lens design and manufacturing is an exact and highly complex science. For the most part, it is not something that a photographer needs to worry about, other than knowing the types of lenses available and which models are generally 'good' or 'bad'.

Types of Lens

Prime Lenses

Prime lenses are fixed lenses. This means they only have one focal length (unifocal), which is fixed. As a general rule, prime lenses are usually of superior optical quality than zoom lenses, as their construction is much simpler and they have fewer moving parts. The prime lens can be accurately tuned to one focal length, rather than making the best of several focal lengths, so it generally produces a sharper image than a zoom lens. As they require fewer optics, prime lenses often achieve a much wider aperture, allowing a shallower depth of field and greater flexibility when shooting in low light, with apertures as wide as *f*1.2. Zooming is not possible with a prime lens, meaning that the photographer has to physically move nearer or further from the subject.

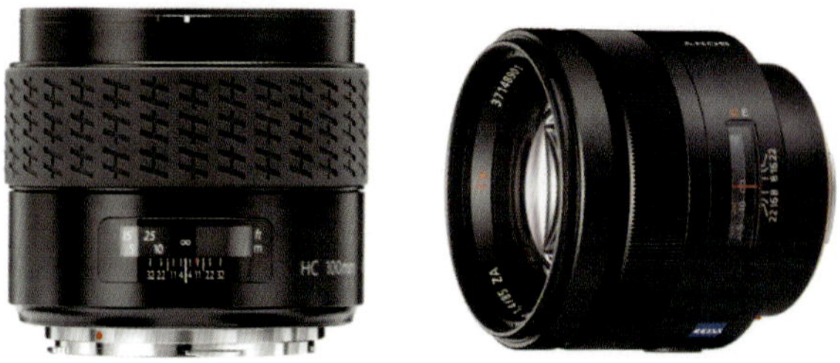

▲ Fig. 1.21
Prime lenses: fixed focal length lenses from Hasselblad (medium format) and Sony (35mm).

Zoom Lenses

Zoom lenses allow the photographer to alter the focal length of the lens, zooming in and out from the subject, without having to move physically from their current location. Zoom lenses tend to consist of a number of different optics inside the body, some of which slide backwards and forwards as the lens is physically zoomed in and out. They are known as either parfocal, meaning that they retain the focus on the subject whilst being zoomed, or varifocal, which means that the focus is lost when the lens is zoomed and the photographer will need to refocus.

Zoom lenses offer maximum convenience for photographers, allowing them to get close to a subject and flatten perspective when they need to. However, they tend not to be as consistently sharp as prime lenses and will often have a 'sweet spot', where the lens is at its sharpest at a given focal length and aperture. Given the number of optics within the zoom lens, they tend to be fairly bulky compared to a prime lens and will only offer maximum apertures of around *f*2.8, even in the most expensive lenses.

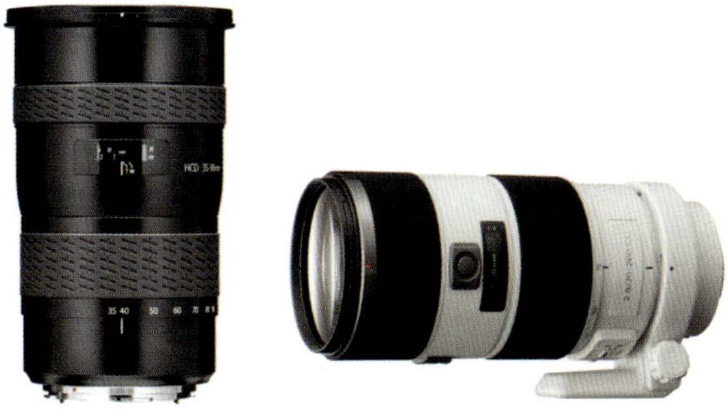

▲ Fig. 1.22
Zoom lenses: Hasselblad 35–90mm (medium format) and Sony 70–200mm (35mm format).

Telephoto Lenses

A telephoto lens is a long-focus lens where the physical length of the lens is shorter than the prescribed focal length, so for example, where the focal length of a lens is 300mm but the physical length of the lens body is shorter than 300mm. Telephoto lenses incorporate a group of lenses, known as a telephoto group, which effectively extends the light path, creating a long-focus lens that can be fitted into a much shorter lens body. They can be zoom or prime lenses and are usually defined and put into groups depending on their focal length. As a rough guide, a short telephoto will have a focal length of around 60–100mm, medium telephoto 135–300mm and super telephoto 300+mm.

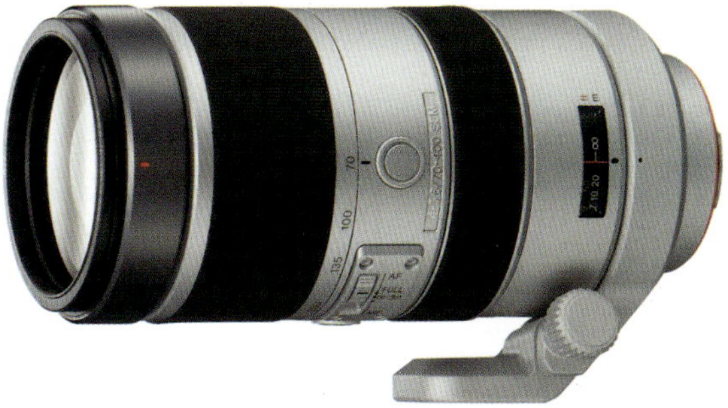

▲ Fig. 1.23
Telephoto lens: 70–400mm from Sony.

Wide-angle Lenses

Wide-angle lenses are lenses that offer a much shorter focal length than a standard 50mm lens, normally 35mm and less. Whilst a telephoto lens will compress the image perspective and offer a shallow depth of field, a wide-angle lens will increase the appearance of distance and offer a greater depth of field. Wide-angle lenses are most commonly used in architectural photography, landscapes and interiors. They tend to distort perspectives, causing parallel lines to converge and on occasions barrel distortion. Some lenses are available with focal lengths of less than 10mm, which are most commonly known as fisheye lenses.

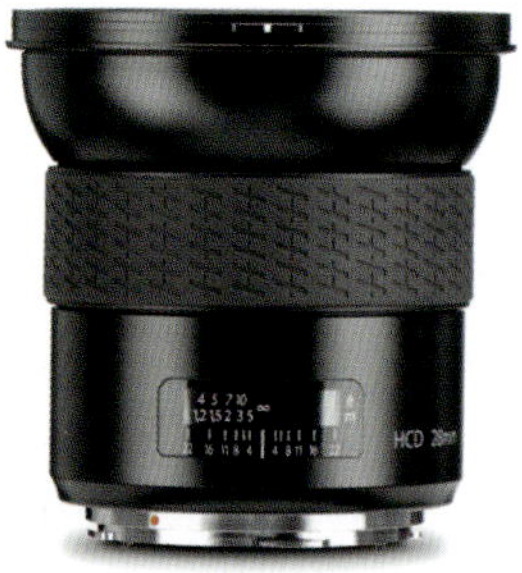

▲ Fig. 1.24
Hasselblad 4/28mm wide-angle lens: studio use is more limited with wide-angle lenses, but they are useful for distorting perspectives.

The choice of lens is a very personal one. It can be based on several factors including subject matter, focal length, sharpness, bokeh, personal preference or even budget.

Tilt and Shift Lenses

Tilt and shift lenses are essentially based upon a similar idea to the large format based camera system, that operates using the Scheimpflug principle, allowing asymmetric tilts and swings to bring the subject plane, lens plane and sensor plane to meet at a virtual point (Scheimpflug intersection). What this means is that the lens can be tilted, allowing the photographer to correct converging lines and perspective-associated issues. Manufacturer-specific tilt and shift lenses available for SLR and DSLR systems are portable prime lenses mounted on a tilting and shifting lens body affording some control over perspective. Tilt and shift lenses are commonly used in studio product photography, interiors and architectural photography.

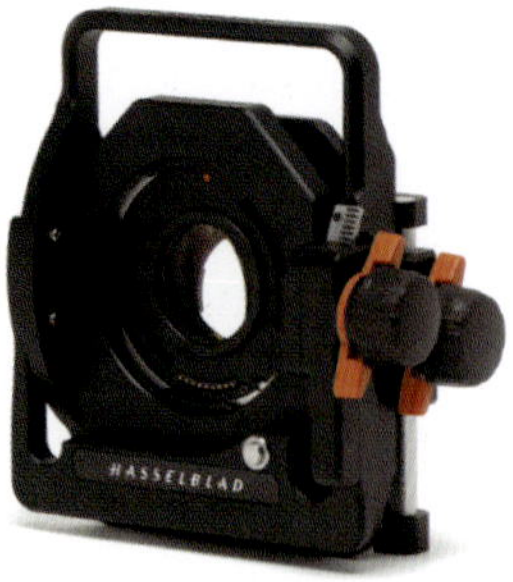

▲ Fig. 1.25
HTS 1.5 Tilt and Shift Lens Adapter from Hasselblad, giving the photographer more control over perspective.

Macro Lenses

Macro lenses are primarily designed for macrophotography, also known as close-up photography. You will probably have seen many incredible macro images of plants and insects that allow you to see every minute hair and detail. These are shot with macro lenses and they allow the photographer to focus very closely on their subject.

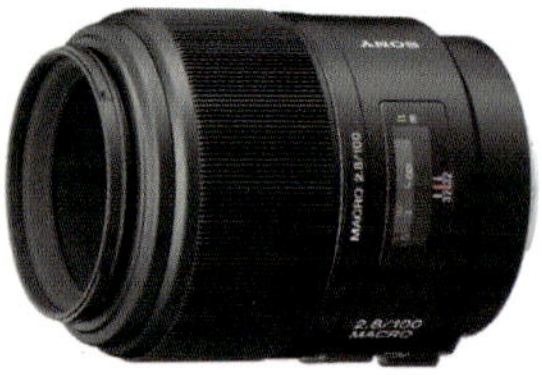

▲ Fig. 1.26
Hasselblad 4/120-II Macro Lens (medium format) and the Sony 100mm 2.8 Macro (35mm format): ideal for getting in close and maximizing shallow depth of field.

Traditionally, macro lenses look similar to a short telephoto lens and will focus within a few centimetres of the subject. They are specifically optimized for high reproduction ratios, usually 1:1 or 1:2, and their use normally depends on the focal length of the lens. Shorter focal lengths will be used for stills and product photography, whereas the longer focal lengths will be more useful for insects and applications where it is not possible for the photographer to get close to the subject without disturbance.

Macro lenses can be used in the same way as any other lens, and their excellent optics produce very sharp results, which makes them suitable for both portraits and products.

Which lens to choose?

The choice of lens is a very personal one. Many photographers swear by certain lenses and have used them for so long, they know exactly how to predict the results. Certain genres of photography have specific lenses that are more widely regarded as suitable for studio work, whether it is portrait, fashion or beauty.

It is widely accepted that a good starting point for portrait shooting would be a focal length between 85mm and 150mm (35mm equivalent). Remember that the longer the focal length, the flatter the perspective and the tighter the crop on your subject. Not only does a longer focal length help flatten the perspective, but it also tends to be more flattering for the subject. In contrast a wide-angle lens would require you to get closer to your subject, distorting the perspective and making your subject look larger – and very few people want to be larger in a photograph! Generally, 85mm is the standard, moving into 100mm and 150mm for half-length and headshots respectively.

Another consideration is the size of your studio or the dimensions of the space you are working in. If you are going to be shooting within a confined space or small home studio, then a 130mm lens may well prove to be too long, as you will be unable to step far enough away from your subject when you need to fit more of them in the frame; whereas with an 85mm, you will have a wider field of view, yet it will still be possible to move closer for a tighter crop when needed. The zoom lens has brought about a handy solution and is very popular with studio photographers. Essentially, the zoom lens does all of the work of moving in and out, allowing the photographer to remain in the same position if necessary. For the most part, studio portraits are shot between *f*8 and f16, and zoom lenses stopped down to this aperture will still prove to be fairly sharp.

It is important to stress that there are no rules, and experimentation with shorter focal length lenses can lead to some very interesting shots; however, unless you are shooting large groups, focal lengths wider than 50mm tend to distort perspectives, creating barrel distortion, which is not very flattering to the subject and will offer little control over the depth of field. It is worth considering the important factor about depth of field, as not all portrait and fashion work is photographed within a studio environment. The longer the focal length and wider the aperture, the shallower the depth of field and the more you will be able to blur the background. A blurred and out-of-focus background is often desirable for studio portraits, helping to provide separation between it and your subject.

All lenses will render light differently, and you would be forgiven for thinking that the most important part of the image is the sharp details of your subject; however, even the out-of-focus areas of your photograph are important and will be affected by the type and quality of lens you are using. Many portrait photographers prefer to have sharp subjects and blurred backgrounds, because it places the emphasis on the subject. Bokeh is the term used to describe the out-of-focus areas of your image. Good bokeh would ideally be described as a milky and undefined background, whereas poor bokeh would have defined edges. Some lenses actually have a defocus control, allowing the photographer to manipulate spherical aberration and improve the bokeh.

As for your choice of lenses a selection of prime lenses (50mm, 85mm, 100mm and 130mm) are a good start, allowing working in different studio environments. Alternatively, a smaller selection of zoom lenses, such as 24–70mm and 70–200mm, will prove to be worthy alternatives.

When selecting lenses for product photography this depends on the product; the true purpose of the photograph is usually to capture a product in the best and most appealing way possible. As a rule, it needs to be accurate, as the intended market will need a clear representation of what is being sold. For some products, say those that have been engineered, the photograph will need to be a clear and scaled representation, whereas other products, such as cosmetics or food, may rely on the photograph being more representative of a lifestyle.

As a whole, the product needs to be seen in its best light and without distortion, so you will find, as with portraits, lenses with a longer focal length tend to be most suitable. Of course, products can be anything from cars to computer processors, so each subject will require its own approach and its own lens considerations.

As a standard for tabletop products, anything from 80mm would be suitable. It is worth remembering that the longer the focal length of the lens, the shallower the depth of field, which is an important consideration should you need to photograph an arrangement of products and keep them all in focus. The addition of a good quality macro lens is also a worthwhile investment, allowing high-quality close-up shots of product details.

Although more costly, tilt and shift lenses and large format camera systems are used frequently in product photography due to their ability to correct parallax and perspective issues, and this can open up a whole new world of lenses. It is not only medium format systems that can be used with this type of system as there are third-party products, from reputable studio equipment manufacturers, such as Cambo, that will allow many DSLRs to be connected to a set of tilt and slide bellows, which may be adapted to take many of the precision lenses used on the large format system.

It is worth keeping an open mind with product photography, whilst considering the effects that certain lenses will have in terms of distortion and depth of field.

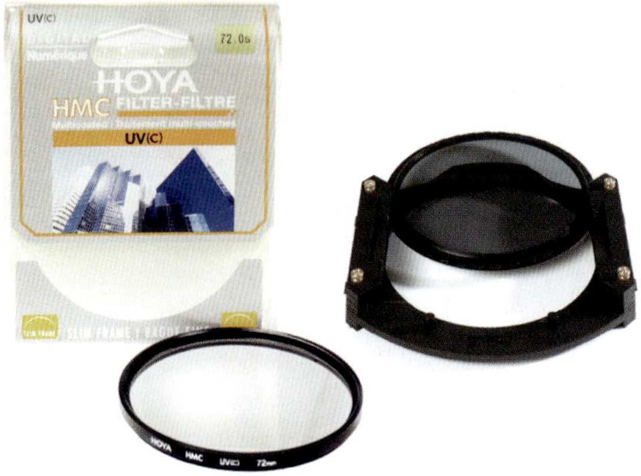

▲ Fig. 1.27
Lens filters by Hoya.

Lens Filters and Bellows

A lens filter is basically an optical filter that is placed on the front of your lens. They are available in a variety of different systems from several manufacturers; the most recognizable being the screw-in filter, available in different diameter sizes from 30.5mm to 127mm, depending on the size of the lens they are intended for. The ⌀ symbol is normally followed by the filter diameter, for example ⌀49mm. There are several plastic filter systems available, such as those made by Cokin and Lee Filters, which comprise of small Perspex sheets made to slide into a filter holder that is attached to the front of your lens.

It is easy to forget about the importance of lens filters now that most of us are in the digital age. For film users, lens filters are still very much a necessary part of the photographic kit, whereas many digital photographers have resorted to the use of post-processing techniques to correct issues. Post-processing may work fine as part of your workflow for the occasional photograph, but may prove to be highly inefficient when you have shot several hundred images. It is safe to say that regardless of your photographic genre, it is important to get the exposure, composition and colour balance as accurate as possible 'in camera', and this is where lens filters may help you achieve that.

Polarizing Filters

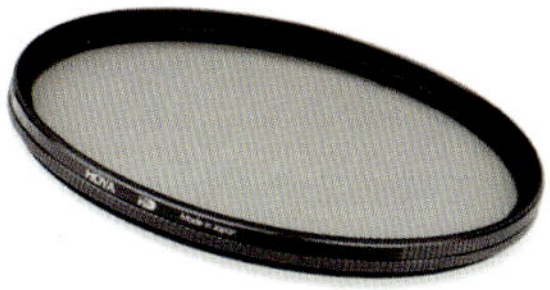

▲ Fig. 1.28
Polarizing filter: ideal for reducing reflections.

There are two types of polarizing filter: linear and circular. Circular polarizers are the most common, as they do not interfere with the camera's inbuilt metering system. Polarizing filters are as useful with digital photography as they are with film and they can be used regardless of whether you are shooting in black and white or colour. Polarizers do not alter the colour balance of the photograph, but instead filter light that has a certain direction of polarization, such as distracting reflections in glass or shiny surfaces. They also help saturate the colours of the image and are useful for darkening skies in landscape photography.

Clear, UV (Ultraviolet) and Skylight Filters

There is a difference between clear filters and UV filters, although in practice they are used in the same way. A clear lens is a 'flat' lens, in that it filters no light. Its main purpose is to protect the front element of the lens from unwanted marks and scratches – a worthwhile investment for expensive lenses. A UV filter is often used in the same way as a clear filter. It is different from the clear lens as it does actually filter out UV light. Ultraviolet light is invisible to the human eye but visible to film and digital camera sensors. The effects of UV filters are fairly neutral and as such they can remain on the front of your lens indefinitely, especially in the studio, as most studio lights have UV coated flash tubes. The effects are more obvious when shooting outside, where they help filter out the haziness caused by UV light.

Skylight filters are commonly mistaken for UV filters and have no real place within a studio environment. They are most commonly used with film and when shooting outdoors, their purpose being to remove the bluish tint often found when shooting on colour film during the day, thus improving the colour accuracy and warming up the photograph.

Colour Correction Filters

Colour correction filters are most commonly used by those photographers that shoot on film. They have several uses, such as correcting colour casts from various lighting sources such as tungsten or adding coloured effects to photographs. Their use is not restricted to coloured film however; they have an important role to play in black and white photography for contrast enhancement, where colours such as yellow help darken skies and foliage. There is no universal system for naming coloured filters, although some manufacturers make use of Wratten numbers, a system introduced by Kodak, for example: CC30R (CC meaning colour correction, 30 indicating the strength of the filter and R for the colour; in this case red). On the whole, most manufacturers will produce a series of filters, each one graded in relation to the last.

The effects produced by coloured filters can often be reproduced fairly quickly in digital photography, so they are seldom used within a colour temperature managed studio environment.

Neutral Density (ND) Filters

There are two types of ND filters: the solid ND and the graduated ND filter. A solid neutral density filter helps to equally attenuate (block out) light of all colours. It is most frequently used in landscapes to facilitate a longer exposure in natural daylight, where the lighting cannot be controlled. A graduated neutral density filter will attenuate light at different points on the filter. The most common graduated ND filter is where the filter is darker on one side. This is useful for controlling bright areas of the photograph, such as skies, to maintain a more consistent exposure across the frame. They are not in common use within the photo studio where the lighting can be consistently controlled; however, they may prove useful when shooting outdoors or on location.

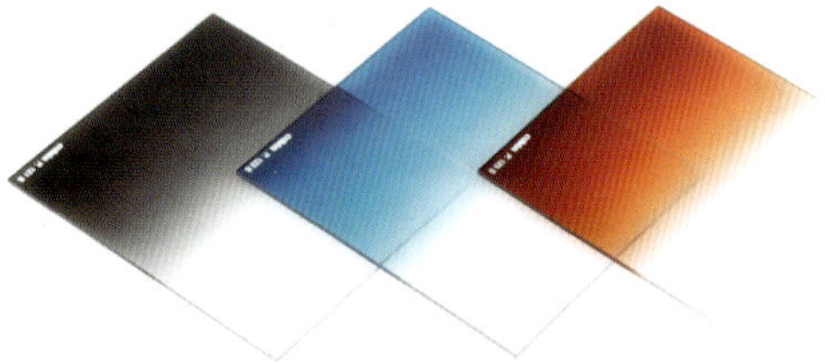

▲ Fig. 1.29
Neutral density and colour graduated filters.

Diffusion/Softening filters

The diffusion lens is popular with portrait photographers as it softens subjects and gives the image a more traditional 'hazy' effect. To some extent, these lenses have been replaced by the capabilities of modern software, which can recreate the effect; this requires more post-processing but affords you the option of removing the effect. Too much computerized blur tends to blow highlighted areas of the photograph, leading to unsightly white blurred masses, and for this reason some photographers prefer to use a diffusion filter to create a more precise and genuine effect.

Close-up filters/ Extension Bellows/ Teleconverters

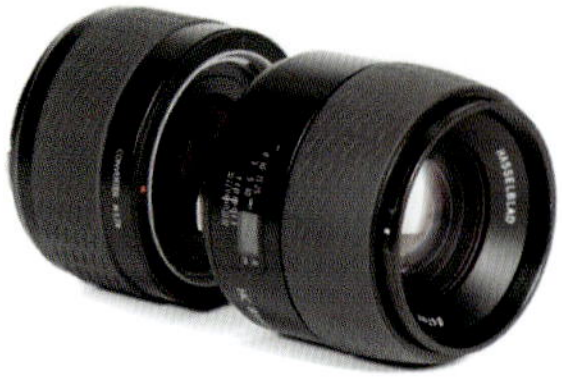

▲ Fig. 1.30
Teleconverter by Hasselblad (medium format).

The close-up filter is essentially a converging magnifying lens built into a screw-in filter housing, so it is not technically a filter. It works in a similar way to a lens found in a pair of glasses which has been placed in front of the camera's lens to magnify the subject further. Close-up lenses come in a variety of different magnifications, such as +1, +2, +3 and so on, and can be stacked (used together) to increase their magnification further. The intended market is a cost-effective alternative to the macro lens, although the optical quality is not comparable.

A cheaper alternative would be bellows, and if you have worked within a darkroom bellows will be instantly recognizable. On 35mm SLR format camera systems, an extension bellows is intended to work in the same way as the darkroom enlarger. The pleated bellows are attached to the lens mount of the camera and allow the lens to be attached to the opposing end. The bellows then allow the lens to be moved back and forth along a rail, creating an extension of dark space between the lens and sensor/film. The net result of this is increased magnification. Bellows were originally designed for manual focus 35mm film cameras and as such have no metering or autofocus capabilities, and as they make the viewfinder significantly dimmer, focusing may become more difficult, especially in the smaller viewfinders found in modern DSLRs. Manual metering needs to be compensated for by several *f* stops (depth of field).

The modern DSLR equivalent to extension bellows/extension tubes are otherwise known as teleconverters. The benefits are that they allow autofocus and metering. The principle is the same, in that spacer 'tubes' are added between the lens and camera body. In the same way close-up lenses can be stacked, and additional tubes can be added to further increase the magnification. The more tubes you add, the less light gets to the sensor/film, so if you are manually metering, you will need to adjust the camera's settings accordingly to allow for the reduction in light (usually by 'stopping up').

All of these systems are suitable for studio product photography, especially when photographing smaller products. Always take into consideration that the longer the focal length and the closer you get to your subject, the shorter the depth of field.

TRIGGERS AND LIGHT METERS

Triggers

There are two common types of triggers, namely infrared triggers and radio triggers. Infrared triggers are still in existence, although they are now somewhat dated. Basically, the infrared trigger was connected to the camera (normally via the camera's hot shoe) and projected a beam of infrared light the moment the shutter on the camera was pressed. The beam of light was instantaneously picked up by an infrared slave-cell connected to the studio light, which fired the flash.

▼ Fig. 1.31
Two-way radio triggers.

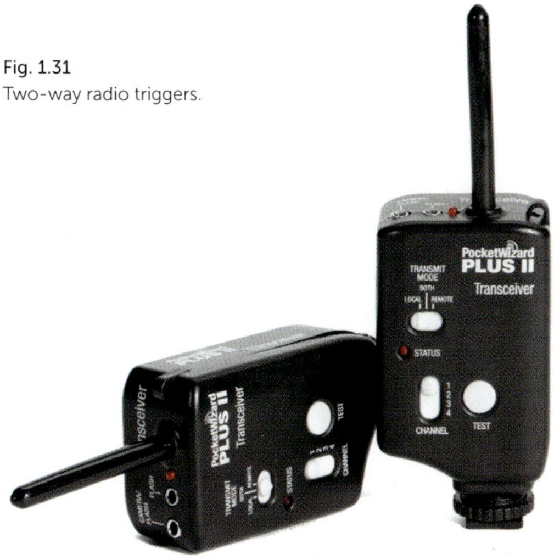

Radio triggers work in exactly the same way, although they are controlled digitally and offer a greater degree of flexibility than infrared. Most lighting manufacturers offer their own radio triggering system, plus some manufacturers also offer compatibility with third-party radio triggering systems. The radio trigger comprises a 'sender' and a 'receiver'. The sender is placed directly onto the camera's hot shoe and the photographer then sets the channel or frequency of the sender. The receiver(s) are then connected to the studio lights and set to the same radio channel or frequency as the sender. These will trigger the studio lights as soon as the camera's shutter is depressed. Setting the trigger frequency allows the photographer to control groups of studio lights independently of each other, or prevents accidental misfires if shooting in a busy studio complex, where other photographers may be shooting on the same triggering system and the same channel.

The benefits of using a radio triggering system are huge, in that they do not suffer from mechanical breaks, restrict movement or allow physical barriers such as walls to obscure the trigger signal as in the case of infrared.

Triggering for some photographers is a key issue, especially when they need to capture movement. As well as their connection to the flash heads, triggers can also be used by the light meter or can be programmed to fire lights in sequence and even trigger several cameras remotely.

Motion and Sound Triggers

It is quite possible to rely just on regular radio triggers and intuition for timing. On the other hand a much more reliable and predictable way would be to utilize a sonic or infrared triggering device to fire the shutter the moment the photographer triggers the sensor. This in turn fires the shutter on the camera and then triggers the flash via the regular radio triggers. It sounds complicated but is actually very simple using the right device. For quite some time, these triggers have been a bespoke order that have been especially constructed for certain professionals. Luckily, they are now becoming available for the average photographer. The trigger can be activated sonically or via an infrared beam, which in turn may be timed and delayed for several fractions of a second to trigger the camera just at the right time. With a little practice, it is possible to time an event precisely. In [Fig. 4.3] to capture the water at the right moment a sonic sensor was used to activate the shutter on the camera at the moment of impact, proving to be far more reliable than simple guesswork.

▼ Fig. 1.32
Motion and sound triggering system by Flaghead Photographic Ltd, allowing control over flash timing and delay.

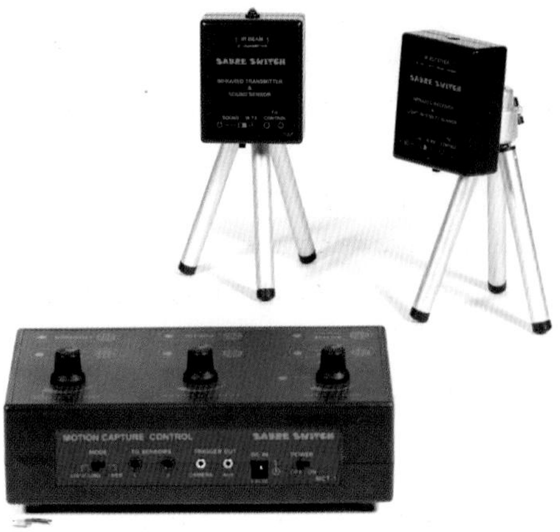

Sync Speed and Leaf Shutter

You would be forgiven for thinking that you can set your camera's shutter speed to any value when using studio flash, but you would be wrong. Even modern DSLRs need to sync accurately with the flash, so will be limited as to the shutter speed they can use. Much of this depends on the camera model itself, so it is advisable that you check the recommended settings for your camera.

The majority of modern DSLR camera systems utilize a focal-plane shutter. It is not the intention of this book to go into too much depth about shutter technology, as it would require an entire chapter of its own; however, it helps to be aware that the camera uses metal blades/curtains that travel across the frame of the sensor to correctly expose the image (either vertically or horizontally, depending on camera model). So, if we take for example the horizontal focal-plane shutter; the moment the shutter is depressed, the first curtain will travel across the sensor, followed by the second curtain a fraction of a second later. Depending on the desired shutter speed, both curtains may travel over the sensor at the same time, leaving a small slit to allow the light through. The timing between the two curtains depends on the shutter speed. The faster they travel, the faster the shutter speed, the closer together they will be. Focal-plane shutters can accurately and reliably achieve shutter speeds of 1/8000sec and above. Their Achilles heel is studio flash. The second curtain is unable to cross the sensor until the flash has fired, and if it does, it will become exposed on the image as a dark vignette towards the edge of the frame. The sync speed is therefore limited to the maximum speed that these shutters can travel across the film/sensor whilst allowing the flash to fire. Typical focal-plane shutters are limited to sync speeds of around 1/200–1/250sec, although there are some models that can sync at faster speeds.

The exception to this rule is the leaf shutter. The leaf shutter resides within the lens rather than the

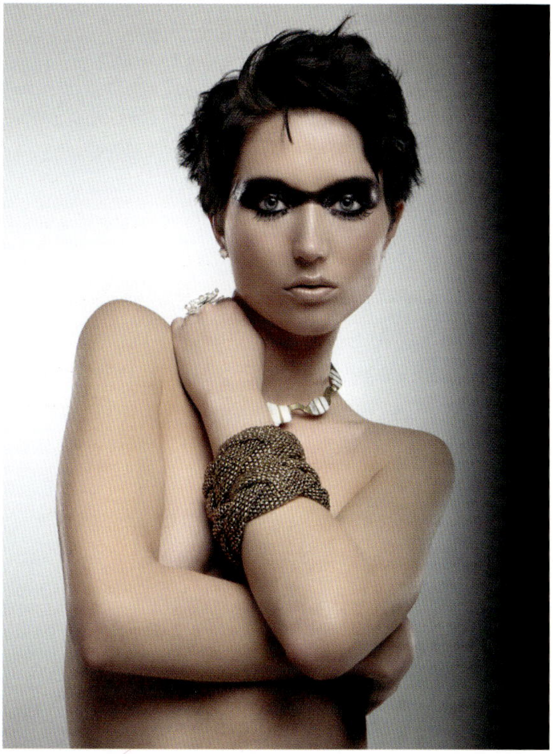

▲ Fig. 1.33
Focal-plane shutters can themselves appear in the photograph when used in excess of the manufacturer's recommended synchronization speed.

camera and consists of several 'leafed' blades that overlap each other and form a diaphragm. When the shutter fires, the leaf shutter opens, allowing light through the centre. Modern leaf shutters can be accurately computer controlled, such as the highly acclaimed and popular system designed and employed by the high-end camera manufacturer Hasselblad. Leaf shutters facilitate much higher synchronization speeds of around 1/800sec because the shutter can remain fully open. The leaf shutter also offers several advantages to photographers when using professional flash systems, allowing them to control ambient light more effectively and make several exposures on the same frame. The downside to the leaf shutter is that it generally makes lenses more expensive, as the shutter mechanism has to be built into each lens.

Light/Flash Meters and Metering

Depending on whether you are shooting with continuous light or flash your method of metering will differ, and it will for the large part influence your choice of reflective or incidental meter readings. Continuous lighting is certainly more intuitive than flash, in that you can immediately see the lighting levels and ratios of each light, and for this reason there are many studio photographers that use reflective meter readings with simple setups, either via spot readings or their camera's inbuilt TTL (Through The Lens) metering system. There are of course times when a light meter will be necessary, even with continuous lighting, especially when you need to ensure consistency of lighting on a large set.

Flash lighting on the other hand is different in many ways. Firstly, it requires a flash meter and not a light meter, so it will not work with the camera's inbuilt metering system. Secondly, it requires the photographer to take an incidental meter reading and not a reflective meter reading. The difference is clear and significant. A reflective meter reading measures the light reflecting/bouncing off a subject (similar system to TTL metering). An incidental meter reading measures the light landing on the subject, which proves to be more accurate as the meter readings are not distorted by the differences between shiny and matt surfaces.

A flash meter will measure the incidental light through the white plastic diffusion dome found on the meter. It makes the measurement in the fraction of a second it takes for the flash to fire and then displays the corresponding meter reading, ready for the photographer to dial the settings into the camera, the key settings being only the aperture and ASA/ISO. The shutter speed within a pure studio environment is the least relevant of the three settings, providing it is used within the camera manufacturer's flash synchronization tolerances. Sync speeds are usually around 1/125sec on SLR, 1/200sec on 35mm DSLR and up to 1/800sec on Medium Format systems that employ a leaf shutter system. This is because flash duration (normally the time it takes for the flash to peak and dissipate) is significantly quicker than the shutter speed. In a theoretical pure studio environment, it is assumed that there is no ambient light and the subject is lit only by the flash, so a moderately slow shutter speed would not make a difference. In reality, ambient light is often present from a mixture of daylight and incandescent light, making shutter speed more relevant.

The flash meter remains an important piece of studio equipment, even with the availability of instant previews and histograms on digital systems. It allows the photographer to measure accurately lighting ratios with absolute consistency. With time and practice, most studio photographers develop an almost intuitive and instinctive approach to their lighting equipment and metering, enabling them to dial in settings based on experience and understanding gained through their use of a meter. Histograms on the other hand are a useful tool for judging the tonal information captured in a given photograph and whether the information captured is within the camera's dynamic range. A histogram cannot tell you about lighting ratios, the most suitable balance between flash and ambient lighting or whether the subject within the scene is properly exposed. The histogram is only a guide, whereas a meter reading is an accurate measurement of the lighting falling on the subject.

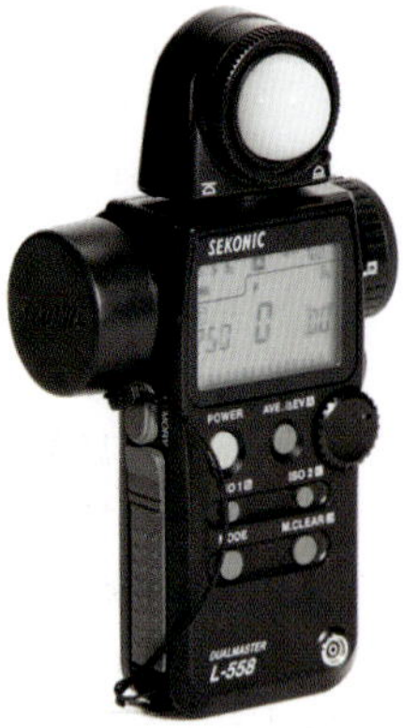

▲ Fig. 1.34
Sekonic flash meter.

GENERAL STUDIO EQUIPMENT

Studio Stands and Tripods

Studio stands and tripods are key pieces of equipment when shooting in the studio, more so when shooting products. They are less commonly used when shooting portraits and other model based studio work, as the subject and the photographs tend to be more dynamic, so the photographer cannot always afford to be rooted to one particular spot with a tripod. As to whether you need to use a tripod or studio stand, this will to some degree depend on what you are shooting and the camera system you are using. Products are fairly static, and there are times when it is important to remain consistent with height and angle when shooting a series of products, which is where a support of some description lends itself.

So what are the differences between a studio stand and a tripod? Studio stands are not designed to be very portable. They are large and heavy articulated stands that glide around on wheels within the professional studio. The arms and joints of the stand are usually designed for precision positioning and engineered with ball bearing and hydraulic joints. They are ideal for large format and heavy camera systems, where small and precise movements are necessary, and they have enough weight to allow cameras to be placed directly above products, like with a boom arm.

In comparison, tripods are considerably smaller, lighter and designed for portability. There is a broad

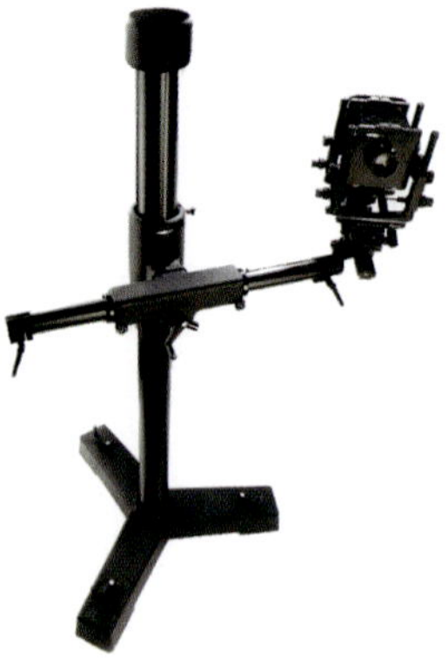

▲ Fig. 1.35
Sturdy studio stand from Cambo.

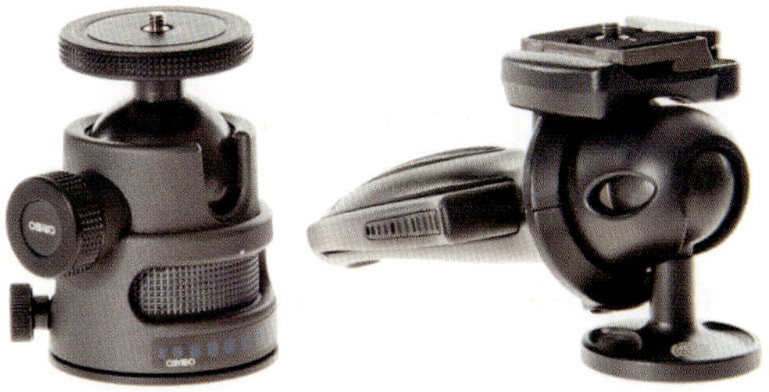

▲ Fig. 1.36
Tripod heads from Cambo and Manfrotto.

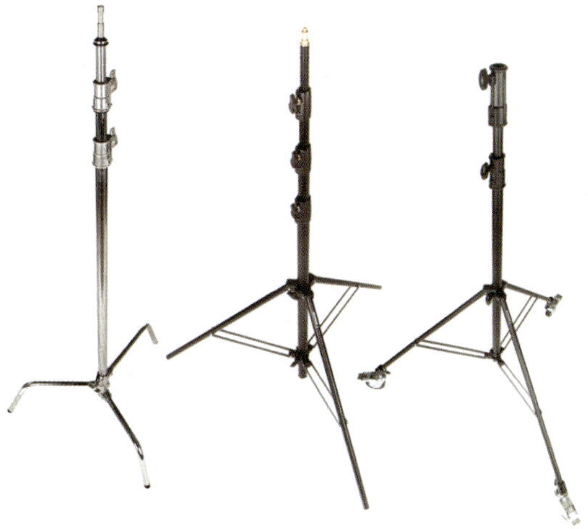

▲ Fig. 1.37
Common lighting stands: (left) C-Stand, (middle) air-cushioned stand, (right) heavy duty stand.

range of tripods available that can support different weights, and they are considerably cheaper than a studio stand. It is really a matter of workflow and personal preference. If you are working from a permanent studio and shooting a lot of product photography, then a studio stand would be a good investment. If you need to work light and remain flexible, then a tripod would prove more suitable.

Lighting Stands and Clamps

Lighting stands are the stands that support your studio lights. There are several different brands and types available, designed for different uses. The most common lighting stand is the type normally supplied with lighting kits. They are a lightweight extending tubular design that fold away for maximum portability and have been adapted for several different purposes, such as backlight stands and floor stands. For the majority of photographers and day-to-day shooting, these stands are perfectly adequate and ideal for smaller heads, small-to-medium-sized softboxes and parabolics.

There are times when heavier support stands are needed, especially when using heavy lighting heads as big modifiers. For this, Century Stands (most commonly known as C-Stands) produced by several companies, are more adept at taking weight, as they are fitted with counter-balances and their legs partially buried in soft earth or sand. Century stands are heavier and more expensive than the standard tubular stands, so are able to support more weight at a greater height, without bowing or flexing.

Boom arms and boom stands are essentially lighting stands with an extending arm that can be rotated at an angle. A studio head is placed at one end of the extending arm and a counterbalance at the other. They allow photographers to place lights and other equipment directly above subjects without the stand straying into the camera frame. Booms are available in several forms, from small extending arms that can be attached to lightweight stands right though to purpose-built, heavy-duty, fully articulated gear-operated stands. A boom is an essential piece of equipment for people and product photographers, and consideration should be given to the weight of heads and modifiers in use before purchasing. Boom arms that are not strong enough to support the weight of the equipment in use will fail with fairly catastrophic consequences.

As you would expect, to accompany the stands there are a range of clamps. These are most utilized in the professional studio, frequently by product photographers to support products, lighting and props in specific positions. Clamps are available in different sizes and designs for many different applications from joining overhead lighting support systems to clamping background paper. It is generally recommended for all photographers to carry several small grips and clamps in their kit bag, including people photographers, as they have many uses, such as clipping together baggy clothing on models and attaching coloured gels to studio lights.

Tethered Shooting

Tethered shooting is still a mystery to many digital photographers, yet once they have utilized it, they rarely want to return to using the camera's LCD. All photographers have shot directly to card or directly to film, depending on whether they are shooting digital or film. It is flexible, portable and very quick.

Tethered shooting is just as quick, although slightly less portable, as the camera is connected (tethered) directly to the computer or laptop via USB or Firewire cable. The camera's functions can be controlled either on the camera or via the software, and a storage card is no longer necessary as all images are stored directly onto the computer's hard drive. The great benefit is that you get a much larger image on the computer screen than you do on the camera's LCD, enabling you to see much more detail in the images as you are shooting, plus it can be useful for checking the accuracy of the white balance and exposure when using a calibrated system.

For product photography and high-end medium format camera systems, tethered shooting is a must. It reduces the need for the photographer to constantly strain to look down the viewfinder when the camera is placed in an awkward position and to constantly change media card. Focusing, camera settings and storage can all be done conveniently via the software on the computer.

Common Reflectors/Shapers

Umbrella

There are several types of umbrella, which vary in size and occasionally in shape. The two most common and readily available types of umbrella are reflective and shoot-through. As the names suggest, reflective umbrellas reflect the light back towards the subject, whereas shoot-through umbrellas are

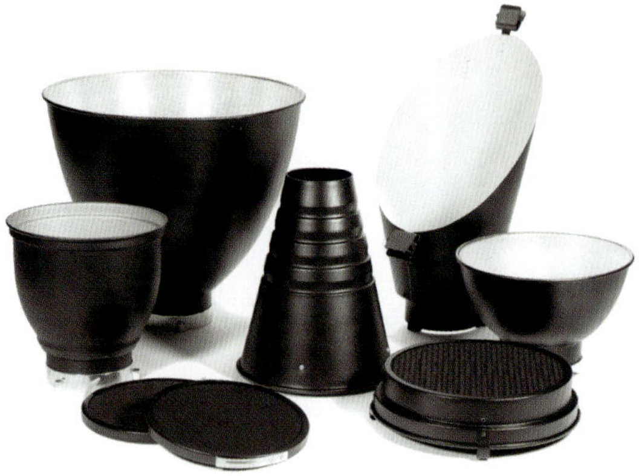

▲ Fig. 1.38
Various reflectors.

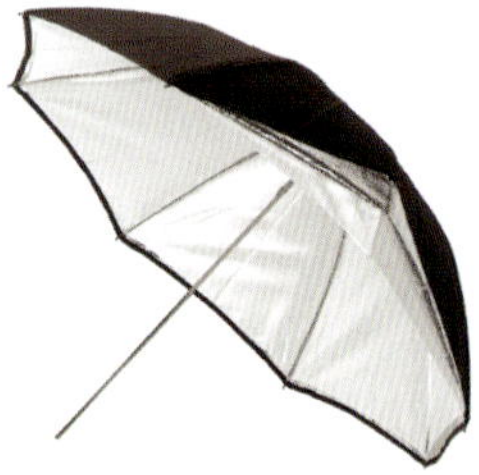

▲ Fig. 1.39
Umbrella.

made from translucent fabric and allow the light to pass through the umbrella. Umbrellas create a broad spread of light, with the contrast depending on the type of umbrella and reflective surface used. More expensive two-metre umbrellas are available for larger subjects, such as groups and automotive photography.

Softbox

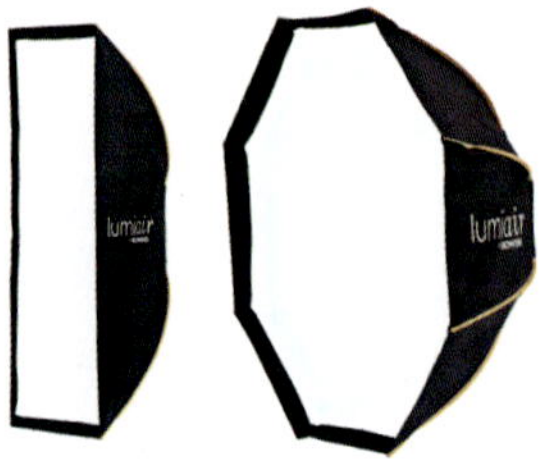

▲ Fig. 1.40
Stripbox and Octabox.

As the name suggests a softbox is essentially a box that produces soft light. Softboxes come in many different sizes and shapes, with the shape of the box forming part of the name, such as Octabox (eight sides), Hexbox (six sides) and Stripbox (thin softbox). The box is erected using flexible rods that shape the covering (reflective on the inside and black on the outside). Once constructed, a white nylon diffuser is fixed to the open aperture of the box to soften the light. The most common type of softbox fits directly to the front of the studio head, allowing the light to pass directly out of the front diffuser. More expensive models allow heads to be inverted within the box, allowing the light to bounce off the internal surfaces before travelling out of the diffuser, thus creating a flatter and more even light. Softboxes have a broad range of uses and afford more control over the light. They are often used for portraits but less so for professional beauty work due to the square shape and catchlight.

Beauty Dish

Beauty dishes come in several sizes and are ideal for single portraits and beauty style photographs. The dishes are equipped with a centralized diffuser built into the dish. The diffuser bounces the direct light back into the bowl of the reflector, helping to reduce proximity hot-spots and create a softer light that is more flattering. They occasionally come with additional diffusers and 'shower-caps' to further soften the light. Beauty dishes are favoured by beauty photographers, as the round reflector is more flattering to the shape of the face when in broad lighting. They produce a slightly harder and more defined light than a softbox.

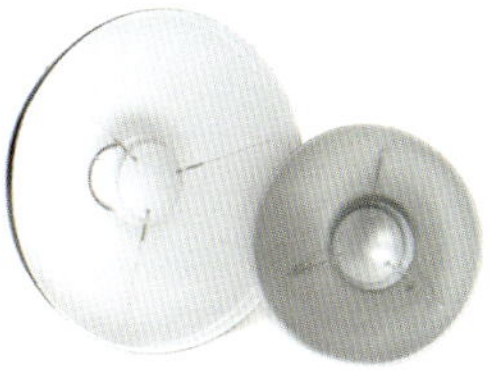

▲ Fig. 1.41
Different size beauty dishes from Bowens.

Narrow Reflectors (Snoots): 10–20 Degree Spread

Reflectors this narrow are usually in the form of snoots. These are cone-shaped to deliver a controlled spot of light. Snoots create defined hard shadows and can be coupled with honeycomb grids to concentrate the light further, lighting small areas.

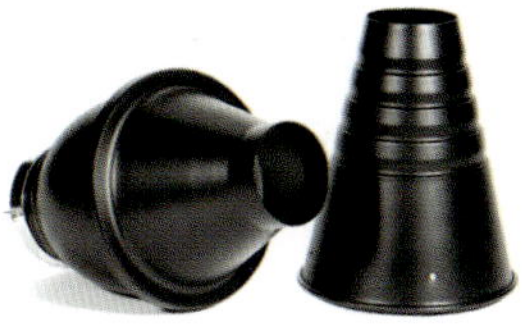

▲ Fig. 1.42
Snoot.

Directional Reflectors: 25–50 Degree Spread

A directional reflector is designed to project the light forwards and usually take on more of a parabolic shape. The longer and narrower the reflector, the tighter and more directional the light will be. Their use is varied and will depend on how much control is needed over the light and the amount of power you want to place in a particular area. When used as key lights, they tend to produce long, well-defined shadows with high-contrast. The coverage will depend entirely on the size of the reflector. Many photographers find them useful for projecting light and maximizing output. They can also be useful for lighting specific areas with honeycomb grids and background scenery/paper. As with all reflectors, the internal coating will directly affect the intensity of the light.

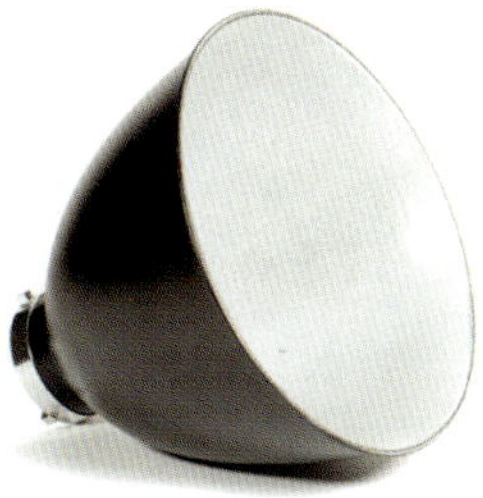

▲ Fig. 1.43
Directional reflector: projecting more light forwards.

Standard Reflectors: 50–60 Degree Spread

Medium-angled reflectors sit in between wide-angled reflectors and directional reflectors. They create a medium amount of spread of light and can be used in a wide variety of lighting situations. They are normally shorter and broader in design than directional reflectors and less open than wide-angled reflectors. They are particularly useful when fitted with honeycomb grids and barn doors to help control and direct the light in specific areas. As with all reflectors, the internal coating will directly affect the intensity of the light.

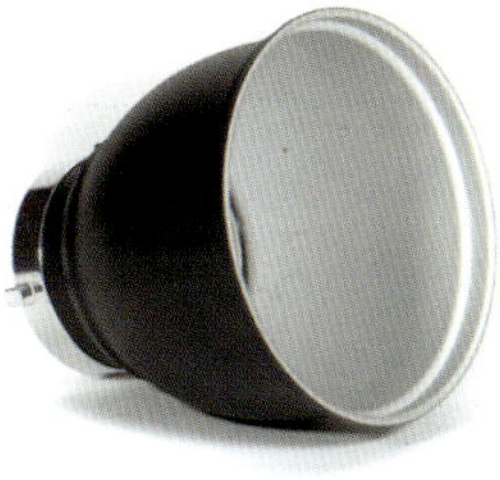

▲ Fig. 1.44
Standard reflector offering medium projection and spread of light.

Medium- to Wide-Angle Reflector: 60–70 Degree Spread

There is no absolute definition of a medium- to wide-angle reflector as it depends entirely on each individual manufacturer and how they classify them. Some manufacturers classify 65 degrees as a standard reflector, whilst others will market them as medium- to wide-angle. They basically spread the light more than a standard reflector and are used to cover a larger area. They can be ideal for replicating sunlight when placed at a distance or for using with gels to colour a broad area. The internal coating will directly affect the intensity of the light. As with standard reflectors, they are particularly effective when used with honeycomb grids and barn doors to control the light.

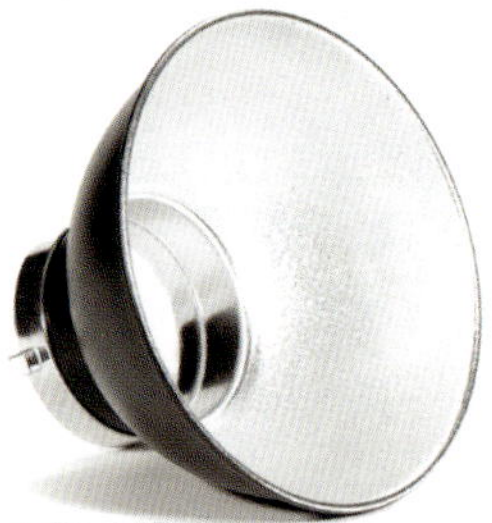

▲ Fig. 1.45
Medium- to wide-angle reflector: a slightly greater spread of light than a standard reflector.

Wide-Angle Reflector: 70+ Degrees

The wide-angle reflector allows the light to cover a larger area. The most common use is larger beauty dishes and umbrella reflectors. They are usually shallow in depth, allowing the light to spread out quickly. Wide-angled reflectors may also prove useful for bouncing light off surfaces within smaller environments. Surfaces for umbrella reflectors are normally glossy to maximize light output, whereas beauty dishes are coated to help diffuse the light.

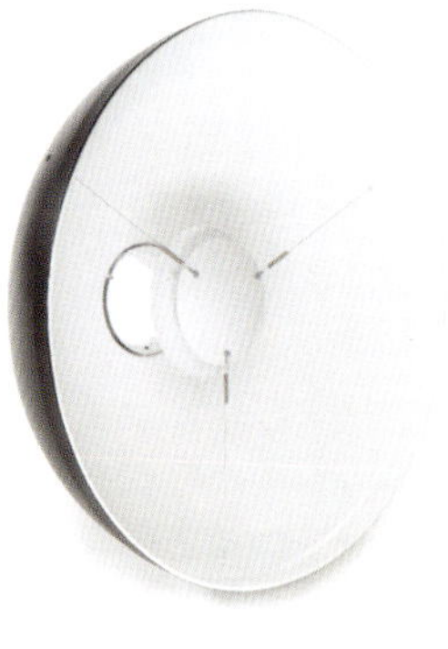

▲ Fig. 1.46
Wide-angle reflector: offering a broad spread of light with less control.

Honeycomb Grids

Honeycomb grids are perfect for controlling the direction of the light, increasing contrast and shadow definition. The larger the honeycomb, the wider the spread of light and vice-versa. They do not have universal fittings and are designed to fit specific reflectors, simply push-fitting or clipping into the front of the reflector. Honeycomb grids have a broad range of uses and are particularly useful when utilizing several different light sources to highlight different areas.

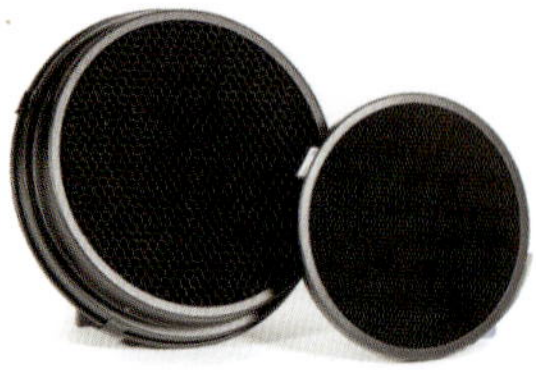

▲ Fig. 1.47
Honeycomb grid: used with reflectors for controlling the spread of light.

Egg Crates

Egg crates are for use with softboxes. They fit into the front of the softbox over the diffuser panel. Their job is similar to that of the honeycomb grid, in that they are there to help restrict the spread of the light, giving you more directional control and less spill, whilst still maintaining a soft light. Egg crates are usually designed to fit specific softboxes and are not necessarily a universal fit.

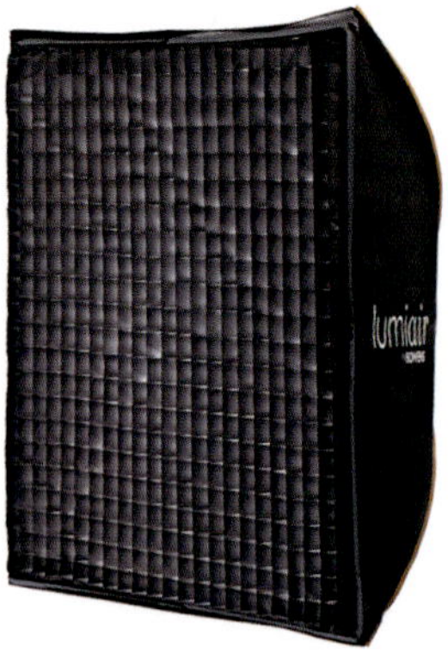

▲ Fig. 1.48
Egg crate: used in softboxes to help control the spread of light.

Fresnel Lens

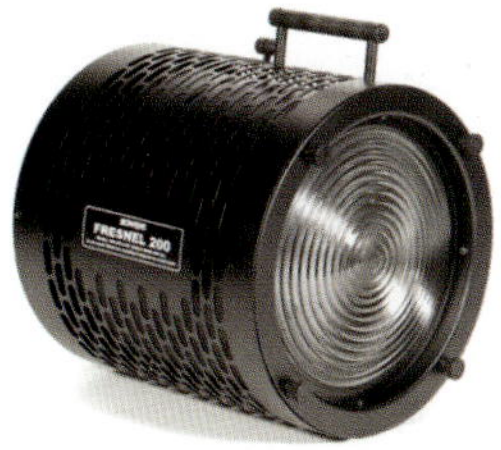

▲ Fig. 1.49
Bowens fresnel attachment: focused and controlled light, ideal for Hollywood lighting.

The Fresnel lens (pronounced Fray-nel) is similar to that seen in a lighthouse, named after the French scientist Augustin-Jean Fresnel. It consists of a series of concentric angular sections to focus the light. Apart from lighthouses, the Fresnel lens has been made instantly recognizable by the use of HMI stage lighting and Hollywood-style lighting. Many lenses include a built-in iris to help narrow the beam of light and produce a central spot effect with defined shadows, with a gently feathered outward gradient. The Fresnel is ideal for portrait and fashion photography, offering a large amount of control over the spread of the light.

Spotlights/Attachments

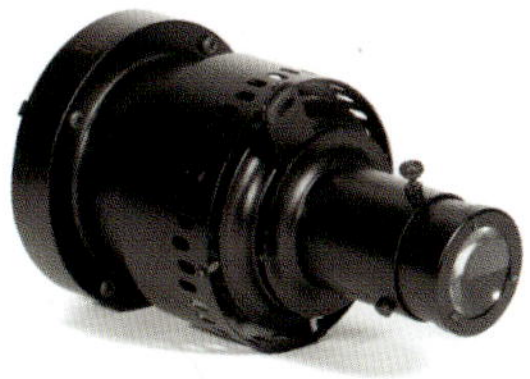

▲ Fig. 1.50
Bowens spot attachment: ideal for gobos and lighting small areas.

A spotlight produces a defined spot of light. It is different to the snoot because the light is projected through a series of lenses, allowing the photographer to focus and defocus the spot, intensifying or softening the shadow edges. The focus light also allows them to be used with gobos, masks and patterns to project shapes. Spot attachments with multiple lenses may be adjusted to change the spread of the light.

Barndoors

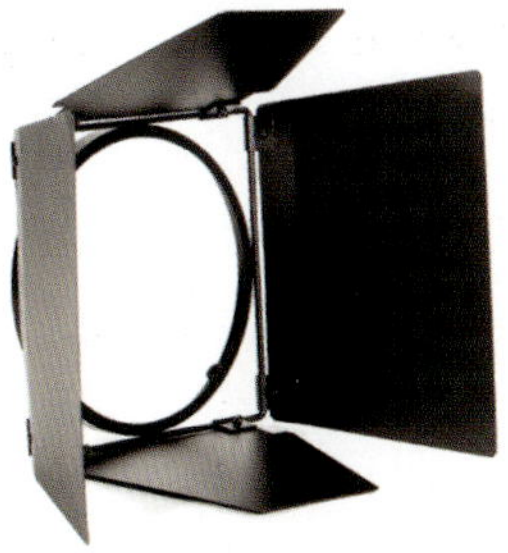

▲ Fig. 1.51
Barndoors: ideal for flagging light and reducing unwanted spill.

Barndoors are useful pieces of studio equipment. They fit onto the front of various reflectors and allow the photographer to flag the light, helping to control unwanted spill. The doors may be moved to increase or reduce the amount of light spilling onto other parts of the set. They are particularly handy when controlling gelled lights.

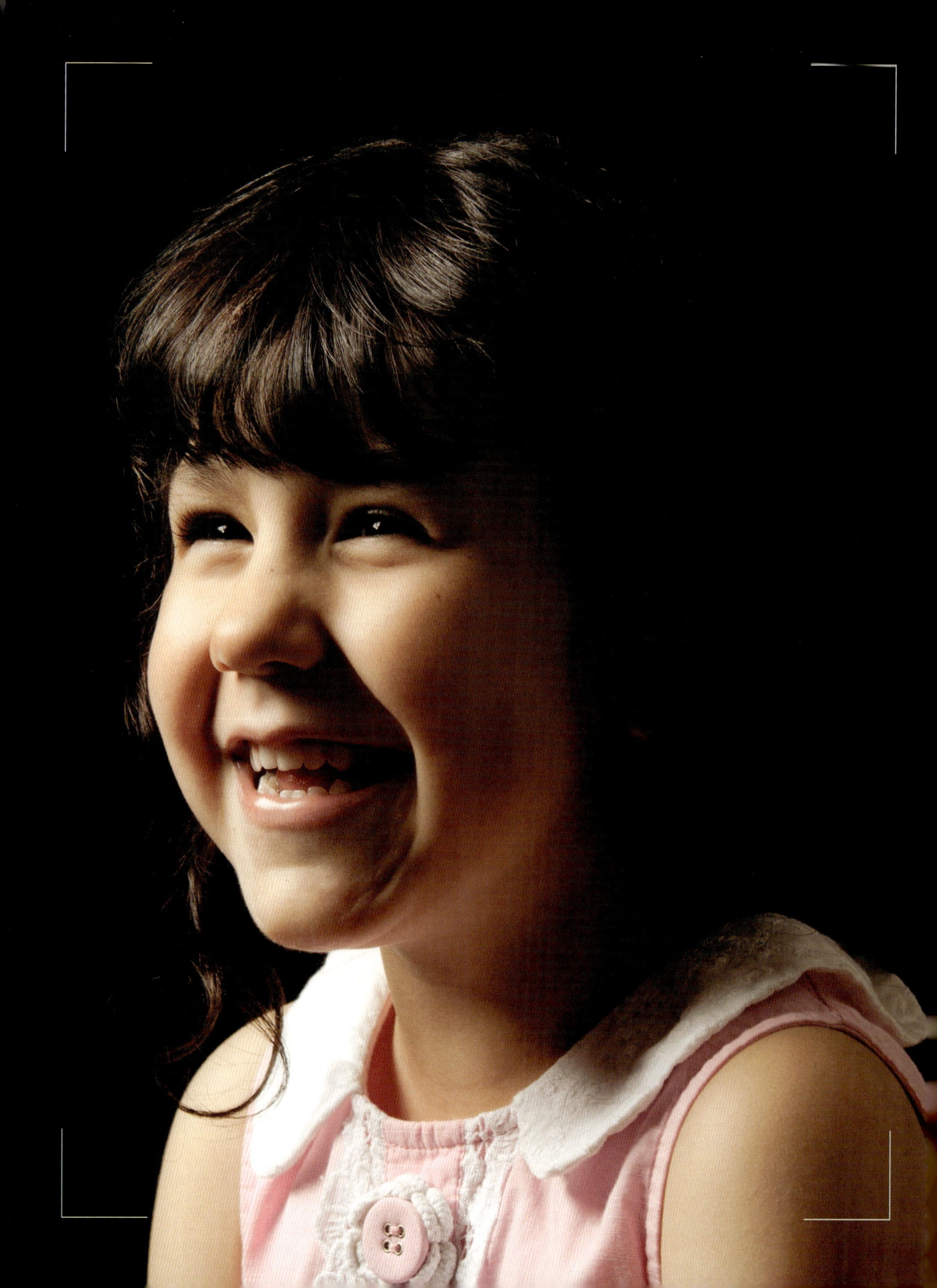

Chapter 2

Basic Skills

SHAPING THE FACE

Shaping the face is one of those important things that many photographers (whether amateur or professional) frequently neglect, yet it can instantly transform a photograph from an average shot into a good one. Everything revolves around the positioning of the face in relation to the light. Slight movement of the key light or the face is all that is required to shape the face. Controlling the light and the shadows in this way remains one of the underlying principles all studio-based photography.

In terms of photographing people, the four most commonly known principles are Short Lighting, Rembrandt Lighting, Broad Lighting and Butterfly Lighting. Other lighting styles that can be derived from these setups are Loop Lighting and Split Lighting. Understanding the basics requires a little practice, but will help you achieve the best possible results every time.

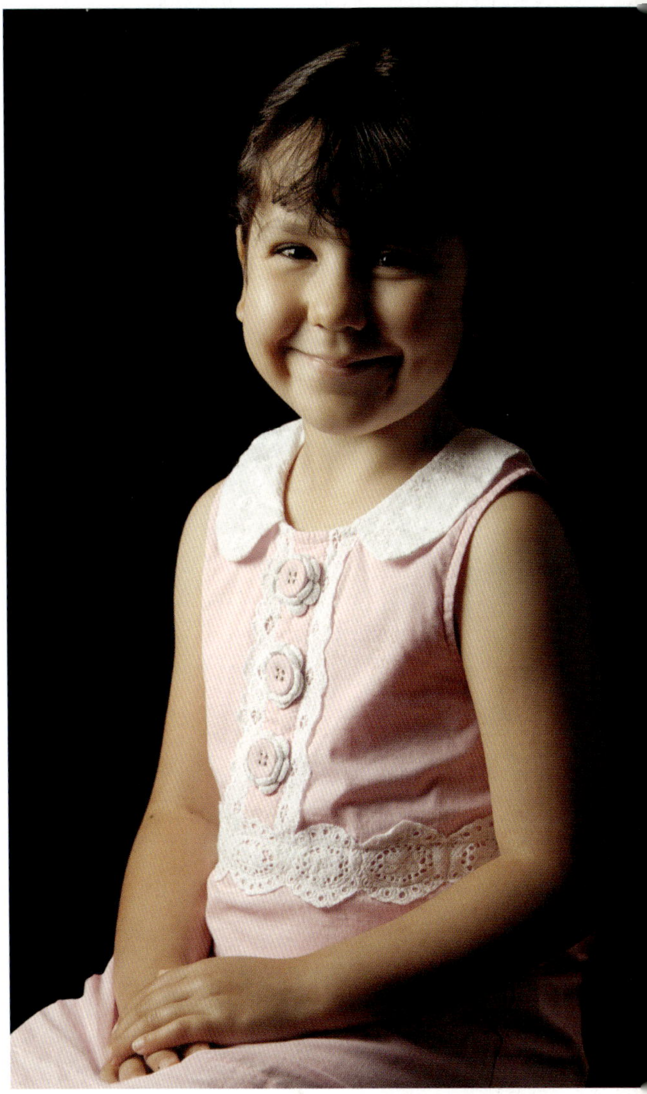

▲ Fig. 2.1
Portrait. Model: Grace Hough.

◄ Image © Christian Hough. Model: Grace Hough.

Short Lighting

Short lighting lights the shortest side of the face, which is further from the camera (normally from cheek to cheek). If you examine the photograph [Fig. 2.2], you will see that the broadest side of the face nearest the camera (ear to chin) is in the shadows. Short lighting makes the face look slimmer and frequently brings out the shape of the mouth and cheeks. Quite often short lighting is the most flattering, especially when photographing people with rounder faces.

However, short lighting techniques are not always suitable for all subjects. For example, if your subject has a tall or long face, you may find that short lighting will make them look too thin. It also requires your subject to remain fairly static, because small movements of the head will change the lighting dramatically as the face moves in and out of the shadows.

HOW IT'S DONE

Sit your subject in front of the camera, positioning at a slight angle, so that the ear is facing the camera and the far eye is still visible.

Now move your key light so that it is approximately 90 degrees to the camera and raise it between 50cm and one metre higher than the subject, so that the catchlight still remains in the eye. The height you position it will depend largely on the face of the subject and the size of the modifier you are using. The idea is to cast the shadows downwards, so that they shape the chin and the nose.

To fine-tune the lighting ask your subject to pose, then move the light around so that it lights the nearside cheek (cheek nearest the camera).

You will find that if your subject subsequently turns to face the camera completely, most of the front of the face will now be in the shadows, and only the ear and cheek will remain lit.

▼ Short lighting.

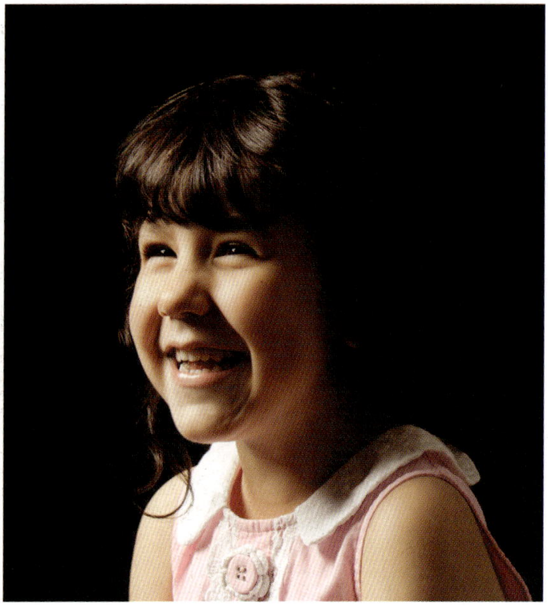

▶ Short Rembrandt lighting.
▶ Split lighting.

Short Rembrandt Lighting (including Split Lighting)

Rembrandt lighting takes its name from the paintings of Rembrandt, in which he used to paint a small inverted triangle of light under-eye on the shaded side of the face. This is caused by the light passing diagonally across the face, over the top of the nose and onto the cheek, creating the inverted triangle shape. In the first image, the Rembrandt lighting is derived from a short lighting technique. When used in this way it is particularly flattering to rounder faces. However, it requires more control than standard short lighting as the small movements of the face towards the light will quickly result in a standard short lighting pattern, whilst movements away from the light will result in a split lighting effect.

Split lighting, on the other hand, is a little more dramatic and merely involves moving the light directly to the side of the subject, to light one side of the face only. This is sometimes achievable by getting the subject to directly face the camera within a short lighting setup. Its applications are somewhat limited, but it can be used to good effect on dark backgrounds, making the face disappear gradually into the shadows on the far side.

HOW IT'S DONE

To achieve the short Rembrandt lighting effect, sit your subject in front of the camera, positioning them at a slight angle, so that the ear is facing the camera and the far eye is still visible.

Now move your key light so that it is approximately 90 degrees to the camera and raise it between 50cm and 1 metre higher than the subject. The idea is that the catchlight is at the 10 or 11 o'clock position in the eye if the light is positioned to camera left (or the one or two o'clock position if the light is positioned to camera right).

This will naturally throw the light downwards and across the face. The nose should shadow the cheek, whereas the light travelling over the bridge of the nose will light the area just under the eye.

It is of course possible to retain this effect even if your subject is facing directly towards the camera, and it requires you only to move the light when your subject changes position.

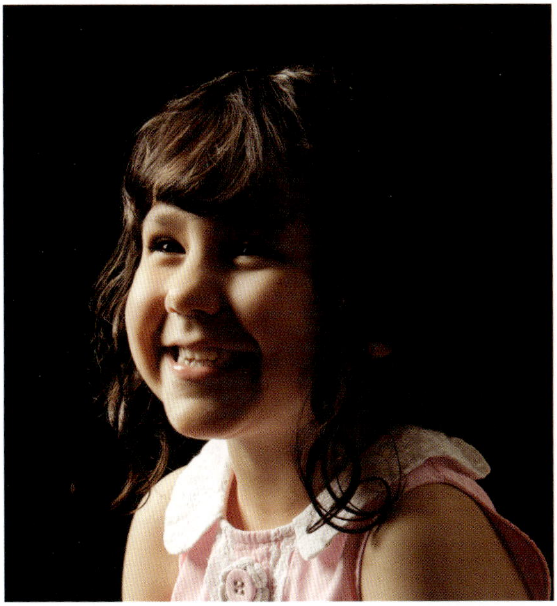

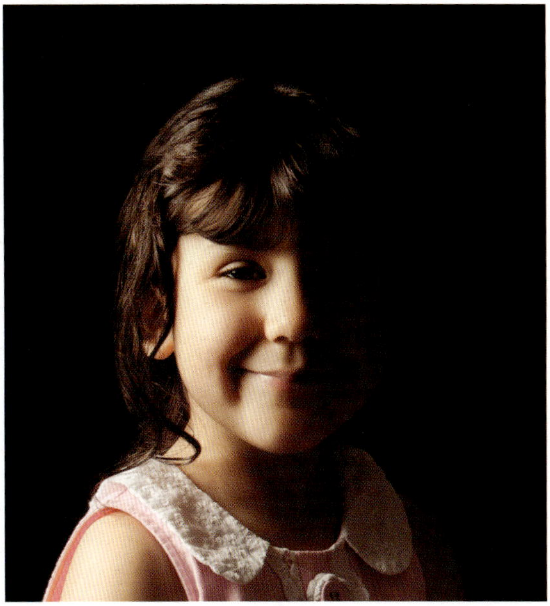

Broad Lighting (including Rembrandt Lighting)

Broad lighting is by far the most common form of lighting. It lights the broadest side of the face nearest the camera, that is, from ear to chin. Broad lighting setups are very flexible, in that they allow a subject to move more freely in front of the camera without the face being lost in the shadows. However, it is not always the most flattering of lighting and has a tendency to make people with rounder faces look much larger as it lights a greater area of the face. On the flip side, it is good for individuals that have tall or thin faces, which is why it is frequently used with professional models. You will also find it utilized in family portraits, especially with boisterous children that are difficult or impossible to keep still long enough to make use of any form of short lighting. Changes in position of the subject will easily change the broad lighting into a broad, head-on Rembrandt lighting pattern, also known as 'loop lighting'.

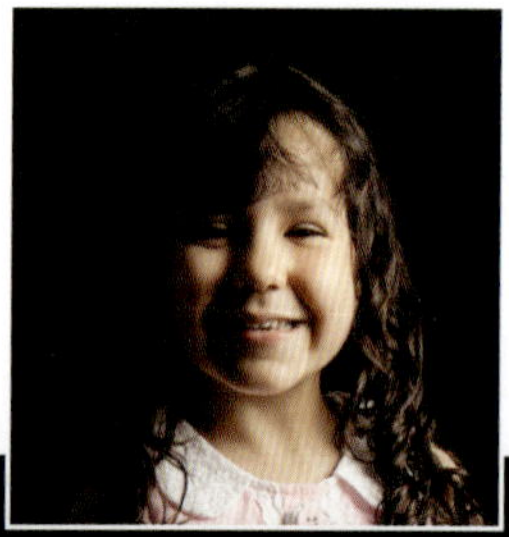

▶ Broad Rembrandt lighting.

▼ Broad lighting.

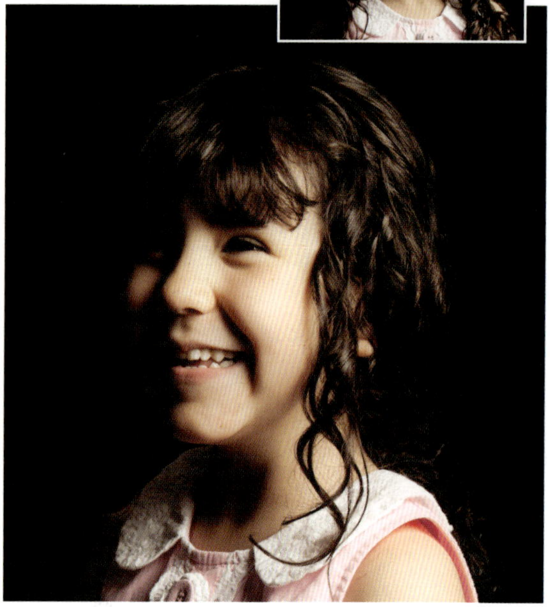

HOW IT'S DONE

Broad lighting is by far the most common approach to portrait photography.

Begin by positioning the studio light approximately 45 degrees off-axis to the camera and meter to approximately *f*11. To shape the face with more shadows, simply move the light left or right around the camera axis. The further around to the side you move the light, the further into the shadow the far side of the face will be.

It is a good idea to start with the subject facing head-on to the camera and adjusting the light until the catchlight is at the 10 or 11 o'clock position in the eye if the light is positioned to camera left (or the 1 or 2 o'clock position if the light is positioned

to camera right). You will find that by doing this, the light will be flattering whether the subject is broad lit facing side-on or head-on.

By keeping the light in the same position and moving the subject, we can instantly change the shape of the face. As the subject moves and faces directly towards the camera, the shape of the face changes and the broad lighting can instantly become loop lighting, where the nose creates a looped shadow on the far side of the face.

By moving the light just a little further around the side of the subject, you can achieve a face-on Rembrandt lighting effect. The key to this remains the height and position of the key light.

Butterfly Lighting

Butterfly lighting refers to the shape of the shadow that is created under the nose. It is known for producing very dramatic lighting and is frequently used in fashion photography. It is perhaps controlling the length of shadows that will make the greatest difference to this type of lighting. You will find that as the subject moves either left or right, the butterfly lighting actually becomes a broad lighting technique, so it is more suitable to subjects with a taller and slimmer face.

Lighting takes practice, but it should be fully understood if you are to build a solid foundation for your photographic career. It is also important to work quickly and professionally so that your subject doesn't lose interest and your shoot doesn't lose its impetus.

HOW IT'S DONE

In an ideal world, using a boom arm/stand makes your life a lot easier as it allows you to place the light closer to the subject without the stand blocking the field of vision between the camera and the subject. However, it is possible to use a regular lighting stand and place it directly behind you and the camera, although you will find that you have less flexibility over controlling the light and shadows as movement of the light stand is more restricted.

The light should be placed centrally to the subject if possible, so that it will cast the shadows downwards, resulting in more symmetrical lighting.

Aim to get the catchlight just under the eyelid or on the top of the cornea. You will find that the higher and closer the light source, the longer the shadows will be and the greater the risk of losing the catchlight in the eye.

▼ Butterfly lighting.

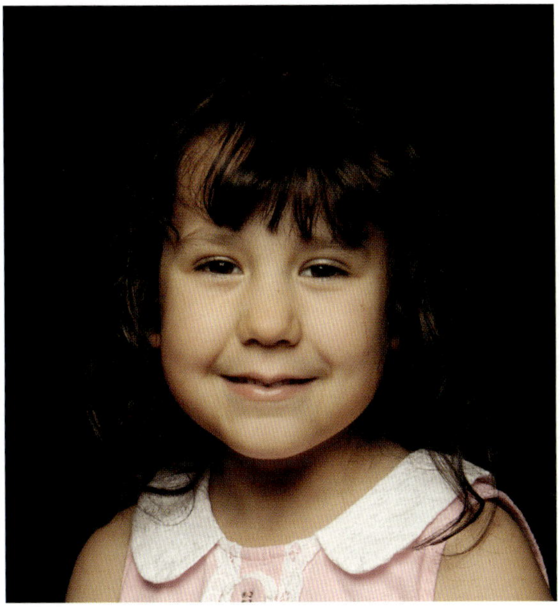

▼ Fig. 2.2
Short lighting.

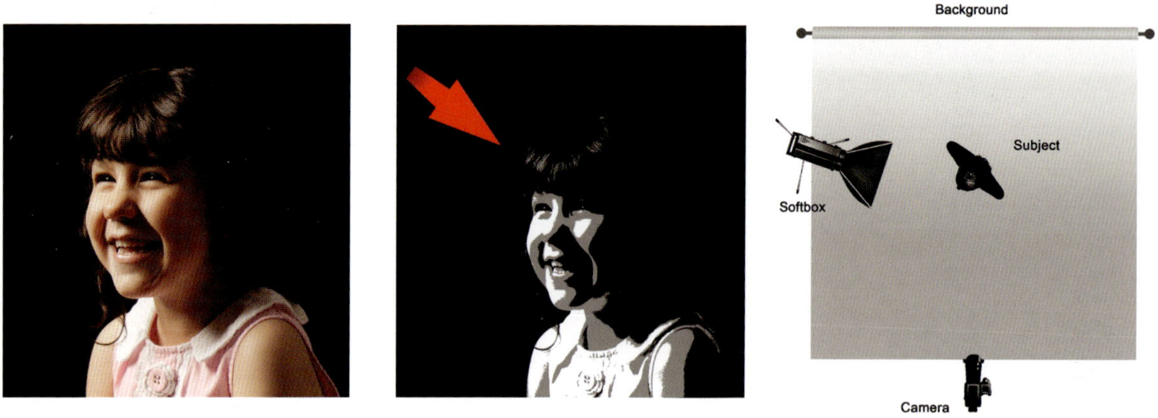

▼ Fig. 2.3
Short Rembrandt lighting.

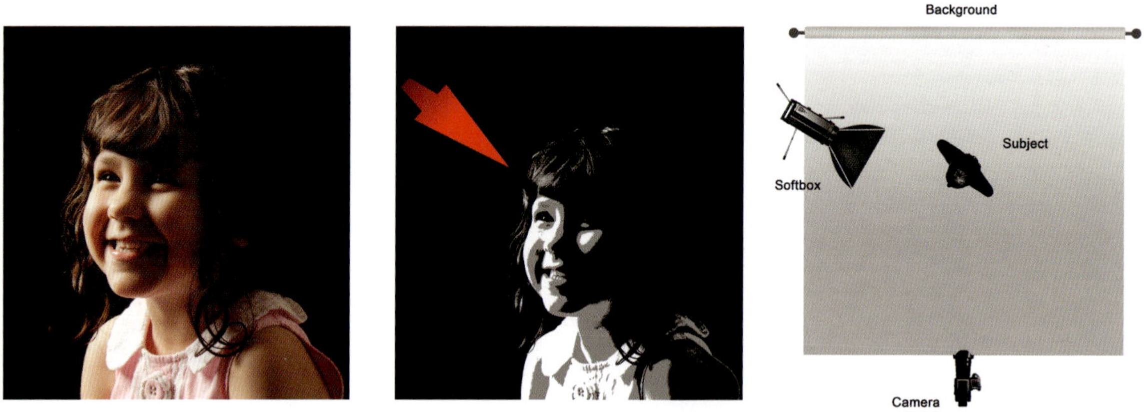

▼ Fig. 2.4
Split lighting.

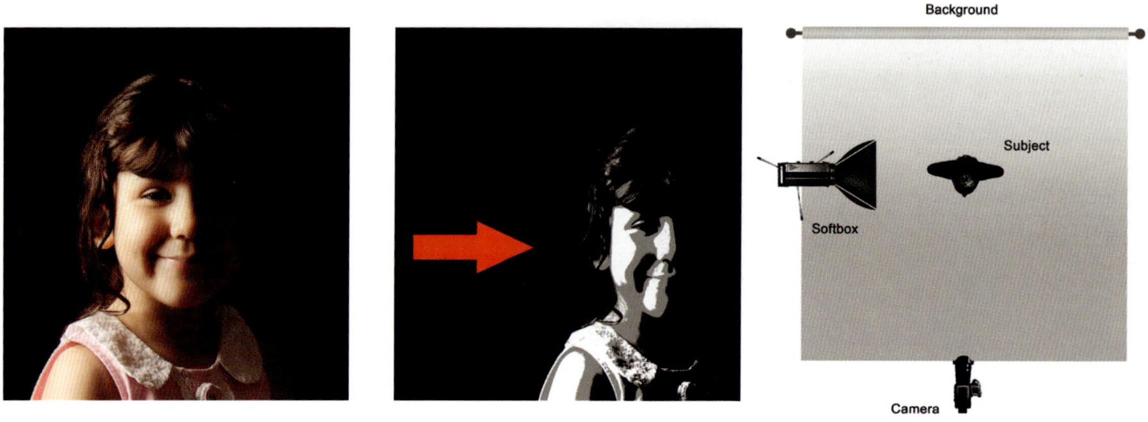

▼ Fig. 2.5
Broad lighting.

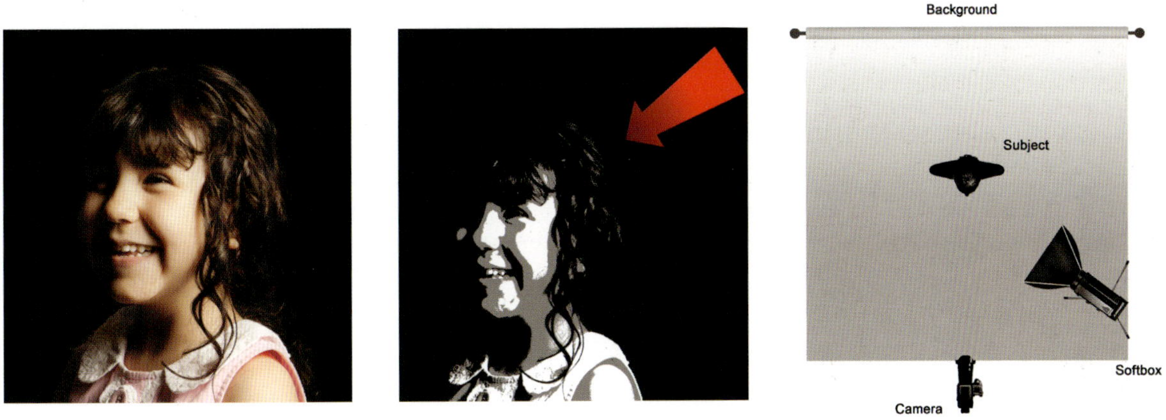

▼ Fig. 2.6
Broad Rembrandt lighting.

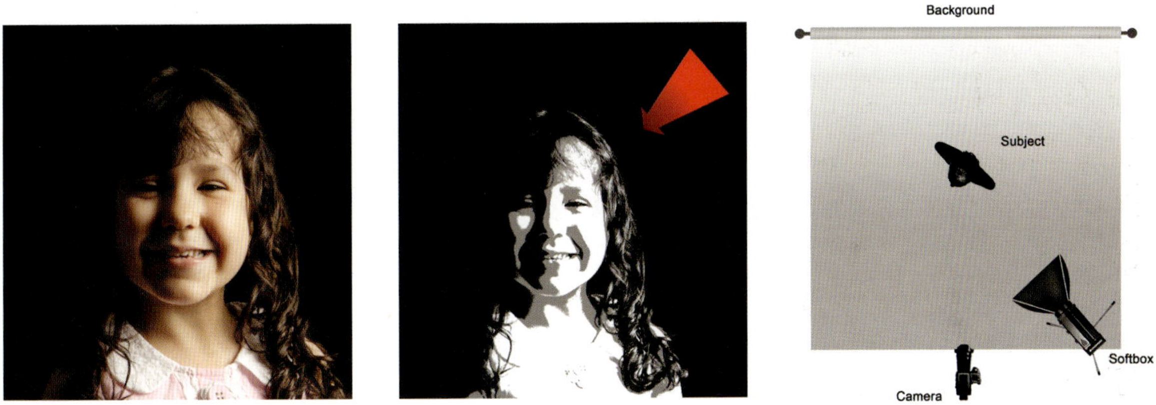

▼ Fig. 2.7
Butterfly lighting.

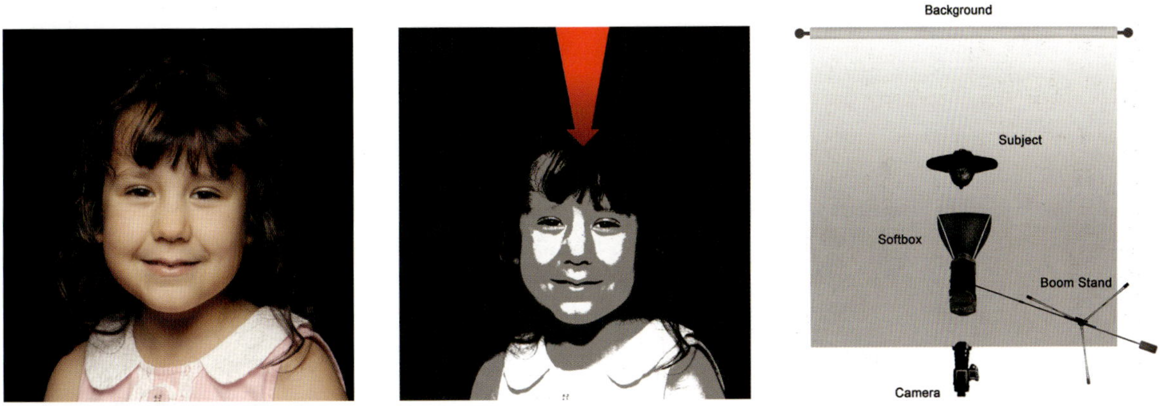

ONE HEAD LIGHTING TECHNIQUES

To illustrate the effects of shaping with light, I have used a single head fitted with a softbox, so that the light on the face may be clearly seen. It pays dividends to practise these techniques so that you are familiar with them when you are working on a commissioned shoot. You will find that friends and family will make willing subjects, and to prove that point, I have used a very fidgety five-year-old! It is one of those occasions where you have to work very quickly if you are to maximize the relatively short attention span of a young child. To help you visualize the light, I have also included a posterized image, clearly illustrating the highlights and shadows. Arrows have been added to indicate the direction of the light along with a schematic of each setup.

Using a single head can at times prove to be quite liberating for studio photographers, in as much as it affords them the ability to work simply, quickly and concentrate on the subject as opposed to the lighting. Relatively new photographers can be forgiven for thinking that working simply in this way undermines the technical prowess associated with studio lighting, yet it can achieve some stunning results.

It is the shape of the light and what you do with it that is important, and there are many different shapers and modifiers available to help you achieve different effects, from snoots to softboxes. Hard light sources will help bring out sharp angles and increase the depth of shadows, whereas softer light sources will produce a more naturally flattering image. It is all about experimentation. Using a single light can help you concentrate on what is really important; drawing out the shapes and contours of your subject from all available angles.

The light and shadows are two contrasting opposites, which become more apparent when using a single light source. It is down to the photographer to control these elements and consider the overall tonality of the photograph. Dark photographs with too many contrasting highlights can detract from subtle tones, whereas overly bright and specular photographs can lack both depth and tonality. With the help of some of the most basic pieces of equipment, such as the studio polyboard or bounce reflector, the photographer can help control the depth of the shadows and reduce the overall dynamic range of the photograph.

One Light Setup 1

The power of this photograph [Fig. 2.8] lies in the contrast and posing of the model. It is lighting at its absolute basic, yet the shot has shape, passion and an erotic feel about it. The strong shadows draw out the shape of the hair, chin and breasts, whilst the highlights bring out the gloss of the hair and lips. The lighting and shadow detail has been controlled to retain the important midrange skin tones whilst the studio wall is quite literally the prop for the model.

SETTINGS AND EQUIPMENT

Camera Settings

Aperture: *f*13.0
Shutter: 1/250sec
ISO: 100
Focal Length: 135mm

Lighting Equipment Required

- Single flash head with a single conical/directional reflector to project the light forwards.
- Bounce reflector or polyboard to fill the shadow detail.
- Flash meter.
- Radio trigger or sync lead to trigger the flash.

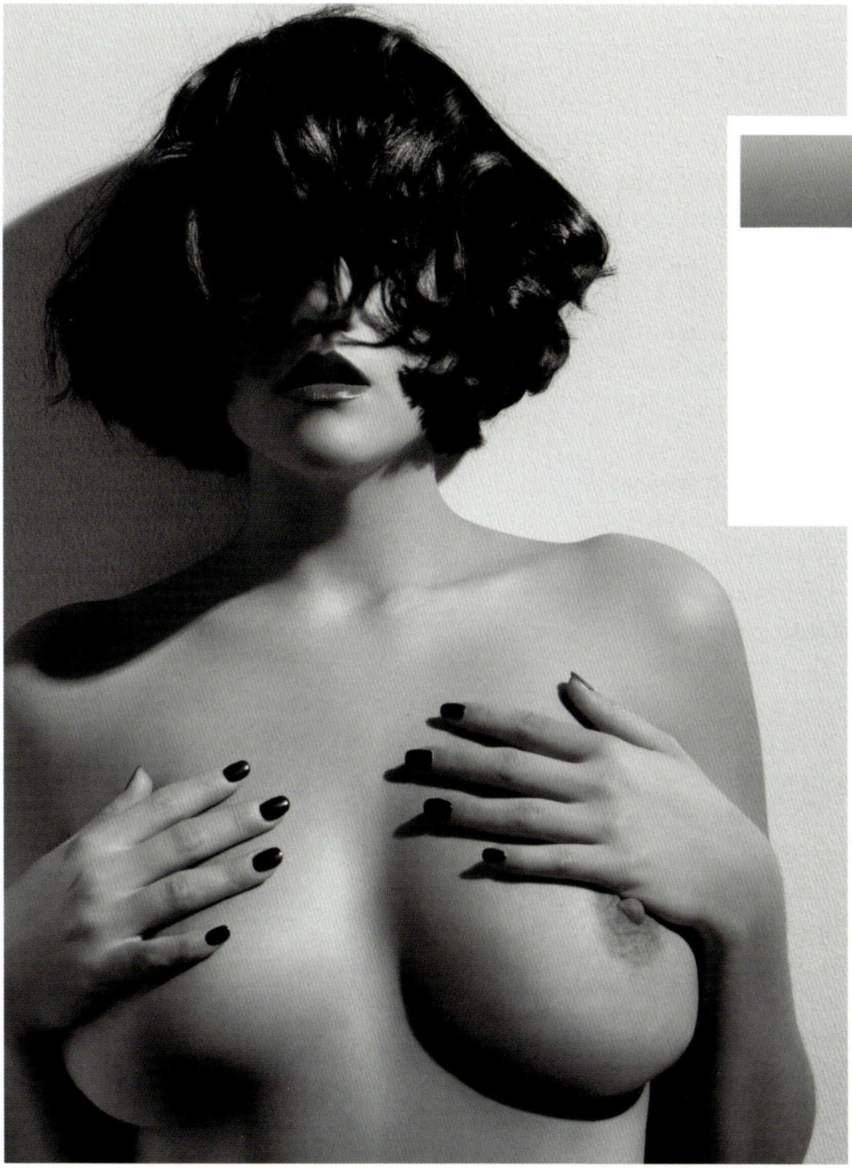

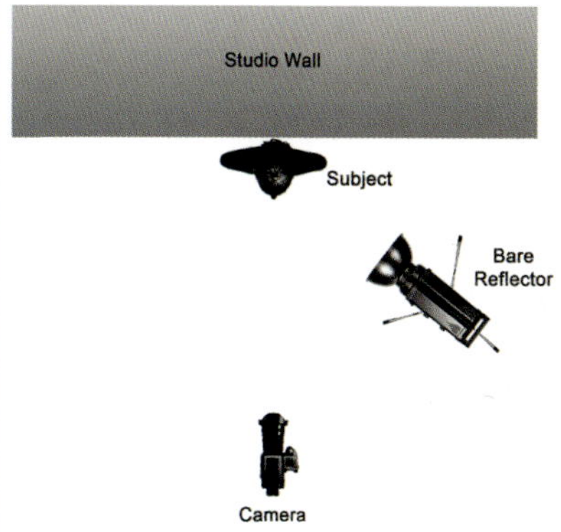

Fig. 2.8
Image © Christian Hough.
Model: Tessa Kuragi.

In this photograph a large conical reflector has been used to throw out as much light as possible and cover at least two thirds of the model and the wall behind. The reflector was positioned to allow it to cover a broad area and by placing it further away to increase the edge definition of the shadows. Although the light is not particularly precise, it has been considered. The broad light source allows enough space for the model to move and pose freely, creating different shapes and movement against the wall, without the need to continuously adjust and move the light. The shadows have been controlled, drawing out the tonal detail and adding shape to both the breast and arm of the model. The shadows have been considered, and casting them downwards under the chin allows just enough light to shape the face, neck and bust but without creating too much of a shadow on the shoulders and chest area so as to become a distraction.

Getting Started

Start by finding yourself a clean white wall. The size of the wall is not an issue here as the crop is fairly tight on the model. If you intend to shoot a full length, then you will need a much larger white wall to work with and may need to reconsider the type of reflector you are using.

Using a single light, add a medium-sized directional reflector and turn on the modelling light. Move the light back far enough to ensure that you are covering a large enough area of the model, and use the modelling light to see where the light is falling. Now move the light around the model, altering its height and direction to create different shapes and shadows. Try and consider the shadows and look where they are cast. Are they distracting or too long? Moving the light further away from the model will make the shadows harder and improve edge definition, whereas moving the light higher will throw the shadows in a more downwards direction, which will add more shape to the face. Positioning the light is important, so it is worth spending a little time to consider the face-shaping techniques covered above. In this example, the lighting leads to more of a split lighting pattern.

Once you are satisfied with the positioning of the light, adjust the power and meter to between *f*11 and *f*16, dial the settings into your camera and take a test shot. Firstly, check the overall exposure and the highlight detail. If you are losing the highlights on the model, then you may need to stop down to compensate or reduce the power of your light. Once you are satisfied with the exposure, pay close attention as to where the shadows are falling and how the light has shaped the body. If you are not happy with them, simply move the light and then re-meter if necessary; after all it pays to experiment! Remember, if you keep the light the same distance from the model, then there will be no need to re-meter.

If you feel that the image has too much contrast, you may wish to use a studio polyboard or bounce reflector to lift the shadow details. Think about where you want the extra light to bounce. Placing a reflector more to the front will make the image flatter and fill more shadow detail, whereas placing the reflector to the side of the model will lift the detail on the side furthest from the light, providing some shape to the body, without filling in too much of the shadow detail.

Common Issues

BLOWN HIGHLIGHTS/TOO MUCH CONTRAST

Blown highlights are a common problem, especially for those shooting digitally, as the dynamic range of many cameras resides around 9 *f* stops. This can often result in blown highlight detail or very dark shadows. There are, however, a few basic steps you can take to help alleviate this problem.

- Use a bounce reflector to help fill in some of the shadow detail and reduce the overall dynamic range of the scene.
- Shoot in RAW. Much of this highlight detail can be recovered with minor adjustments in post-processing using the highlight recovery tool, whereas the blown highlight detail will be lost forever in JPEG.
- Move the light source closer to the subject to produce softer shadows. Conversely, the further the light is from the subject the harder the shadows.
- Consider using a broader reflector or a softer light source. Hard light creates hard shadows and increases contrast. If this is too much, try changing to a more diffused or softer reflector or modifier, such as a shoot-through umbrella or softbox.

One Light Setup 2

Low-key baby shots can be difficult to pose and light, as children and babies traditionally suit lighter and softer photographs. The traditional child pose is eyes at camera and smiling or laughing – after all, this is the way parents prefer to remember their children. Getting a natural and more serious expression from a child or baby within a studio can be difficult, due to their natural enthusiasm and general excitement, so more considered lighting often gets forgotten in favour of something more flexible.

The choice of light modifier is what makes this photograph work. A soft broad light traditionally suits children and babies as it brings out their more rounded features and soft skin tones. This photograph retains the necessary softness, but also draws out a sense of determination from the young baby. The short lighting setup and low-key background concentrates the viewer's attention on the face, making them connect with the outward gaze of the child, whilst the sense of scale is increased by the lower angle at which the photograph has been taken.

Getting Started

Before we even consider lighting, one of the first things you need to deal with when photographing babies is safety. It goes without saying that babies are unaware of danger, so it is the photographer's responsibility to ensure that there are no hot lights, cables or other hazards close at hand that may fall or be pulled over.

Small babies cannot support themselves very well and frequently topple over, which makes photographing them difficult. It is recommended that you support the baby using a baby poser, such as the one from Lastolite used in [Fig. 2.9]. The baby poser consists of several padded cushions that are secured together with Velcro, with a raised section at one end, to make the baby naturally rise up. Don't worry if you do not have a baby poser, as several heavier cushions can also be used, but it may require more attention to keep them in place if you are photographing a particularly active baby. Once you have arranged the baby poser or cushions into position, place a black cotton or velvet sheet over the top.

Try placing the baby poser on a low and wide table (no more than 50cm high is advisable) and secure to prevent it from sliding off. This will enable you to photograph the baby from a slightly lower angle, adding to the sense of perspective. Ensure that you place plenty of cushions and padding on the floor to cushion any fall, and ensure that a parent is immediately to hand to restrict movement.

Before you place the baby in front of the camera, it is recommended that you get all of your lights and equipment set up and metered, as a baby's attention span is very small and they quickly lose interest. For the background a black velvet sheet has been suspended from a portable background support system and placed approximately two metres behind the baby. This helps reduce the amount of light hitting the background and facilitates the movement of the parents in and out of the frame without the risk of them pulling over any equipment.

This shot makes use of the short lighting technique with a single large softbox. The short lighting concentrates the light onto the face of the baby, but does not directly light the baby's body, so retains the overall low-key feel of the photograph. If you don't have a large softbox, a smaller softbox or shoot-through umbrella will also suffice; however, if you are using a smaller light source, it may require you to adjust the light more frequently if the baby moves.

Start by placing the studio light to the side or slightly behind the baby and directing it back towards the baby's face, but not directly into the lens of the camera. Meter the light between *f*11 and *f*16 and dial the settings into your camera. Place something light onto the baby poser and take a test shot to see where the light is falling. If you find that you are getting a lot of light falling onto the black background, then you may need to consider moving the background further back or altering the angle of the light.

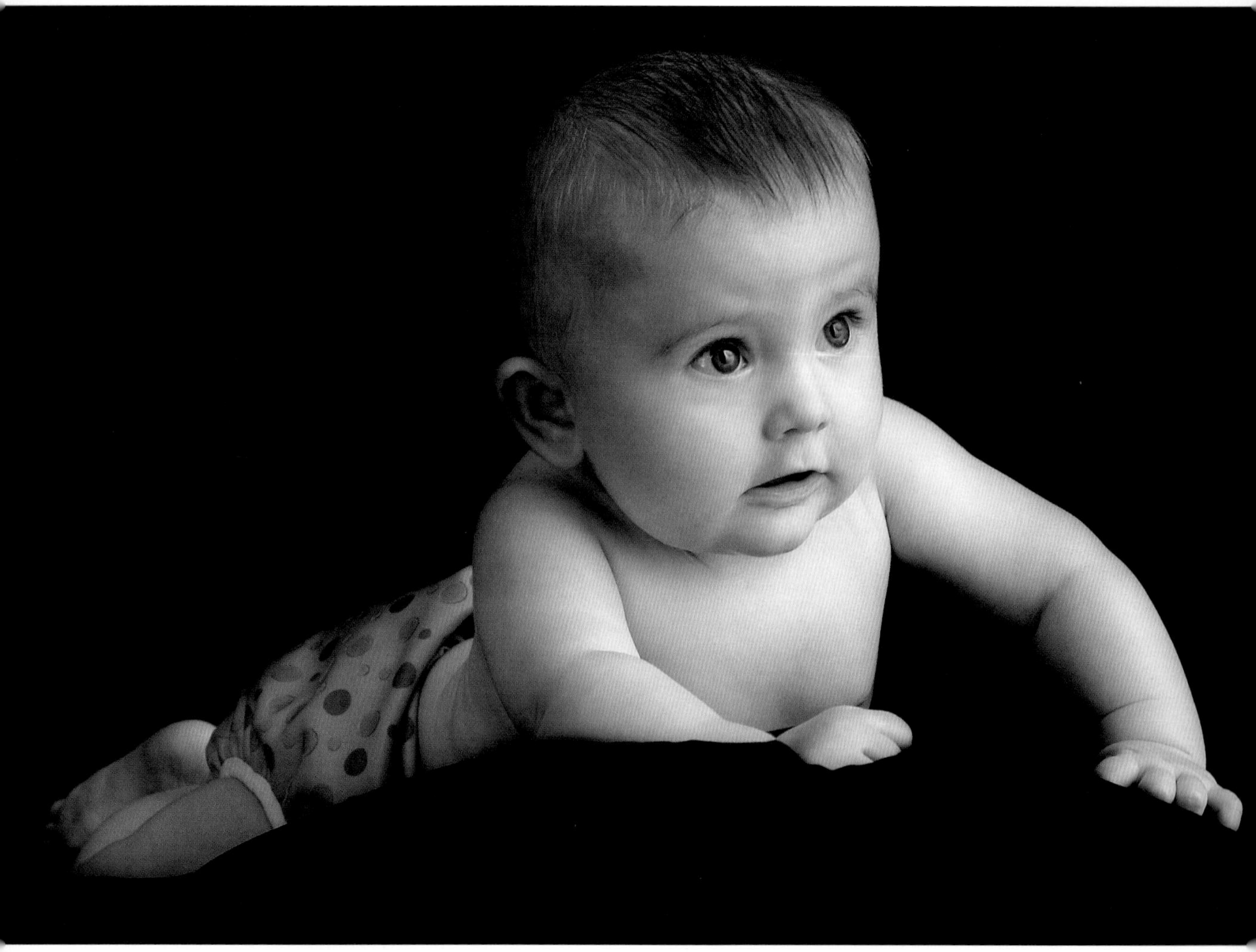

▲ Fig. 2.9
Image © Christian Hough. Model: Tabetha Wydymus.

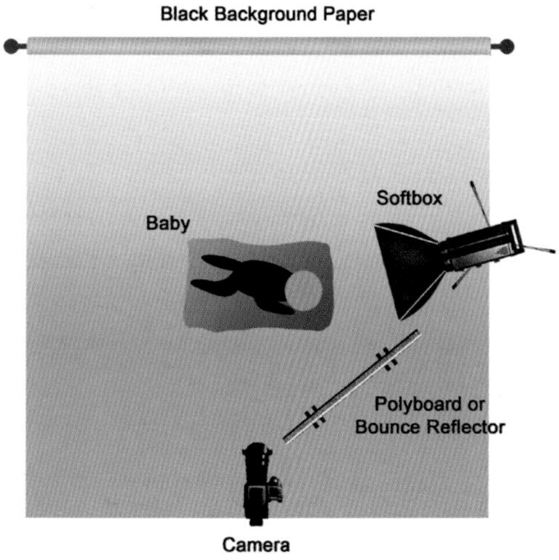

Once you have set up, it's time to get your young subject in front of the camera. Ask a parent to place the baby on the baby poser. The company of the parent will help the baby feel more secure and less likely to begin crying. Help the parent to move the baby into position and take a few test shots with the parent in situ. Now is the time to fine-tune your lighting. Use the modelling lights to see how the light falls onto the baby's face, and don't be afraid to move the light back and forth, until you have the effect you are after, as small movements can make a big difference. Once you are happy, it's time to start shooting. It is possible that with a single light you find the image too dark and you may begin to lose all detail on the near side of the baby. The simple solution to this is using a bounce reflector or poly-board to lift the shadow details and soften the image. It only takes a few seconds, but can dramatically alter the dynamic of a photograph. Take the time to consider which part of the image you want to lift and ensure that the bounce reflector/polyboard is bouncing the light in that direction.

You may find that you have to shoot many frames before you get an expression that you and the parents are happy with. It is also beneficial to invite the parents to view the images while you are shooting as the feedback can be valuable to you both in achieving the right lighting, pose and expression. Work swiftly and take regular breaks, as it is not uncommon for babies to get tired very quickly.

SETTINGS AND EQUIPMENT

Camera Settings

Aperture: *f*13.0.
Shutter: 125sec
ISO: 100.
Focal Length: 105mm

Lighting Equipment Required

- Single flash head with a large softbox or diffused light source.
- Bounce reflector or polyboard to fill the shadow detail.
- Baby poser or heavyweight cushions to support and lift baby.
- Black fabric to place over baby poser/ cushions.
- Background support and black fabric or pop-up background.
- Flash meter.
- Radio trigger or sync lead to trigger the flash.

Common Issues

LIGHT FALLING ONTO BACKGROUND

If you are using a black cotton background, then it is possible that this will pick up unwanted spill light and appear as dark grey as opposed to black. There are several solutions, which will depend entirely on the modifiers you are using and the space you have available.

Move the background further back or flag the light; moving the background reduces the intensity of the light hitting the background, whilst flagging the light will also help prevent unwanted spill light.

- Move the position of the light, directing it away from the background.
- Change the reflector/modifier on the light for a smaller or more directional light source to control the light more and reduce the amount of spill light.
- Use a black velvet background to minimize reflected light, as velvet naturally absorbs light, so will appear black, even when close to the subject.

KEEPING BABY'S ATTENTION

It is difficult at the best of times to keep a baby's attention, let alone when you are trying to photograph one, and the last thing you need is tears, which will inevitably delay things further. Try keeping the whole atmosphere light and joyful. Some gentle background music will help the baby settle into its surroundings. The idea is to make the whole thing fun, especially the flashing and popping of the flash, so fully brief and engage the parents from the outset so they know what to expect and how they can help. It can be worthwhile investing in some toys to dangle near the camera whilst making silly noises, which will help grab and keep the baby's attention and encourage a smile. Keep shooting and waiting time down to a minimum, and take regular breaks to prevent the baby from becoming too tired.

One Light Setup 3

Propping your photographs can really add interest to your shot, and this portrait of a saxophonist is very simple and good example. The image works, simply because the viewer's eye is drawn immediately to the two subjects: the musician and his instrument. There is an interaction between them both, and the angle of the saxophone flows naturally with the angle of the head and body. The dark clothing enables to subject the blend into the dark background avoiding making the image too busy, and the soft, clean and simple lighting draws your attention directly to the subject. Finally, there is sufficient light to separate the hair and far side of the face from the background blackness.

A medium-sized standard softbox can work wonders for single portraits. It is versatile, portable and quick to set up, plus it can be controlled more easily in a confined space, reducing unwanted spill light, yet remains broad enough to facilitate the effective use of a bounce reflector or studio polyboard to lift the shadows. The medium-sized softbox was used to create a Rembrandt-type lighting pattern on the face, leaving a small patch of light under the eye furthest from the light.

Getting Started

This shot could not be easier to set up and requires a softbox, dark background and bounce reflector only. Begin by attaching black paper, a black cotton sheet or black velvet to a background support system or wall behind the subject. In front of the background, place a stool, small step or backless chair for your subject to sit on, leaving approximately two metres of distance from the background. The exact distance from the background will depend entirely on the size of the softbox you are using and the type of background material. If you are using a paper background or larger softbox, then you may well need more distance between your subject than with a velvet background.

Meter the light to anywhere between *f*8.0 and *f*16, depending on the depth of field you prefer, and then get your subject to pose. Once they are in a comfortable position, move the studio light and use the modelling facility to ascertain where the light is falling on the face. To obtain a Rembrandt lighting pattern, the key light needs to be higher than the subject, so it picks up the cheek on the far side as it shines across the bridge of the nose. A good starting point would be to place the light between half and one metre higher and then make fine adjustments once your subject is comfortable and has begun posing.

Once you get started, take a couple of test photographs and examine your lighting. Check to see how the light is shaping the face. If the far side of the face is too dark, you may need to move the light further around to the front of the subject; alternatively, if the face is too light, then moving the light more towards the side of the subject will reduce the amount of light on the far side of the face.

As you keep shooting and your subject keeps moving, continue to check the light, either using the modelling light or the camera's LCD to see if it is shaping the subject's face in the way you intend. If you are happy with your key light then you may want to consider lifting some of the shadow detail by using a bounce reflector. This will depend entirely on the subject's wardrobe and skin tone. If your subject is wearing light clothing and is very pale, then it may not be necessary to fill the shadows, unlike in the photograph of the saxophonist, where without a reflector, the black clothing absorb most of the light, causing him to disappear into the background.

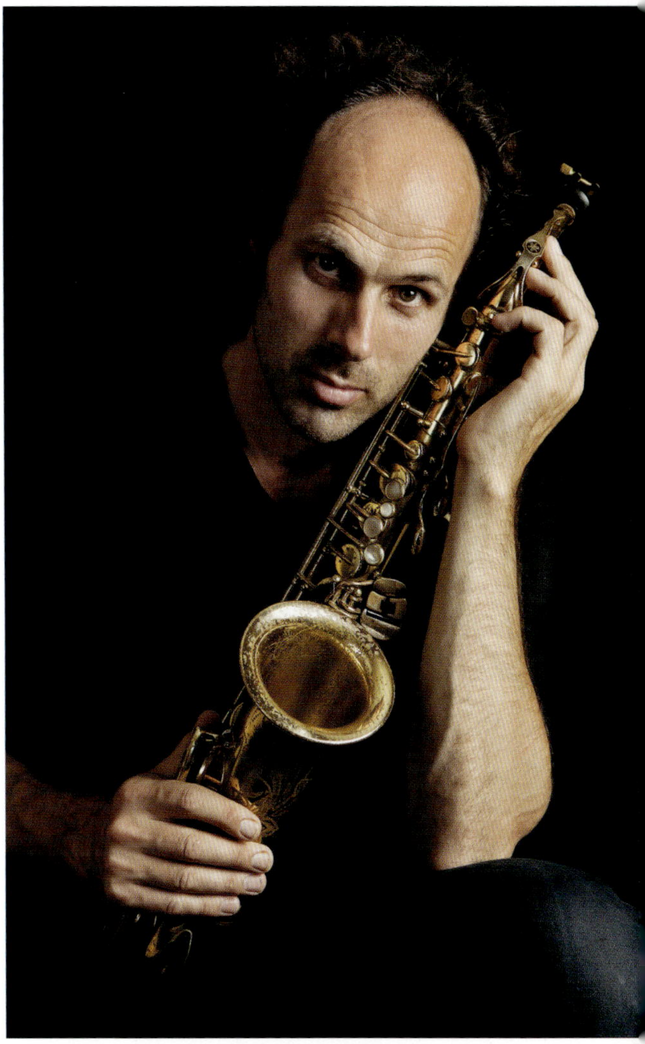

Fig. 2.10
Image © Christian Hough.
Model: Gavin Randle.

Common Issues

PROXIMITY HOT SPOTS

Moving such a softbox or reflector into close proximity to the subject can create harsh 'hot spots', most commonly on the forehead of the subject, especially if they have a slightly oily complexion or shiny skin.

- Begin by moving the light source further back so as to even the spread of light out, or using powder/make-up to make the skin more matt.
- You may find that an extra baffle inside the softbox helps diffuse the light more.
- Failing this, place a small flag inside the front baffle of the softbox to reduce the intensity from the flash.

SETTINGS AND EQUIPMENT

Camera Settings

Aperture: *f*8.0
Shutter: 1/125sec
ISO: 100
Focal Length: 110mm

Lighting Equipment Required

- Single flash head with a medium-sized softbox or diffused light source.
- Bounce reflector or polyboard to fill the shadow detail.
- Stool, small step or backless chair.
- Background support and black fabric or pop-up background.
- Flash meter.
- Radio trigger or sync lead to trigger the flash.

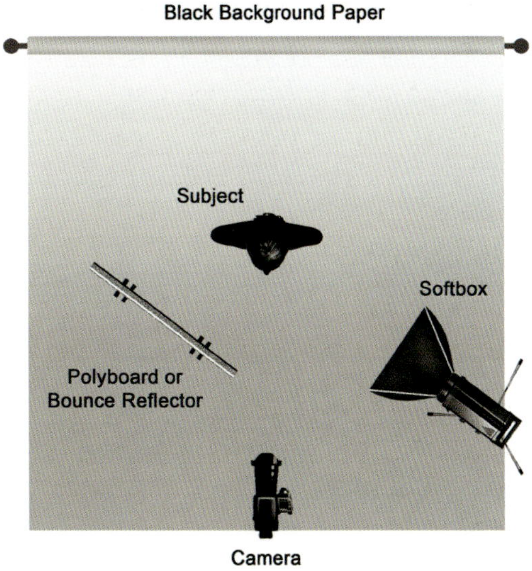

One Light Setup 4

Not all studio photos have to be shot against a studio backdrop. Occasionally it works if you use the surroundings within the studio, such as the wall and the floor. In this shot [Fig. 2.11], the model has moved to the studio floor to create more interesting shapes and fill the frame. This has been accentuated by the use of angles from the camera, filling the frame from corner to corner as opposed to top to bottom. It's the use of angles that make this photograph. The floor-boards of the studio and the model are all travelling in the same direction, which add to the sense of perspective. The shadows are definite, but kept to a minimum. The strong eye make-up contrasts nicely against her pale skin and the white floor, whilst her gaze connects with the viewer.

The photograph is evenly lit, with no obvious sign of vignetting, which maintains the overall contrast. Using a large reflector, such as an umbrella or large softbox overhead, is a fairly indiscriminate way of lighting, but will allow you to cover a much larger area. This will afford greater flexibility and freedom of movement from both you and your model, without the need to continuously adjust your lighting.

Getting Started

This setup requires only a medium-sized silver umbrella, attached to a standard spill kill or umbrella reflector. The umbrella needs to be placed high and above the model, so it is literally throwing light downwards. For this shot the light and umbrella were placed on a boom arm, enabling the light to be placed overhead without the interference from the stand. Don't worry if you don't have a boom, as you can still achieve something similar with clever placement of the umbrella.

Set your light up over a clear area of the floor, where there is no immediate obstruction or clutter. It sounds obvious, but you will be surprised how background unwanted scenery can find its way into your photograph when you are moving around and shooting from different angles. Once you have found a suitable spot, meter your light to about *f*16 as we are no longer working with a flat focal plane. It's a good idea to take the meter reading to the floor, especially if it is white, as this will help you maintain the highlights and keep the tonality fairly even. Dial the settings into your camera and you are ready to go.

As you are shooting, keep an eye on the shad-ows. The more directly overhead the umbrella, the narrower the shadows and the flatter the light. If you want more shadow, move the light further away from the model and place it at more of an angle to create a longer shadow. The idea is to keep moving around and get your model to move too. Experiment with angles, perspectives and framing until you find something that works.

Common Issues

LIGHT TOO FLAT, NO SHADOWS

- Manoeuvre the light away from the camera and above the head of the model. This will shorten some of the shadows, but will still create shadows under the chin and eyes, giving shape to the face.
- For greater shadows, place the light behind the model, throwing the light towards the camera and casting shadows on the nearside of the model.

SHADOWS TOO STRONG OR TOO LONG

- Place the light closer to the camera axis and more in front of the model.

SHADOWS TOO DARK

- Consider using a bounce reflector or fill light to lift the shadow detail.

Be mindful of how your model is moving and the placement of the light. If the model changes position on the floor, then you may need to consider moving the light to control the shadows.

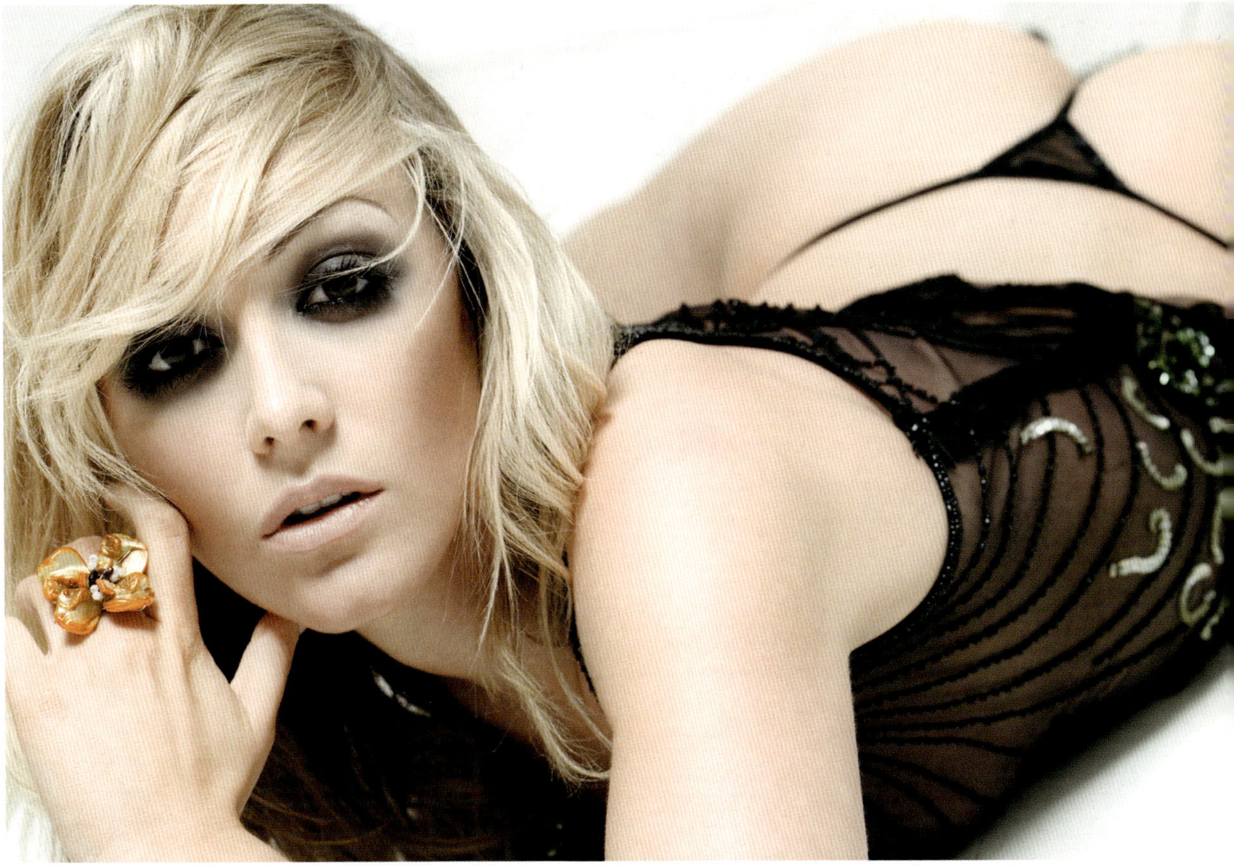

▲ Fig. 2.11
Image © Christian Hough. Model: Kerri Guiney-Donnelly.

SETTINGS AND EQUIPMENT

Camera Settings

Aperture: *f*16
Shutter: 1/100sec
ISO: 100
Focal Length: 100mm

Lighting Equipment Required

- Single flash head with a medium-sized silver umbrella.
- Boom stand and arm.
- Uncluttered area of clean light-coloured floor.
- Flash meter.
- Radio trigger or sync lead

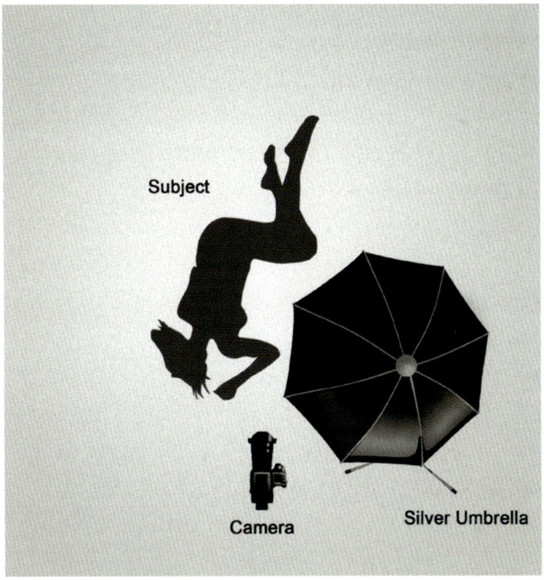

TWO HEAD LIGHTING TECHNIQUES

With two studio heads, photographers can be much more creative and have greater control over the light. The most frequent use of a second studio light is that of a 'fill light', which is used to control the depth of the shadows, whereas the main light or the 'key light' is used as the main light source and toadd shape. The fill light is more cumbersome than the bounce reflector, but allows the photographer much greater control of how much shadow detail they desire. The caveat is that with greater control comes the necessity for more discipline and understanding of light and how it is used, plus the effects of the various modifiers and reflectors that are available.

There are of course many other creative ways in which to use a second light, either as a hair light, background light or even rim light. It's where you place and use it that makes all the difference.

Two Light Setup 1

This image [Fig. 2.12] was a simple public relations shot for profile and website use. Consideration was given to the muscular build of the subject and how to best fill the frame and what lighting to use. The photograph was deliberately kept low key and the subject photographed in dark clothing, against a dark grey Colorama. This ensures that the focus is on the face and not the clothing or body.

Posing also played a key part, in that the subject wanted to appear relaxed and at ease. Most people appear at their most comfortable when they assume a position that is natural to them. Whether they are sat down or stood upright, the key is to get their body to relax naturally. Nowhere is it more obvious when a person is tense than in the shoulders, neck and face. In this shot, the subject felt at his most natural sitting down and using his hand to prop his head, which helped him to naturally relax his neck and shoulders. To facilitate the positioning, a small step was used to allow the legs to be placed at different heights, which in turn helped support the elbow and hand.

A Rembrandt lighting pattern was used to make the broad jaw line look much slimmer, casting only a small amount of light under the eye on the far cheek. This also brought out the shape of the cleft chin adding further interest to the jaw line. A second light was used as a fill light to 'fill' the dark shadows created by the key light, helping to soften the image and reduce the overall contrast.

The positioning of the hand was crucial. Too far forwards and it cast distracting shadows onto the face. Too far back and the pose began to look unnatural. The final positioning added more shadow to the edge of the face, making the shape appear much slimmer.

SETTINGS AND EQUIPMENT

Camera Settings

Aperture: *f*10
Shutter: 1/100sec
ISO: 100
Focal Length: 100mm

Lighting Equipment Required

- Two flash heads and stands.
- Two small/medium-sized softboxes.
- Background support and plain background paper/backdrop.
- Flash meter.
- Radio trigger or sync lead.

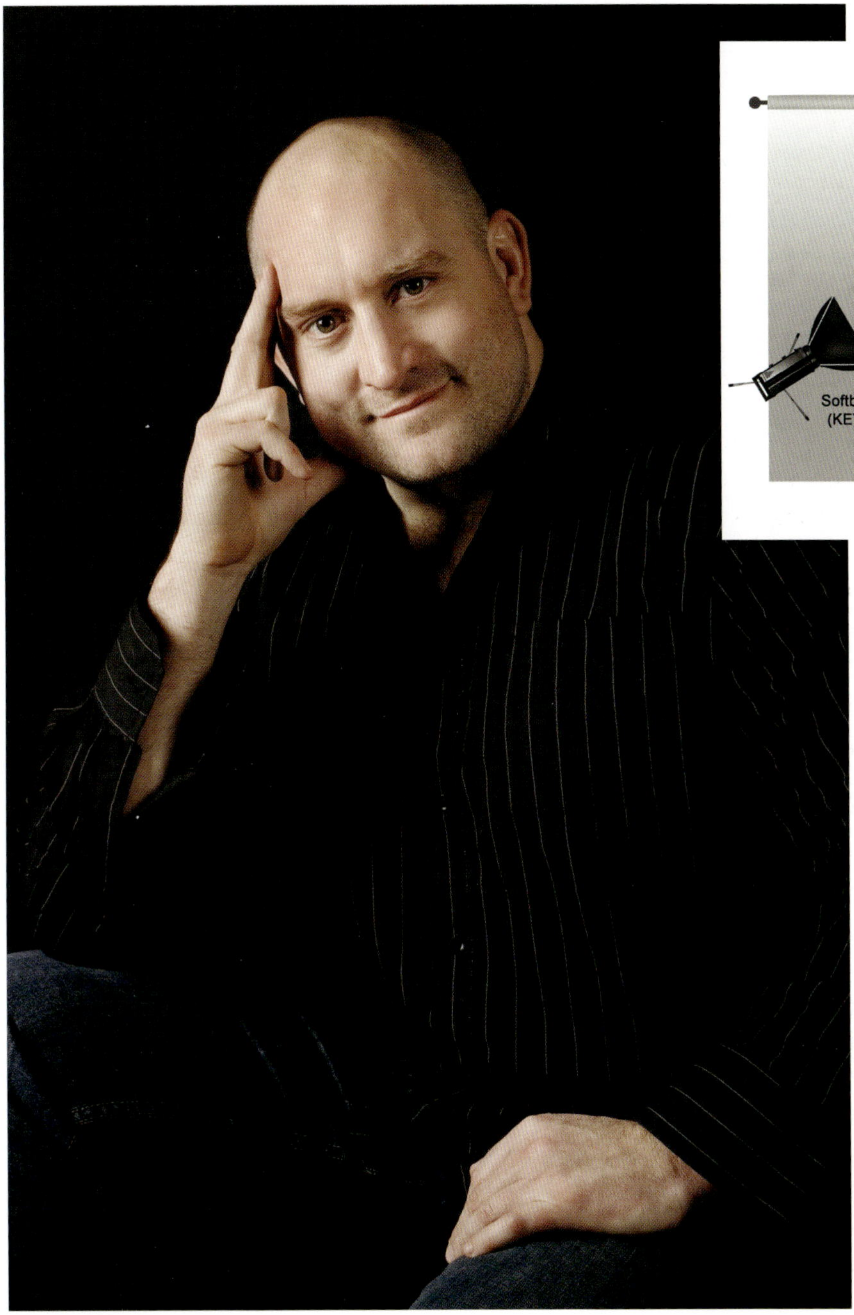

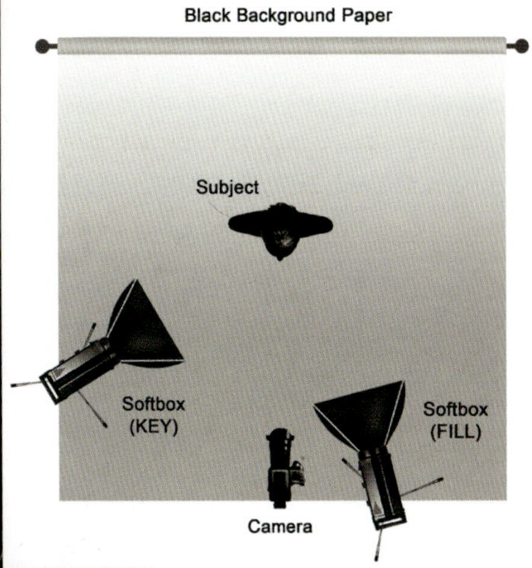

Fig. 2.12
Image © Christian Hough.
Model: Paul Bunker.

Getting Started

If you are looking to achieve a clean and uncluttered finish, it is ideal to use a studio backdrop of some sort. Before you choose the colour, try to consider the clothing and skin tone of the subject you are photographing. Very pale skin tones and light clothes can look very stark against brightly coloured or strong backgrounds, whereas it can be difficult to bring out a full range of skin tones with very dark skin and clothing. Every person is different, so before considering different colours and shades of background it is beneficial to think whether you would be best to go for a high-key or low-key photograph. Once you have decided on the background, get your posing stool or step and place it approximately three metres in front of the background. Positioning the stool is a useful thing to do as it can be used as a metering point without the need for your subject to be continuously sat in front of the camera.

Ideally, softboxes are a flattering and cost-effective choice for small portraits. Start by setting up two studio lights on stands and then placing two small or medium-sized softboxes (approximately 60x80cm) on each light. Move your key light to approximately 45 degrees off the camera axis and meter between *f*11 and *f*16. The key light ideally needs to be around one metre higher than the head of the subject, so that it casts the shadows downwards, under the chin to give the face shape. Now place the fill light close to the camera axis and at roughly the same height as the key light (or slightly higher) and meter between one and two stops less than the key light, approximately *f*5.6 to *f*8.0. The more light from the fill light, the more it will fill in the shadows and the flatter the image will look. Don't worry about getting the meter readings absolutely exact, as small movement from the lights and your subject will cause the readings to fluctuate.

It is now time to get your subject to sit down and assume a comfortable pose. Use the modelling facility on the key light to shape the face, paying close attention to where the light and shadows are falling. Don't be afraid to move the key light around the subject and alter the height until you get the desired effect. Once done, re-meter the key light and take a test shot, and examine the image, looking at the shape of the face and the depth of the shadows and adjust the light as necessary. If the shadows are too dark, simply increase the power of the fill light. If the shadows are too light and the image looks flat, reduce the power of the fill light.

Cross Lighting Woes

Depending on the light modifiers and shapers in use, then the positioning of the fill light can have a big impact on your photograph. Ill-considered placement of the fill light can occasionally cause a phenomenon known as crosslighting, which can occur when the fill light is placed off the camera axis. Cross lighting is most apparent when hard light sources are being used, creating hard and defined shadows. The result is that several distracting shadows appear on the subject, literally crossing each other. Fortunately, it can be easily remedied and the simple movement of the fill light close or onto the camera axis tends to rectify the problem. Cross lighting rarely becomes an issue when using very diffused light sources and modifiers such as softboxes.

Common Issues

CREASES IN THE PAPER AND FABRIC ARE ACCENTUATED BY THE LIGHTS

- Move the subject further from the background to create more separation.
- Reduce the light falling on the background or adjust the position of the lights to try and reduce the light falling on the background.

NOT ENOUGH SPACE TO MOVE THE SUBJECT FROM THE BACKGROUND

- Use smaller/tighter reflectors or modifiers to try and control the light more.
- Flag the background with black pieces or fabric/ studio polyboards.

UNABLE TO UTILIZE SMALLER REFLECTOR IN A CONFINED SPACE

- Consider reducing the power of your lights, using a slightly longer focal length and shallower depth of field to help blur the unwanted details from the background.

Two Light Setup 2

Creating separation from a dark background can help give a photograph a more three-dimensional appeal and add a little more shape to the outline. For this simple portrait [Fig. 2.13], lighter yet textured clothing has helped separate the model from the dark grey background paper. The model has been short-lit by a single key light, leaving the far side of the face and hair in the shadows, which suits the model's slim features. Rather than using the second available light as a fill light, it has instead been utilized as a 'hair light', creating light on the top of the head and around the edges of the hair-line. This helps lift the outline of the hair out of the shadows, detail that would have otherwise been lost against the dark background. The hair light has been controlled to prevent light spilling back into the lens of the camera, and just enough power has been used on the hair light to accentuate the detail on top of the head and the outline, without making it a distraction.

Getting Started

Hair lights can be used in several ways and with several modifiers, but their main purpose is to high-light the hair. There are several reasons for lighting hair, such as highlighting colour, texture or finish, drawing out shape or creating separation from the background. What it is used for is entirely down to the photographer and the subject, but it's how it is used that is important.

Start by erecting your background support and hanging your background paper – for this shot a dark grey paper background was used. Then position a seat approximately two metres in front of the background where you wish the subject to sit, or place a marker on the floor. This will give you a rough position with which to meter, without the subject having to be there.

Attach a medium-sized softbox to your key light and place it approximately 45 degrees off-axis from the camera. Meter this between *f*11 and *f*16. The hair light can be positioned in several ways, depending on the modifiers you have available. For this shot a bare reflector has been fitted with a honeycomb grid to control the direction of the light. Once you have attached the honeycomb and reflector to the light, placed it on a stand and position it high up behind the background support and adjust it until it is pointing in a downwards angle towards the back of the subject's head onto the top of the hair. The placement and angle at which the hair light is pointing is important, as it needs to be positioned directly behind the subject, so that the light is prevented from shining back into the lens of the camera. Ideally, a boom arm will offer you more flexibility when positioning the key light. If you have a boom arm, position the boom behind and above the subject, adjusting the angle until it is lighting the hair; otherwise, placing it behind the background support is a good workaround.

Once you have set up your hair light, meter around one stop lower than your key light. There is no fixed rule about metering, and to a large extent it will depend on the style and colour of the hair of your subject. For example, shiny and very light blonde hair will require much less light than dark frizzy hair. The idea is that the hair light is a subtle accent as opposed to a very bright halo, so it is paramount not to blow the highlight detail. Take a test shot and examine the image carefully, to see if the key light is shaping the face and that the hair light is not too dark or too bright and is lighting the hair. Simple adjustments to power and positioning can make a big difference.

If you have a boom stand, then you will have much greater freedom as to where you can place the hair light, without the stand intruding on the image. It will also facilitate the use of different reflectors and modifiers. Start by placing your boom stand so that the light is approximately 50cm to one metre above the subject and roughly a foot behind. Adjust your light so it is highlighting the hair the top of the head and the shoulders of the subject. It is not always necessary to use a very tight reflector or modifier, and a small softbox may suffice when placed directly overhead. Remember, the closer the light is to the subject, the smaller area it will cover.

Common Issues

LENS FLARE FROM HAIR LIGHT THAT IS POSITIONED BEHIND THE BACKGROUND

- Ensure you are using a tightly controlled shaper or modifier to make the light is as directional as possible.
- Adjust the position of the light so that the light is shining downwards onto the hair and less towards the lens of the camera.

LENS FLAIR AND UNABLE TO ADJUST THE LIGHT FURTHER DOWNWARDS

- Start by moving the model closer to the background so that you can adjust the angle of the light.
- Alternatively, use a longer focal length lens to reduce the field of view and a lens hood to minimize stray light entering the lens.

LIGHT FROM THE HAIR LIGHT SPILLING ONTO THE FACE OF THE SUBJECT

- Move the light further behind the subject and adjust the angle to ensure that the light is lighting only the hair and not the face.

BRIGHT/BLOWN HIGHLIGHTS

- Reduce the power of the hair light to ensure that the highlight detail is not lost.
- Alternatively, change the lighting shaper/modifier to something that is more diffused.

SETTINGS AND EQUIPMENT

Camera Settings

Aperture: *f*11
Shutter: 1/125sec
ISO: 100
Focal Length: 110mm

Lighting Equipment Required

- Two flash heads and stands.
- One small/medium-sized softbox.
- One reflector and honeycomb grid.
- Background support and plain Colorama or backdrop.
- Flash meter.
- Radio trigger or sync lead.

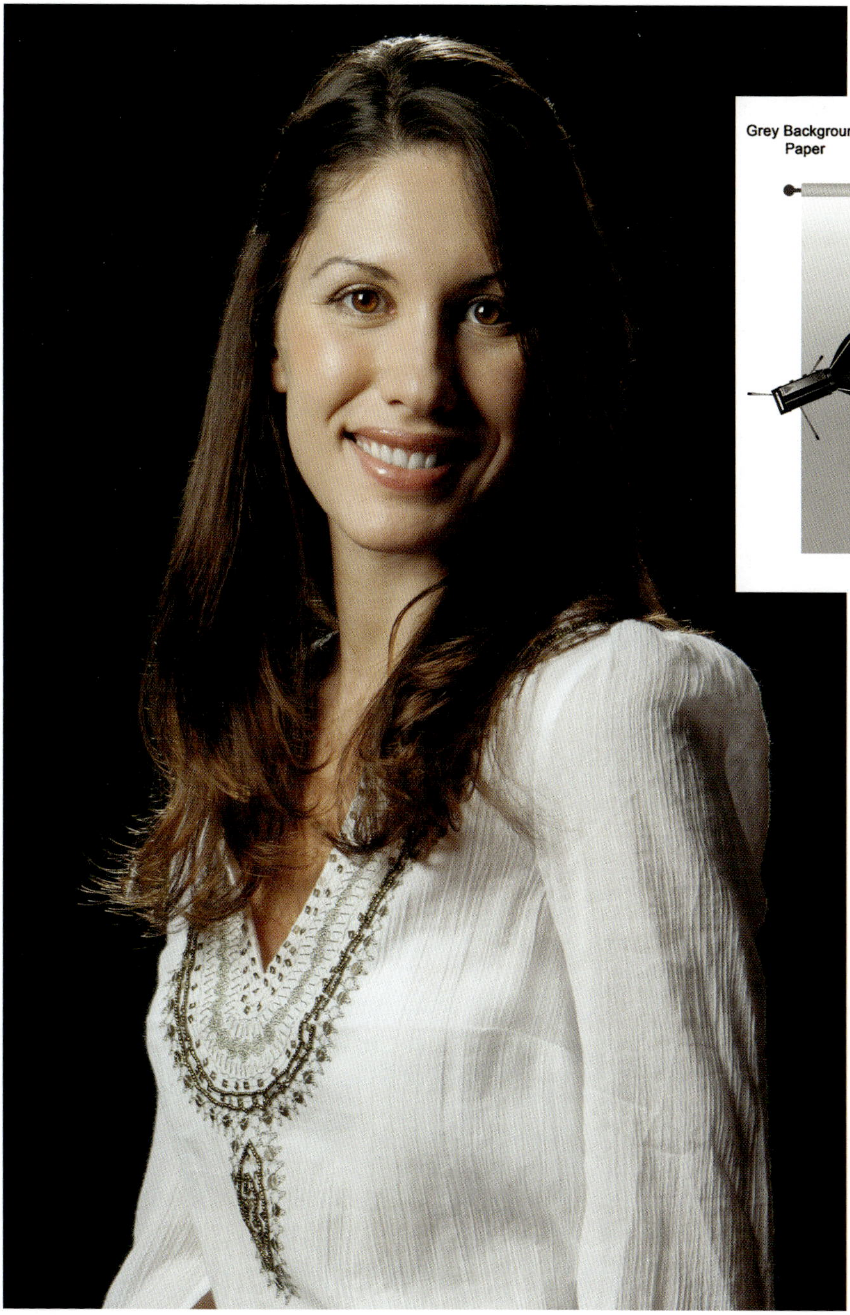

▲ Fig. 2.13
Image © Christian Hough.
Model: Freya Berry.

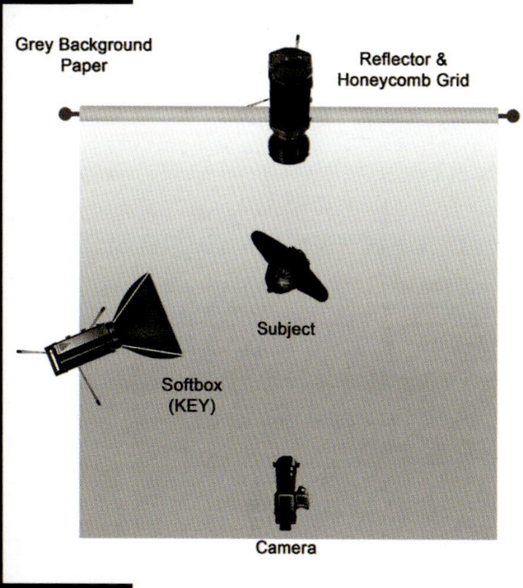

▲ Original

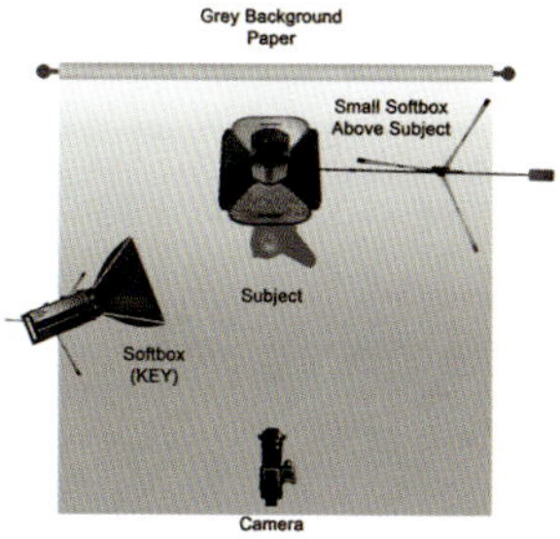

▲ Alternative

Two Light Setup 3

In the same way in which you can use a hair light, a second light may be used to accent other parts of the subject. Here, the focal plane of the photograph [Fig. 2.14] is much deeper than a sitting portrait. The head is very close to the camera and the legs are much further away. The face and the body of the model have been lit by a single head with a small softbox. The softbox provides sufficient coverage to light the face and the torso, before becoming darker towards the legs. The second light has been used to create the highlights on the model's skin, and the power has been increased to make the highlights more specular as opposed to subtle, giving the image a more overall glamorous overtone. Finally, the photograph has been shot at a slight angle to give the image a more editorial appeal, whilst the feeling of being low down and the flatter perspective helps the viewer engage with the model.

Getting Started

Start by setting up a black fabric backdrop or Colorama, so that the train of the backdrop also runs underneath the model. Now attach one small softbox to your main studio head for the key light and a standard stripbox (100x40cm) to the second head. The second studio head with the stripbox will act as the highlight, so ideally needs to be fixed to a boom arm to allow the stripbox to be positioned directly above the subject, to ensure a continuous and balanced highlight is achieved, without the stand protruding into the frame.

Meter the key light to around *f*16. The focal plane is much longer, due to the positioning of the subject, so you will find that you require slightly more depth of field than your normal portrait, depending on your choice of lens. Get your model into position and now manoeuvre the second head so that it is between half a metre and one metre higher than the model and approximately the same distance behind. Using the modelling light, adjust the angle of the light so that it is shining back towards the model, picking up the outline of the buttocks, outside of the legs and mid back area. Once in position, meter the light to around *f*22 at the nearest point, in this shot the base of the spine. This will provide the highlights on the model.

Take a test shot and see how the highlights and shadows are working together; pay close attention to the highlight and ensure that none of them are blown. Depending on the width of the stripbox you are using, you may find that you need to move the position of the light more overhead to increase the amount of light or further behind to decrease the light. Changing the angle of the head so that it is pointing either towards or further away from your model will also help, but care needs to be taken to ensure that that it is not unintentionally lighting the background.

You will find that using a longer focal length of lens, such as a shot telephoto, will allow you to compress the perspectives more, making the image more flattering. Wider lenses will distort the perspectives and make the head look much larger than the legs and torso.

SETTINGS AND EQUIPMENT

Camera Settings

Aperture: *f*13
Shutter: 1/125sec
ISO: 100
Focal Length: 110mm

Lighting Equipment Required

- Two flash heads and stands.
- Small/medium-sized softbox.
- Standard stripbox (40x100cm).
- Background support and plain Colorama or backdrop.
- Boom arm and stand.
- Flash meter.
- Radio trigger or sync lead.

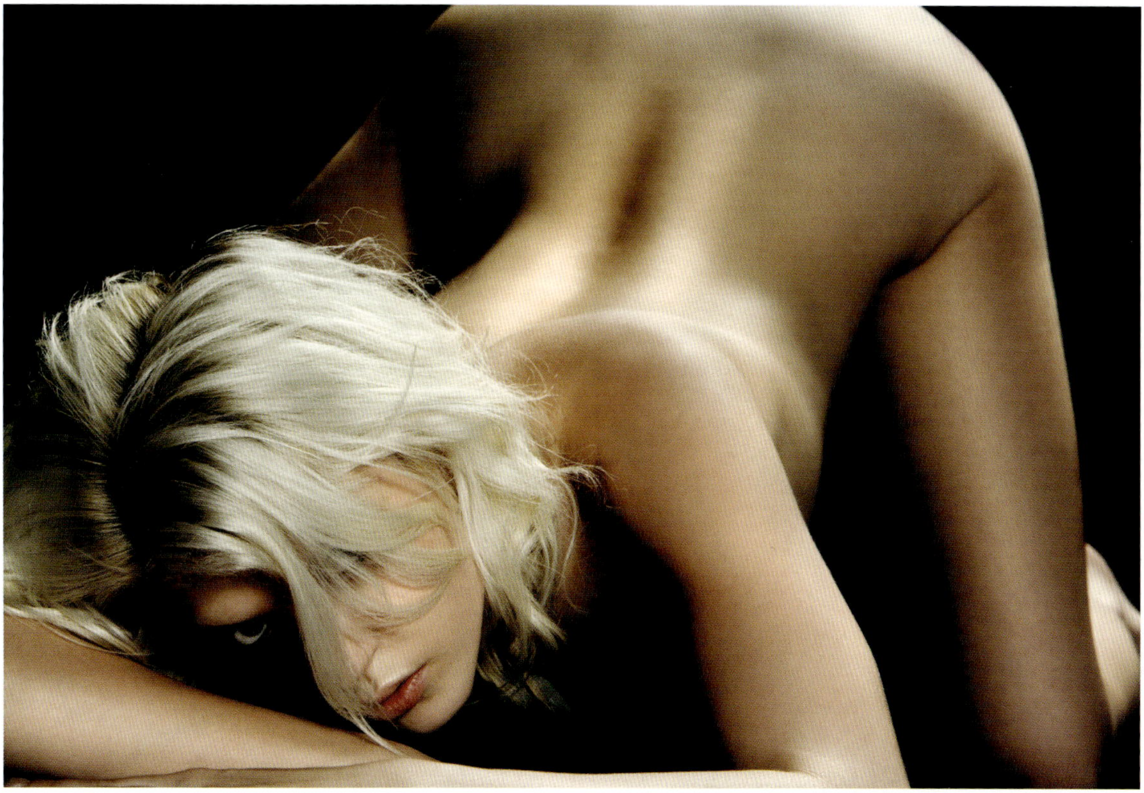

▲ Fig. 2.14
Image © Christian Hough. Model: Ally Andrews.

Common Issues

HIGHLIGHTS BLOWN/TOO BRIGHT

Placing heads very close to subjects with certain softboxes often causes proximity hot spots, meaning that the light hasn't sufficiently 'diffused' and is too concentrated.

- Reduce the power of the head for the highlights, or move it further away, to increase the distance.

POWER HAS BEEN REDUCED/MOVED HEAD, BUT HIGHLIGHTS STILL BLOWN

- Try reducing the ratio of your heads; consider increasing the power of your key light and then stopping down to a smaller aperture to compensate.
- Alternatively, add more material to the front of the softbox to reduce and further diffuse the light.

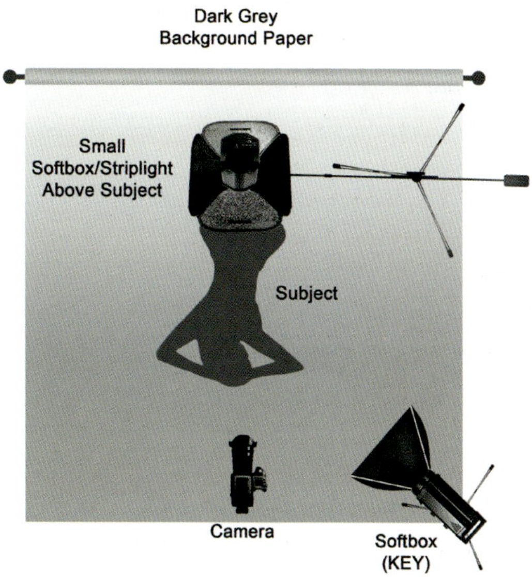

THE SKIN OF THE SUBJECT IS VERY FLAT

- Use a light skin oil or olive oil applied sparingly to increase the sheen on the skin; the more oil you use, the more shine on the skin and the more specular the highlights.

Two Light Setup 4

There are times when you may wish to lift a dark background and create some separation from your subject. Subtly lighting the background is an ideal way of adding interest to your photographs and can be a good way of controlling unwanted spill light from other lights on set.

This photograph [Fig. 2.15] is a commercial shot advertising skin products, yet was shot using very simple lighting techniques. The lighting was set up to deliberately create a lot of shadows, utilizing a butterfly lighting setup. The light was positioned high up and in front of the subject, casting all of the shadows under the brim of the hat, under the chin and below the arms, whilst still drawing out the detail of the product. The objective was to try and maintain symmetry with the light and shadows so that they all fell centrally. The dark grey paper background was subtly lit from behind, to prevent the shadow areas on the subject and the background from blending together, and thus providing an element of separation.

Getting Started

Set up your background paper or fabric on your support system. For this lighting technique, paper generally works best as it can be made to be completely smooth, whereas fabrics tend to crease easily, the creases becoming ever more visible when lit. Once the background is set up, mark a position for your subject approximately two to three metres in front of the background.

For the key light, you need a fairly small and controlled light source to prevent too much spill light falling onto the background. A small softbox (approx 60x60cm) placed on a boom arm will allow you to control the light, but maintain sufficiently soft lighting. Place your softbox on the boom and position it high up above and approximately 60cm in front of the subject. Point the softbox downwards towards the subject and check the position of the shadows. Move the light until the shadows fall centrally when the model faces directly towards the camera. Meter the light to *f*11.

Now set up your background light. For this photograph a single head, fitted with a reflector and honeycomb grid, was attached to a floor stand and placed on the floor directly behind the subject. If you don't have a honeycomb grid, use a directional reflector and aim it directly at the background, adjusting the upward angle so that the light falls behind the back and head of the subject. The spread of the light will depend on the size of the honeycomb grid in use and the reflector, whereas the intensity of the effect will be determined by the material and shade of the background in use, so you will have to adjust your setting accordingly. Meter the light at the background between one and two stops lower than the subject, *f*5.6 to *f*8.

Once you have set up, take a test shot and examine the lighting. Check the positioning and the power of the light behind the subject and adjust if necessary. It is also important to look at the light and shadows from the key light. If the shadows are too long, move the key light further away from the subject and closer to the camera, adjusting the angle of the light once you have finished. This will have the effect of throwing more light directly at the subject and shortening the shadows. If you want to achieve more shadows, then reverse the process and move the light closer to the subject. Don't forget to re-meter once you have repositioned the light.

Common Issues

THE SKIN OF THE SUBJECT IS VERY REFLECTIVE, CAUSING BLOWN HIGHLIGHTS

Increasing the distance between the light and the subject will reduce the risk of proximity hot spots.

- Move the light higher up or further away from the subject.

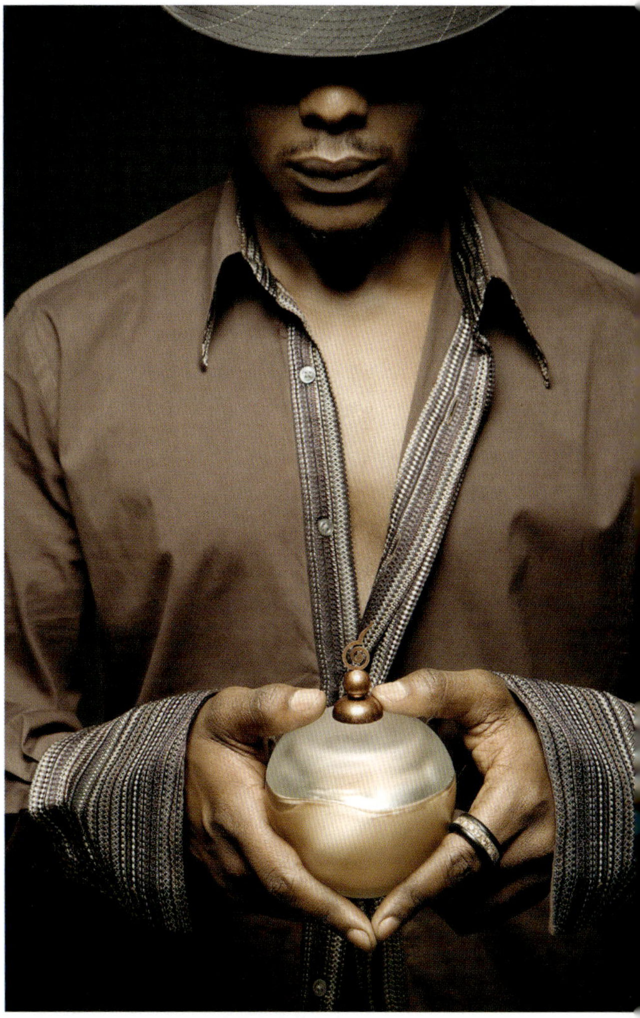

▶ Fig. 2.15
Image © Christian Hough.
Model: Hani Bagedo.

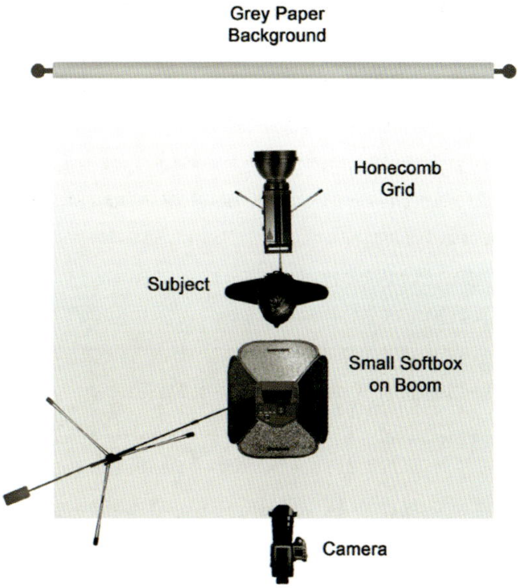

UNABLE TO MOVE THE LIGHT FURTHER AWAY

- Use a powder-based make-up or a skin oil mattifier to reduce the shine on the skin; avoid powders that contain mica as these can make the skin look shiny and add shimmer.

THE KEY LIGHT IS SPILLING UNWANTED LIGHT ONTO THE BACKGROUND

A more controlled light source will greatly reduce spill, but harder light may increase proximity hot spots.

- Adjust the angle of the key light so that it is pointing more downwards.
- Consider moving the subject further from the background to reduce the effects of any unwanted spill.

SETTINGS AND EQUIPMENT

Camera Settings

Aperture: *f*11
Shutter: 1/125sec
ISO: 100
Focal Length: 70mm

Lighting Equipment Required

- Two flash heads.
- Small/medium-sized softbox.
- Standard reflector and honeycomb grid.
- Background support and plain Colorama or backdrop.
- Boom arm and stand.
- Floor stand.
- Flash meter.
- Radio trigger or sync lead.

Two Light Setup 5

The high-key background has become one of the most popular lighting setups used, especially in modern portrait photography and even classic fashion photography, often favoured by photographers such as David Bailey. It is a remarkably simple yet effective technique, providing a clean background, allowing the viewer to concentrate purely on the subject. However, it can also be one of the most overused, so the flip side is to ensure that the photograph itself has something visually interesting. This shot [Fig. 2.16]has been done using only two lights – one for the background and one for the model. Traditionally, a highkey (white) background would be lit with two or more heads to ensure adequate power and even coverage. Here this single head has proved more than adequate for a single half-length beauty portrait.

Getting your subject to pose can be difficult. The model in this shot continuously changed position between each photograph to maximize shapes and poses, thus reducing time and increasing the chances of a successful shot. The end result was this natural-looking image, with a sense of movement and her gazing out of the frame. Together with the mouth remaining partially open and hair over the face and eye, it adds a sense of passion and engages the viewer.

Getting Started

Start by setting up your background paper or fabric and marking a position for your model approximately two metres or more in front of the background. The more space you have between the model and the background, the more control you will have over your lighting, reducing the risk of bleed. Set up a single head on a floor stand positioned behind the subject or on a regular stand to the side and slightly behind the subject. Fit the head with a standard spill kill reflector or small softbox. The idea is to project the light forwards onto the background, directly behind the subject.

For the key light, place a reflective silver or white umbrella onto a head and position this about 45 degrees off the camera axis (either side of the camera will do). Remember, the larger the umbrella, the greater the area it will cover, which will include the background. Start by metering your key light to *f*11. Once done, it is time to meter the background. The amount of power that you need will depend entirely on the background material you are using. Vinyl and paper backgrounds tend to be quite reflective, so will require less power than a matt fabric background. To begin with, meter the background light to between *f*11 and *f*16 and check your LCD. If your background is too dark, then increase the power on the background until you are just blowing the highlights on the background. Depending on the background light reflector you are using, you should find that the highlights will be brighter immediately behind the subject and gradually fall off towards the edge of the frame. The idea is to end up with a properly exposed subject and an overexposed background.

Don't be afraid to readjust your lighting if it is not correct, as working things out so that you get the right results 'in camera' will increase your knowledge and skills, and will also save you hours of post-processing.

Common Issues

THE SUBJECT LOOKS WASHED OUT AND HAZY

This is generally caused by too much power from the background bleeding back into the lens of the camera, causing haze.

- Try reducing the power of the background light.
- Or try increasing the power of your key light to compensate.
- Stopping down to a smaller aperture may also help in some circumstances.

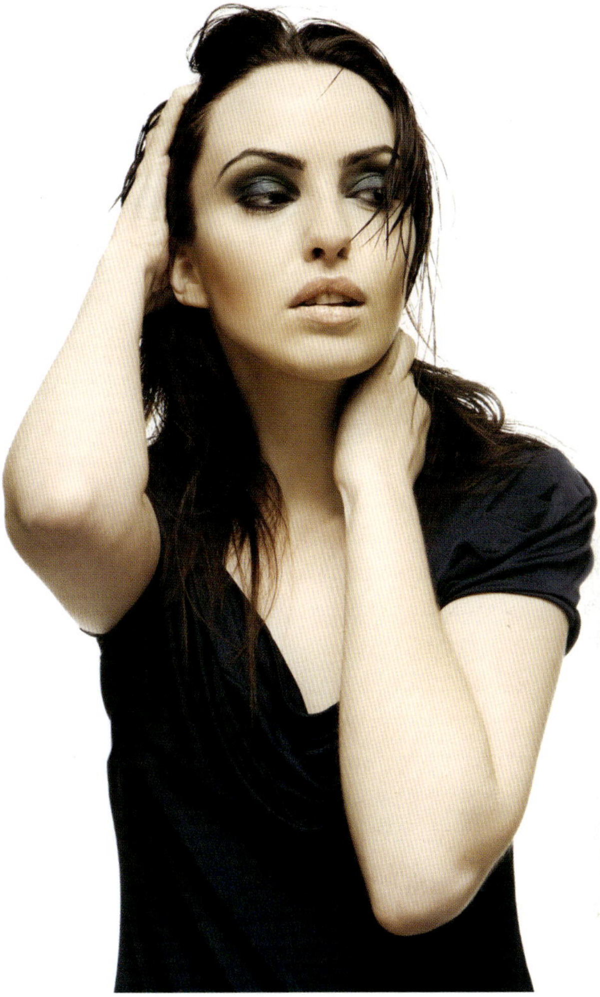

Fig. 2.16
Image © Christian Hough. Model: Christine Hogan.

WHITE HIGHLIGHTS/SPILL LIGHT ON THE SIDE OF THE SUBJECT

Unwanted light on the subject can come from two places and have different terms. Bleed is light bounding back from the background, and this can be resolved by creating distance between the subject and the background. Spill is cause by unwanted light spilling from other heads onto the subject; in this case it will be the background light.

- Simply moving the light further behind the subject.
- Or use a more directional reflector.

SETTINGS AND EQUIPMENT

Camera Settings

Aperture: *f*11
Shutter: 1/100sec
ISO: 100
Focal Length: 70mm

Lighting Equipment Required

- Two flash heads.
- Single directional reflector or softbox.
- Reflective umbrella.
- Background support and plain Colorama or fabric/vinyl backdrop.
- Two stands or one stand and a floor stand.
- Flash meter.
- Radio trigger or sync lead.

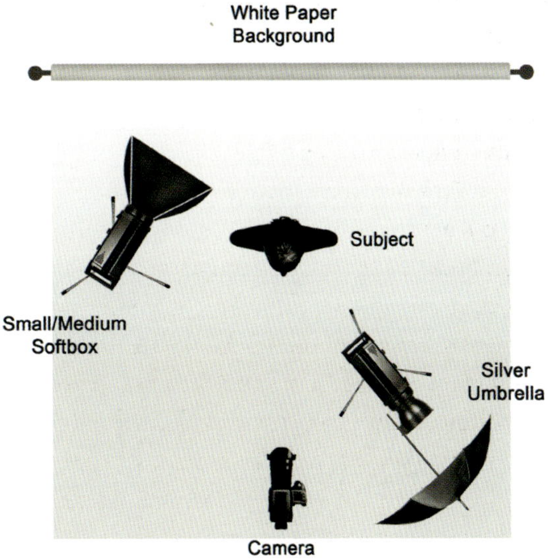

Original

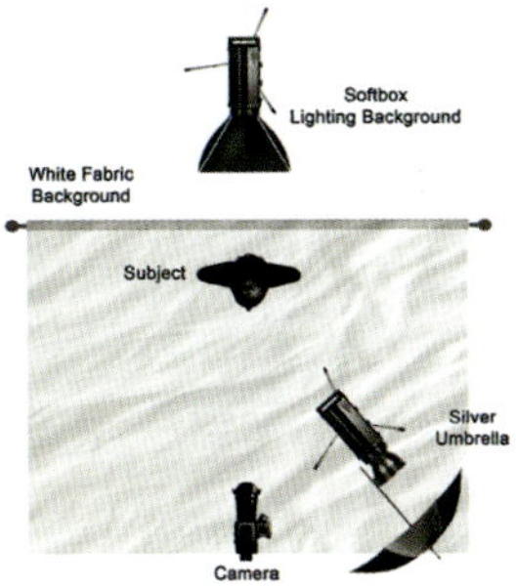

Alternative

Two Light Setup 6

The white highkey backgrounds and black backgrounds have their uses; however, there is more to backgrounds than meets the eye. Using a grey paper backdrop can open up a range of creative possibilities for photographers, which include the use of the gradated and gelled background. When using only two studio heads, your options can be more limited, yet with considered placement of the background light, it is possible to get a nice gradated grey background to contrast well with your subject.

This photo [Fig. 2.17] is a simple portrait, shot as a series for the actor Oreke Mosheshe. This shoot was different from your standard portrait, as it was shot from a higher angle and with a wider focal length to accentuate the perspective and bring out the shape of the face. This naturally made the subject look up towards the camera, instantly connecting with the viewer. A second light was added to light the upper half of the background paper and spill back onto the subject, which created the gradated background and the highlight on the hand. Overall, the dark shadows of the far side of the face contrast with the lighter part of the background, whilst the highlighted hand adds separation from the darker part of the background. Finally, a sepia effect was added in Photoshop.

Getting Started

For this type of background, you really need a thunder grey/dark grey paper background or a grey vinyl background with a matt finish. Background paper is smooth, fairly matt and allows the light to fall off evenly. If you are planning on using a fabric background, you will need to ensure that it is crease-free and positioned with an even cove where it meets the floor; however, the results may still be unpredictable and depend entirely on the type of fabric you are using.

Start by setting up your seamless paper background on the background support and marking a position for your subject to sit approximately two to three metres in front. Now fit a single flash head with a standard spill-kill reflector or small softbox and place it onto a boom arm. Using the boom, position the flash head up above the subject, moving it halfway between the subject and the background.

Once you have set up and roughly positioned the background light it is time to move onto the key light. Attach a small beauty dish or reflector to another head and position this up high close to the camera axis. Depending on the focal length of lens you are planning on using and the angle you intend shooting at, start by metering the key light to *f*11 at the forehead of your subject. It is inevitable when shooting at more extreme angles that you will get some light fall-off, so metering the head or face is a good start and will help reduce the occurrence of proximity hot spots.

Once you have positioned the key light, use the modelling facility on the background light and adjust the boom so that the light is lighting more of the background but also spilling a little onto the back of the subject. This will help create a clean background gradient and a gentle back light to achieve some separation. The rest is now up to you! Remember to continuously adjust the angle of the lights to compensate for the angle you are shooting at. The higher the angle you are shooting in relation to the subject, the more you will need to adjust the background light to light further down the paper towards the ground.

Common Issues

UNABLE TO LIGHT BOTH BACKGROUND AND MODEL

Narrow reflectors will be more directional and therefore cover a smaller area.

- Consider using a broader reflector to throw light out at a greater angle.
- Alternatively, you can try increasing the height of the background light, or sitting your subject slightly closer to the background.

GRADIENT APPEARS TOO HARSH

This can be a common issue with backgrounds within confined environments. Obtaining a smooth background relies partially on the distance of the background from the subject and depth of field.

- Try using a shallower depth of field to blur the background.
- Alternatively, utilize a broader and softer reflector on the background light, spreading the light more evenly.

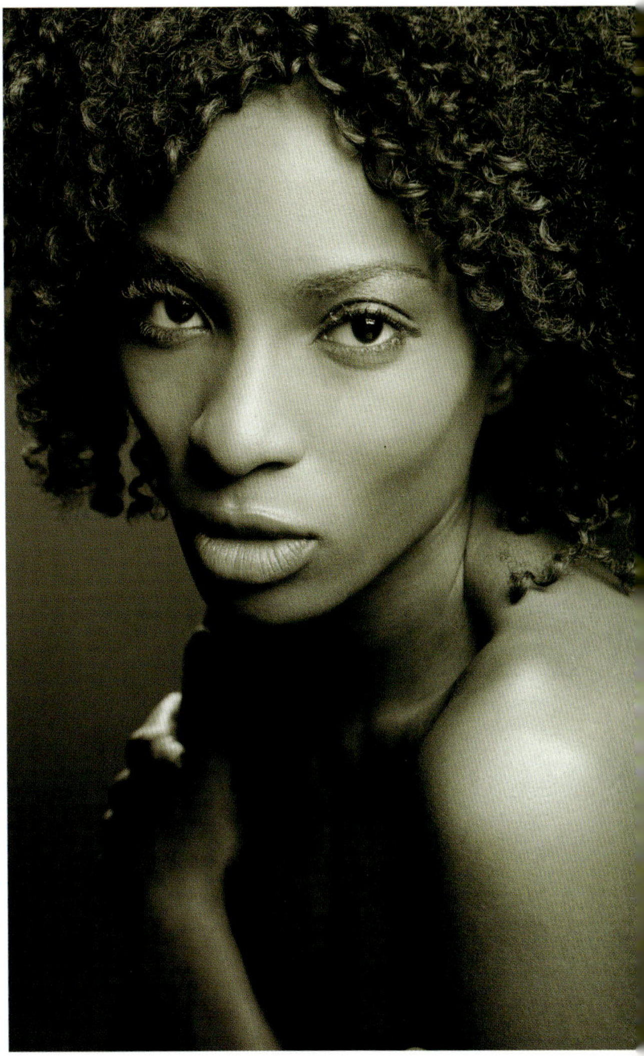

▲ Fig. 2.17
Image © Christian Hough. Model: Oreke Mosheshe.

SETTINGS AND EQUIPMENT

Camera Settings

Aperture: ƒ8.0
Shutter: 1/125sec
ISO: 100
Focal Length: 50mm

Lighting Equipment Required

- Two flash heads.
- Small beauty dish reflector or softbox for key light.
- Wide-angled reflector or small softbox for background light.
- Background support and grey paper or vinyl backdrop.
- Boom stand.
- One standard lighting stand.
- Flash meter.
- Radio trigger or sync lead.

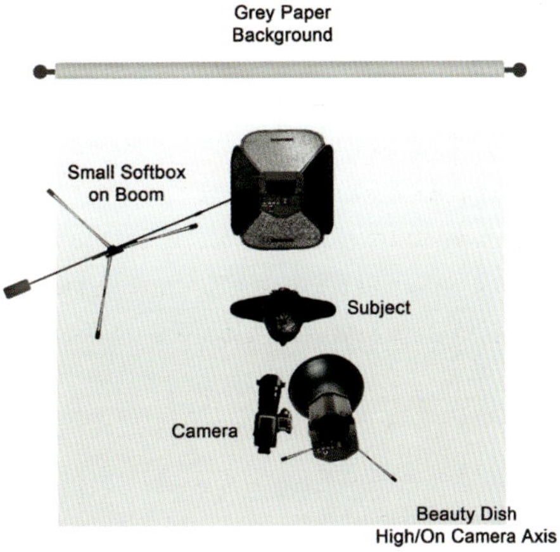

Two Light Setup 7

Getting some movement in images can really add to the overall dynamic of a shot. Not only does it change the energy of a photograph, but it can also change the expression and shape of your subject. 'Movement' doesn't necessarily mean big movements such as running and jumping, but can also mean small movements, such as the slight blowing of the hair from a reflector or small fan. In this photograph [Fig. 2.18] I have sought to restrict the movement to the head only, and worked on the framing and sitting pose of the model to give it a more editorial feel.

The framing and movement are both key to the image. Rather than shoot in the portrait orientation, I have chosen to shoot this landscape and position the bodyline diagonally within the frame. The movement was then created by simply getting the model to throw her head backwards several times until she created the right expression and angle with her face. Capturing movement can at times be hit and miss, so it may take a few more frames for you to get the right shot. Be patient and check your results as you go.

Getting Started

This shot was taken on a painted white infinity cove and required very little power to lift the white background. A 160cm silver umbrella was used on the key light to cover a large area with light, lighting both the model and the background. A secondary light was then used to lift the background, making it white.

Begin by attaching a silver reflective umbrella to your key light and positioning this off-camera. In this shot, the key light is off-axis to camera left. The exact positioning of your key light will depend on the positioning of your subject and the type of movement you want, so it is a good idea to get your subject to practise a few moves so you can find out where and how they are finishing, to enable you to capture the end result and ensure they will be adequately lit. It is also highly beneficial to consider the depth of field, especially if the subject is moving in and out of the focal plane as opposed to traversing it, as a greater depth of field will increase your chances of capturing a properly focused image.

When you have worked out a good position for your key light, meter it to your desired focal length (anywhere between *f*8.0 and *f*16 is generally acceptable). Now it is time to consider lifting the background. In the example, the background light has only been used to lift the shadows further and reduce the fall-off of light from the key light, so its positioning and direction will depend on the area you are in and the angle at which you are shooting. Here a single High Performance reflector has been used to bounce light off the background back onto the floor behind the model. In this instance, the background light was metered to approximately one *f* stop higher than the key light and then bounced off the background onto the floor area. Bouncing the light ensured that it provided a diffused light source and no bleed onto the model. If you don't have a white wall to bounce off, try using a very large piece of card, bounce reflector or even a second umbrella/large softbox, taking time to position it carefully so that it only lights the areas you want it to and doesn't spill onto your subject.

There are no exact settings for metering for this setup and there are so many variables that will affect the settings. Ensure you check the camera's LCD after each shot to see how the movement is working and make use of the blinking highlight facility to see how the background is exposing.

Common Issues

BLURRED MOVEMENT

- Studio photography relies more on flash duration than shutter speed. If you are unable to freeze motion, it is more than likely that the flash duration of your flash heads is not short enough to freeze movement. Increasing your shutter speed will have limited effect.

SUBJECT OUT OF FOCUS

Depending on your camera's focusing system, it is not always possible to track moving subjects that easily within the studio, especially if they are moving towards you.

- For accurate and consistent results, use a motion capture trigger, such as the Sabre Smart.
- Alternatively, for a more unpredictable approach it is possible to pre-focus on a point and then manually depress the shutter when the subject reached that point.

SUBJECT OUT OF LIGHT

Ensure you light the area where you want to freeze the movement.

- Using a broad light source such as a larger parabolic or softbox will help, as it will light a much broader area, whereas a narrow light source will only light a small area, reducing your chances of a properly lit photograph.

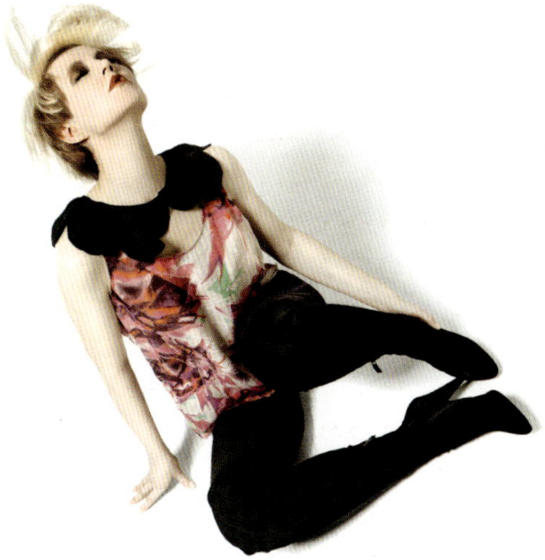

▲ Fig. 2.18
Image © Christian Hough. Model: Lucy Flower.

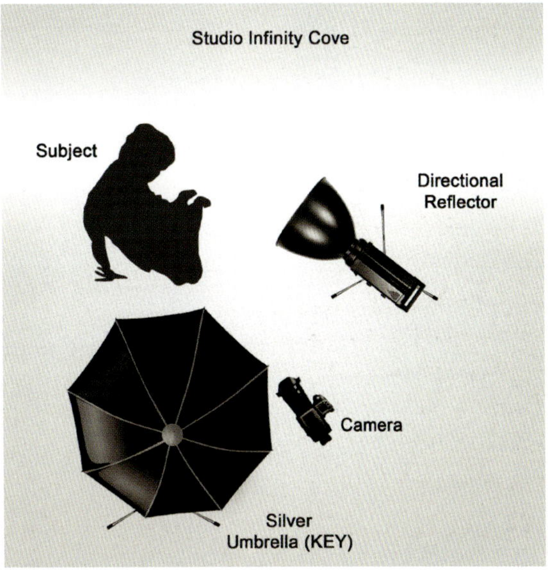

SETTINGS AND EQUIPMENT

Camera Settings

Aperture: ƒ9.5
Shutter: 1/250sec
ISO: 100
Focal Length: 34mm

Lighting Equipment Required

- Two flash heads.
- Silver reflective umbrella or large parabolic reflector.
- High Performance reflector (broad and directional).
- Studio infinity cover or background support and white paper or vinyl backdrop.
- Two standard lighting stands.
- Flash meter.
- Radio trigger or sync lead.

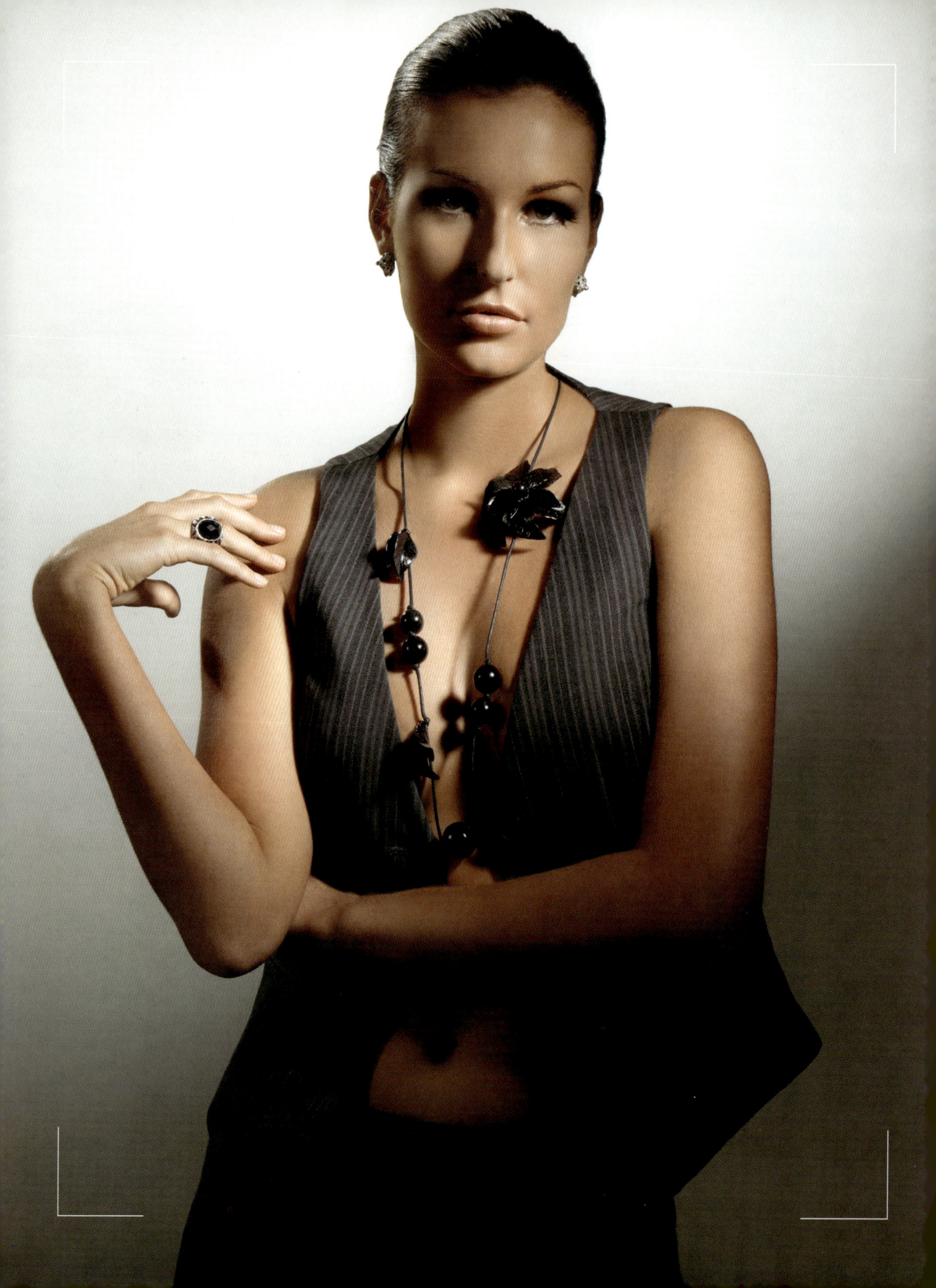

Chapter 3

Expanding Your Skills

THREE HEAD LIGHTING TECHNIQUES

Expanding from two heads to three heads will add a huge amount of flexibility to your setup. It is probably at this point that most photographers begin to fully develop their lighting skills, as the third light can be used to add several effects to both the subject and the backgrounds, without compromising on the use of a fill light when required. Understanding how to use this light effectively takes a little practice and requires more control and forethought. But with experimentation you will soon get to grips with some of the great techniques and effects you can achieve, eventually carving out your own style.

One common mistake made by many is not investing in additional reflectors and modifiers to use on an additional head, finding themselves limited as to how they can use it. It is important to invest in the right reflectors at the same time to help you adequately control and shape the light so your creativity is not hindered. So before you add a third light to your kit bag, factor in the price of some additional reflectors to keep your skills growing and your portfolio fresh.

Three Light Setup 1

There are several creative ways in which we can use a third light in a standard portrait. This example [Fig. 3.1] builds on the lighting from the similar one and two light setups as discussed previously, but now adds a third light by way of a hair/rim light. There are several ways in which we can light hair, using different reflectors and from different angles; however, in this shot I have boxed clever and circumvented the need for a second boom arm by positioning the light further back, concentrating the light on the hair, whilst also providing a slight rim light effect. Setting up in this way requires more control over the hair light to prevent spill and lens flare. Cognizance needs to be given to the style and colour of hair of your subject, as lighting the hair from behind has a tendency to pick out all of the loose strands of hair.

Finally, rather than using the second head as a fill light, I decided to use it to light the seamless background, creating a natural vignette around the subject. This helps focus the viewer's attention on the subject, whilst creating an element of separation from the dark grey background and at the same time reducing the contrast between the hair/rim light.

◀ Image © Christian Hough. Model: Elen Erichson.

Getting Started

Begin by setting up your background and hanging the dark grey seamless paper or background of your choice. A seamless paper background will provide the most pleasing effect, as it naturally creates a smooth gradient when lit, which is much more difficult to achieve with fabric. Try and leave enough space between the rear of the background and the wall of your studio within which to place another stand and studio head. When you have set up your background, mark a position on the floor of your studio, or use a seat, as to where you will be placing your subject. Leave approximately two metres distance between the background and subject.

Now place a studio head on a standard lighting stand and fit the head with a reflector and a honeycomb grid. Place this studio head behind your background and position it high over the top of the paper, pointing it downwards towards the back of your subject. The honeycomb grid will help control the direction of the light, preventing it from spilling over your set. The tighter the honeycomb, the narrower the light will be, so it pays to experiment with different honeycomb grids to see which works best. Ideally, if you have a second boom stand you can use this to place the hair light more directly overhead of the subject, offering more flexibility and control, fitting it with either a broader honeycomb or even a small softbox.

Once you set up the hair/rim light, attach a background reflector to a second studio head and position this on a floor stand immediately behind the subject, positioning it so that the light shines back onto the background paper. If you do not have a floor stand a standard lighting stand can be used from the side, although the lighting on the background will be asymmetrical and difficult to position centrally. It is also possible to use a reflector and honeycomb grid if you do not have a background reflector. Use the modelling facility on the studio light and position the light so it will shine directly behind the subject when viewed through the camera.

Fit the key light with a second honeycomb grid, fixing it to a boom arm, before placing it centrally in front of the subject. Raise it up about one metre higher. The honeycomb grid fitted to the key light will help control the light and prevent spill light from hitting the background. Using the modelling facility on the key light, adjust its position to get the light as symmetrical as possible, throwing all the shadows downwards, whilst ensuring that you are retaining the catchlight in the eyes. Meter your key light between *f*8.0 and *f*16.

There are no exact power ratios for the background light and hair/rim light, as the colour and type of background material and finish and colour of your subject's hair or clothing will all affect the outcome. Dark fabric backgrounds will require more power than lighter paper backgrounds, in much the same way as very dark hair will require more light than very fair hair. It is worth positioning your subject and then making the final adjustments to the direction of these lights using the modelling facility and adjusting the power to taste by using the camera's LCD/computer monitor.

Common Issues

LENS FLARE FROM HAIR/RIM LIGHT

Lens flare is caused by light shining directly down the lens of the camera.

- Start by repositioning the hair light so that it doesn't shine directly into the camera.
- Fit a smaller honeycomb grid to control the light more and reduce the possibility of spill light.
- Adjust your angle of shooting slightly to compensate.
- Fitting a lens hood may also help.

BACKGROUND LIGHT SHOWING CREASES IN BACKGROUND PAPER

- Try positioning your subject further from the background or using a wider aperture, so that the background naturally falls out of focus.

- If you are limited for space and equipment, try diffusing your background modifier using thin tracing paper or fabric. Ensure that the modelling light is switched off and that the fabric or paper is not touching the flash tube to avoid any risk of fire.

SETTINGS AND EQUIPMENT

Camera Settings

Aperture: f11
Shutter: 1/125sec
ISO: 100
Focal Length: 110mm

Lighting Equipment Required

- Three flash heads.
- Background reflector (background light).
- Two reflectors and honeycomb grids (key/hair/rim light).
- Grey seamless background paper.
- One standard lighting stand.
- One boom stand.
- Floor stand.
- Flash meter.
- Radio trigger or sync lead.

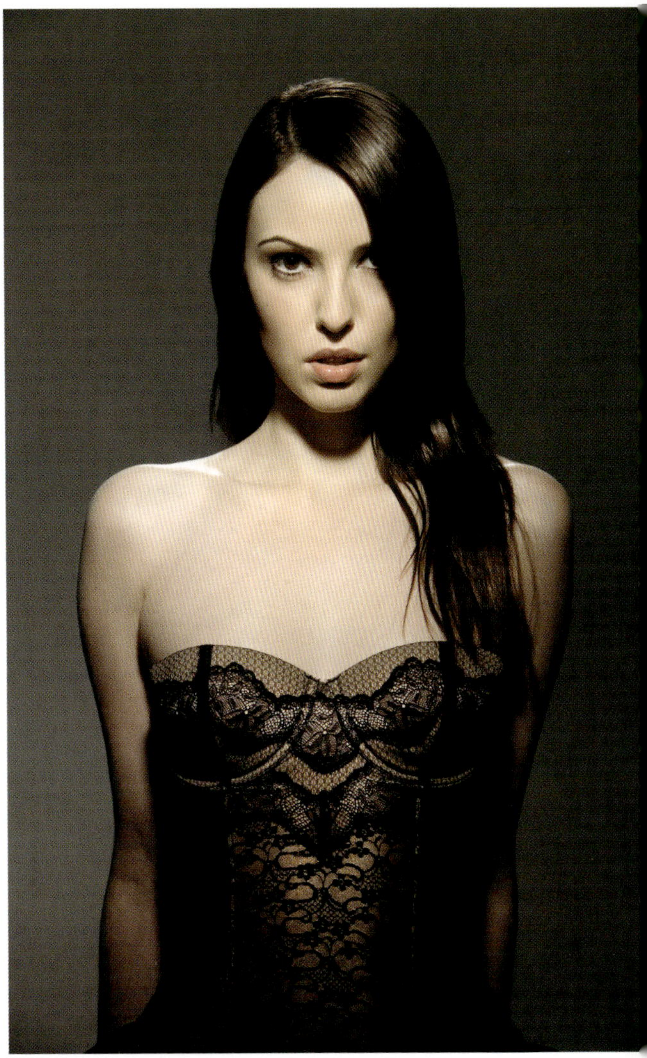

▲ Fig. 3.1
Image © Christian Hough. Model: Christine Hogan.

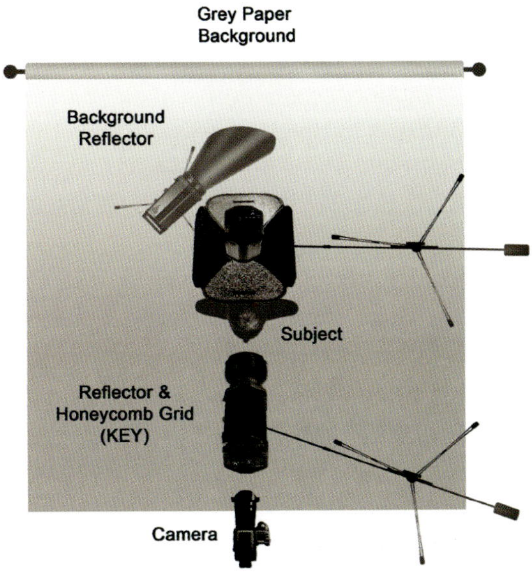

▲ Original

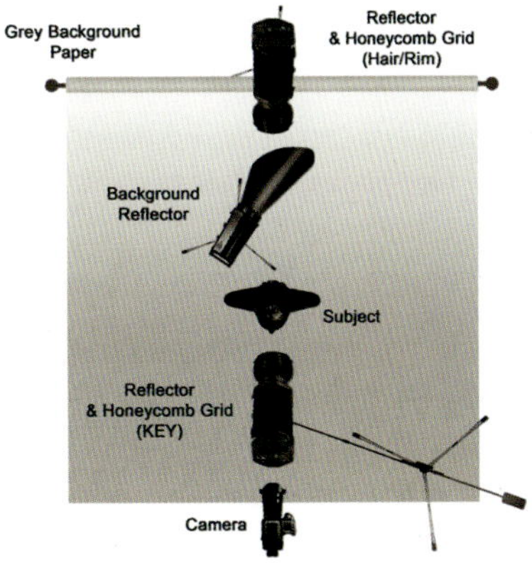

▲ Alternative

Three Light Setup 2

Small adjustments of the lights and the pose can dramatically change the mood of a photograph. In this shot [Fig. 3.2] I have changed the mood from more of a serious fashion feel to that of a softer sitting portrait. The lighting setup is similar to the previous setup but with a few minor adjustments to take into account the position and direction in which the subject is sitting, and to add colour to the background. The idea here is to try and add an element of warmth to the shot by drawing the depth of the red background with a coloured gel. It is entirely possible to use a deep red background paper and light it independently in a similar way to the previous setup; however, using coloured gels can enable you to change the colour of the background very quickly and with the bare minimum of cost. The biggest factor to consider in obtaining a deep colour on a background when using a gel is the colour of the paper; you will find that a thunder grey/dark grey background will hold the colour well, without it looking too light and washed-out.

Getting Started

In a setup similar to the previous shot, start by hanging a dark grey seamless paper roll from your background support. The results from fabric backdrops can be somewhat unpredictable, whereas a dark grey paper background will provide the most pleasing effect, creating a smooth gradient when lit. Remember to leave enough space between the rear of the background and the wall of your studio within which to place another stand and studio head. When you have set up your background, mark a position on the floor of your studio or use a seat so you can judge where you will be placing your subject. If possible, leave at least two to three metres distance between the background and subject.

Now place a studio head on a regular stand and fit the head with a reflector and a honeycomb grid. Place this studio head behind your background and position it over the top of the paper, so that it is pointing back towards your subject. The honeycomb grid will help control the direction of the light, preventing it from spilling over your set. Remember, the tighter the honeycomb, the narrower the light will be, so it pays to experiment with different honeycomb grids to see which works best for you.

As in the previous setup, attach a background reflector or a set of barn doors to a second studio head and attach this to a floor stand immediately behind the subject, positioning it so that the light shines back onto the background paper. Using the clip on the background reflector/barn doors, place a coloured gel over the front of the light, ensuring that

SETTINGS AND EQUIPMENT

Camera Settings

Aperture: *f*11
Shutter: 1/125sec
ISO: 100
Focal Length: 117mm

Lighting Equipment Required

- Three flash heads.
- Small beauty dish or small softbox (key light).
- Background reflector/barn doors (background light).
- Coloured gels.
- Reflector and honeycomb grid (hair/rim light).
- Dark grey seamless background paper.
- Two standard lighting stands.
- Floor stand.
- Flash meter.
- Radio trigger or sync lead.

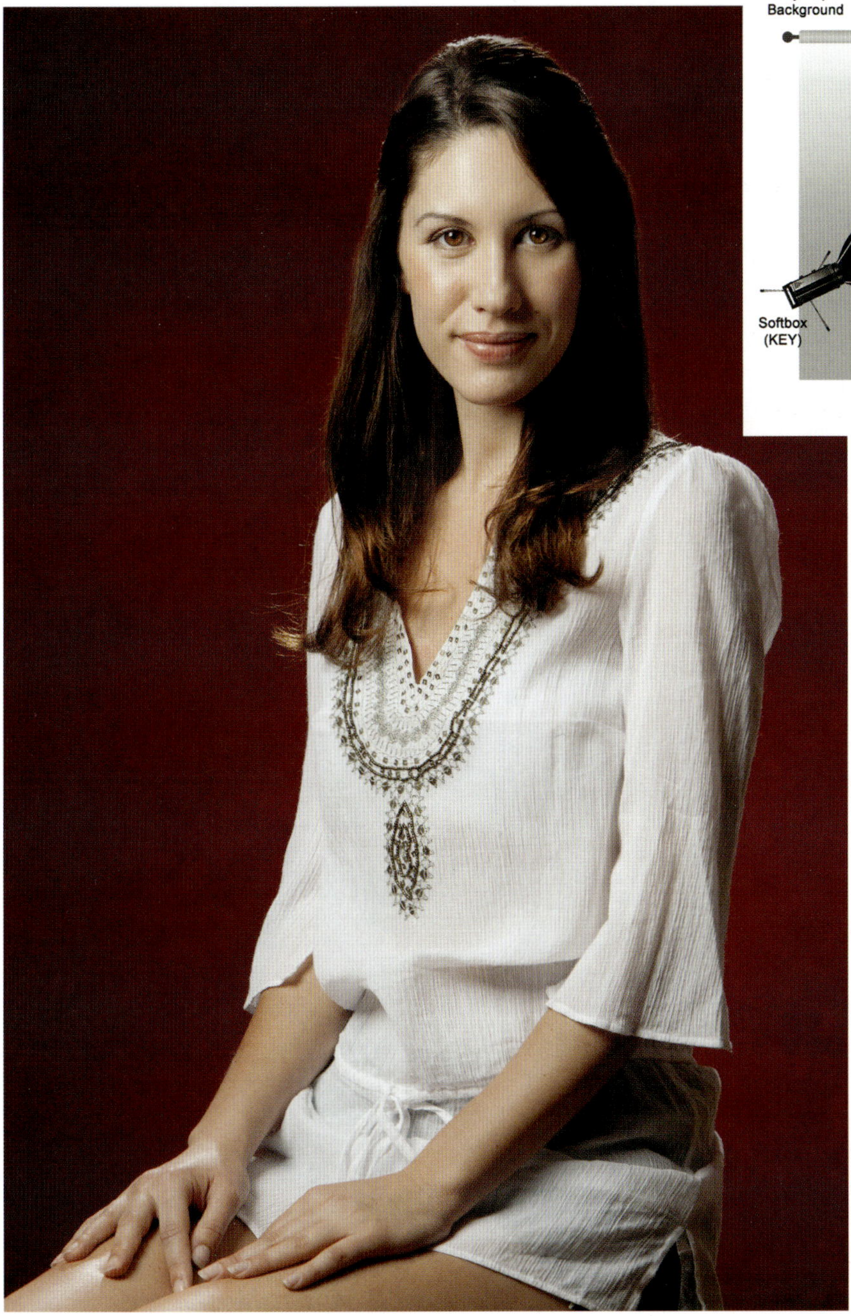

▲ Fig. 3.2
Image © Christian Hough.
Model: Freya Berry.

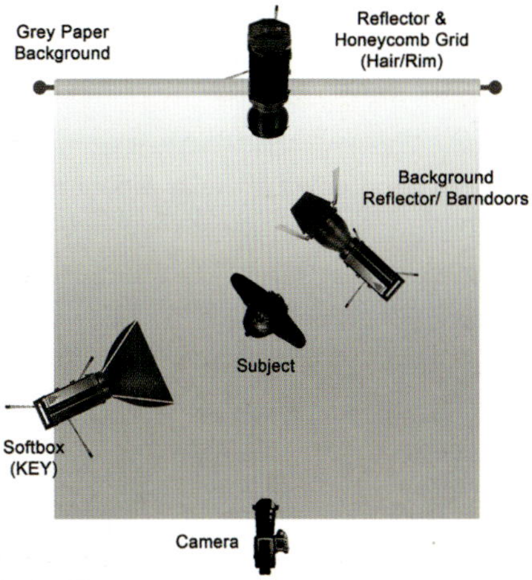

▲ Original

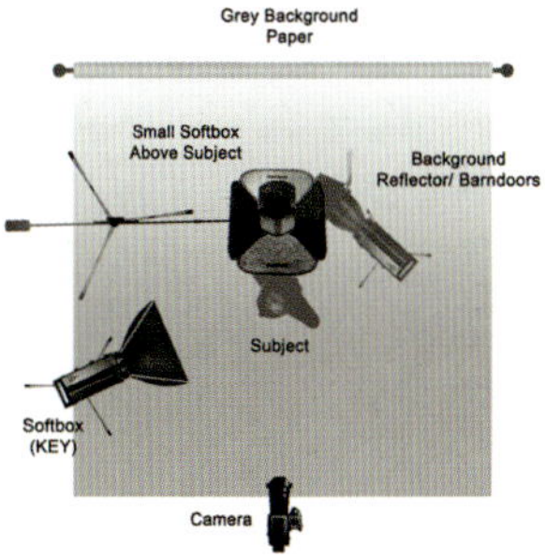

▲ Alternative

it completely covers the aperture of the reflector. If you do not have a floor stand a regular stand may be used from either side, although the colour on the background may be unevenly lit. Ensure that the coloured gel is not resting on the modelling light or flash tube, and ensure that you are using heat rated photographic gels, otherwise you are likely to create a fire risk. Now position the light so it lights the background directly behind the subject. Finally, attach a small beauty dish or softbox to your key light and place it approximately 45 degrees off-camera axis and about a metre higher. Once your subject sits down, you can adjust the positioning of the key light and begin to model the face properly. Meter your key light to approximately *f*11.

As before, there are no exact power ratios for the gelled background light and hair/rim light, as the coloured gel you use will require different amounts of power to light the background. Your subject's hair or clothing will all affect the outcome. Remember dark gels on dark backgrounds will require more power than lighter-coloured gels on lighter backgrounds, in much the same way as very dark hair will require more light than very fair hair. It is worth positioning your subject before making the final adjustments to the direction and power of these lights, adjusting the power to taste by using the camera's LCD/computer monitor. As long as your key light is metered properly, you can be more confident in trusting what you see in the LCD.

Common Issues

COLOUR BLEEDING BACK ONTO SUBJECT

Ensure that the background reflector or any other modifier you are using is pointing directly at the background and not spilling onto the subject.

- Start by increasing the distance between the background and the subject, to reduce the bleed.
- Alternatively, decrease the power of the background light or use a less reflective background.

BACKGROUND LOOKS WASHED-OUT

- If you are using a light grey or white background, start by changing this to a dark grey, so that it gives the coloured gel more depth.
- Alternatively, use a darker-coloured gel.
- You may find that a large reflector or umbrella on the key light will partially light the background, reducing the depth of the colour, so if possible use a smaller light source and change its direction so that it no longer lights the background directly behind the subject.

Three Light Setup 3

Creating a high-key background with three lights is an altogether easier prospect. The use of two heads to light the white background enables you to cover a much greater area, even for a standard full-length shot. The trade-off of course is that this will leave you only a single studio head with which to light the subject, which may not be ideal for the individual or subject you decide to photograph. In the majority of cases choosing the right reflectors for all heads can certainly make your life easier, especially within more confined spaces. It really is a case of using the right tools for the job.

In this photograph [Fig. 3.3], I decided to introduce more movement, by getting the model to move around and by using a fan to lift the hair. It is important to allow your subject to move relatively freely when trying to get shape and expression into a photograph as you will find that both the body and the face will help express the energy. In this shot, the model was made to swing from side to side to music, using the waistband and pockets of the trousers to prop the hands. By moving the shoulders back and the elbows inwards, the hand naturally exacerbates the curve in the hip, whilst the breeze through the hair and expression on the face adds to the sense of passion. You will find that a little music on your set will go a long way to helping relax people and create mood!

The key to this shot is covering a larger area with the key light. A lot of free movement can be difficult to achieve with very tight and precise lighting as the subject will constantly move out of the light. For this reason I deliberately used a very large parabolic on my key light, to cover a broad area.

Getting Started

Start by setting up your background. White seamless paper, vinyl or a studio infinity cove are ideal; and fabric is also an acceptable alternative. Each background will require different amounts of power, depending on the finish and distance from the subject. Remember, shiny reflective vinyl will require less light than an extremely matt finished fabric. Once you have set up your background, mark a position for your subject approximately three to four metres in front of the background. More space between the background and the subject will help you control the light more.

On each side of the subject and about half a meter behind, place a studio head fitted with a broad directional reflector or small softbox, without the front diffusers fitted. These heads will make the background white, so they need to be positioned slightly behind your subject to help eliminate any risk of light spilling back. Use the modelling facility on each light to ensure you are evenly covering the white background behind the subject. There is no need to aim both of the heads at the same spot directly behind the subject. Directing the light on each side of the subject should be enough to offer consistent yet broad coverage of the background.

It is a good idea when choosing a modifier for your key light to think about coverage. A large softbox or umbrella will achieve good coverage of the subject and will also help throw light onto the background, whereas a small reflector with a honeycomb grid will only cover a small and relatively precise area. It is recommended that you use a large umbrella or softbox on the key light. Once you have done this, move the key light in front of the subject, between two and three metres and approximately fifty centimetres to a metre higher. It is not crucial as to where on the camera's axis you have the key light, but it is worth considering that the closer to the camera's axis the key light, the flatter the light. In the example pictured here, the key light was placed around 45 degrees from the camera and was metered to *f*16. If your subject is moving, you will find that *f*16 will increase the chance of you capturing a properly focused image.

With the background lights, it is recommended that you meter these individually to ensure a uniformly lit background. On forums there is usually a lot of debate with regard to the metering of the high-key background, with many photographers professing fail-proof metering for all scenarios. However, in reality, it is not always that clear cut, as factors such as the type of background in use (paper, painted wall, fabric, vinyl and so on), the space within which you are shooting, the distance between the subject and the background, even the key light modifier will all affect the metering. For this reason, I frequently advise photographers to begin by metering the background approximately a stop higher than the key light and then to utilize the histogram or flashing highlights on the camera's LCD to ascertain how much of the background they are overexposing, and increasing or decreasing the power as necessary. It is important to consider all of the studio environment to reduce undesirable effects, such as flare, bleed and spill.

Once you have metered your key light and background, be sure to test the settings on your subject and utilize the key light to shape the face and body properly. Get your subject to move about, and get an assistant to waft the hair with a reflector or fan to add a little more movement.

Common Issues

LIGHT BOUNCING ONTO THE SUBJECT FROM BACKGROUND (BLEED)

- Start by moving your subject further from the background, to reduce the intensity of the light bouncing back.
- If this is not possible, reduce the power of the background lighting until the bleed is reduced.

INSUFFICIENT COVERAGE OF THE BACKGROUND

- Begin by adding a broader reflector to the background lights.
- Or move the background lights further away from the background so that they cover a wider area. The further away from the background you move the lights, the more power you will need to compensate.

UNABLE TO MAINTAIN CONSISTENT BACKGROUND

If you are using a fabric background, you will possibly find that it can be more difficult to retain fully blown highlight detail towards the outer edges of the frame, depending on how wide you are shooting. This is because fabric absorbs light and can result in a yellow discoloration towards the edge of the frame.

- Try repositioning the background lights so that they cover a broader area.
- Using a larger reflector on the key light will also help light the background.

SETTINGS AND EQUIPMENT

Camera Settings

Aperture: *f*16
Shutter: 1/125sec
ISO: 100
Focal Length: 97mm

Lighting Equipment Required

- Three flash heads.
- Large umbrella or softbox (key light).
- Two high performance/broad directional reflectors (background lights).
- White seamless background paper or infinity cove.
- Three standard lighting stands.
- Flash meter.
- Radio trigger or sync lead.

Fig. 3.3
Image © Christian Hough. Model: Jannica Klingborg.

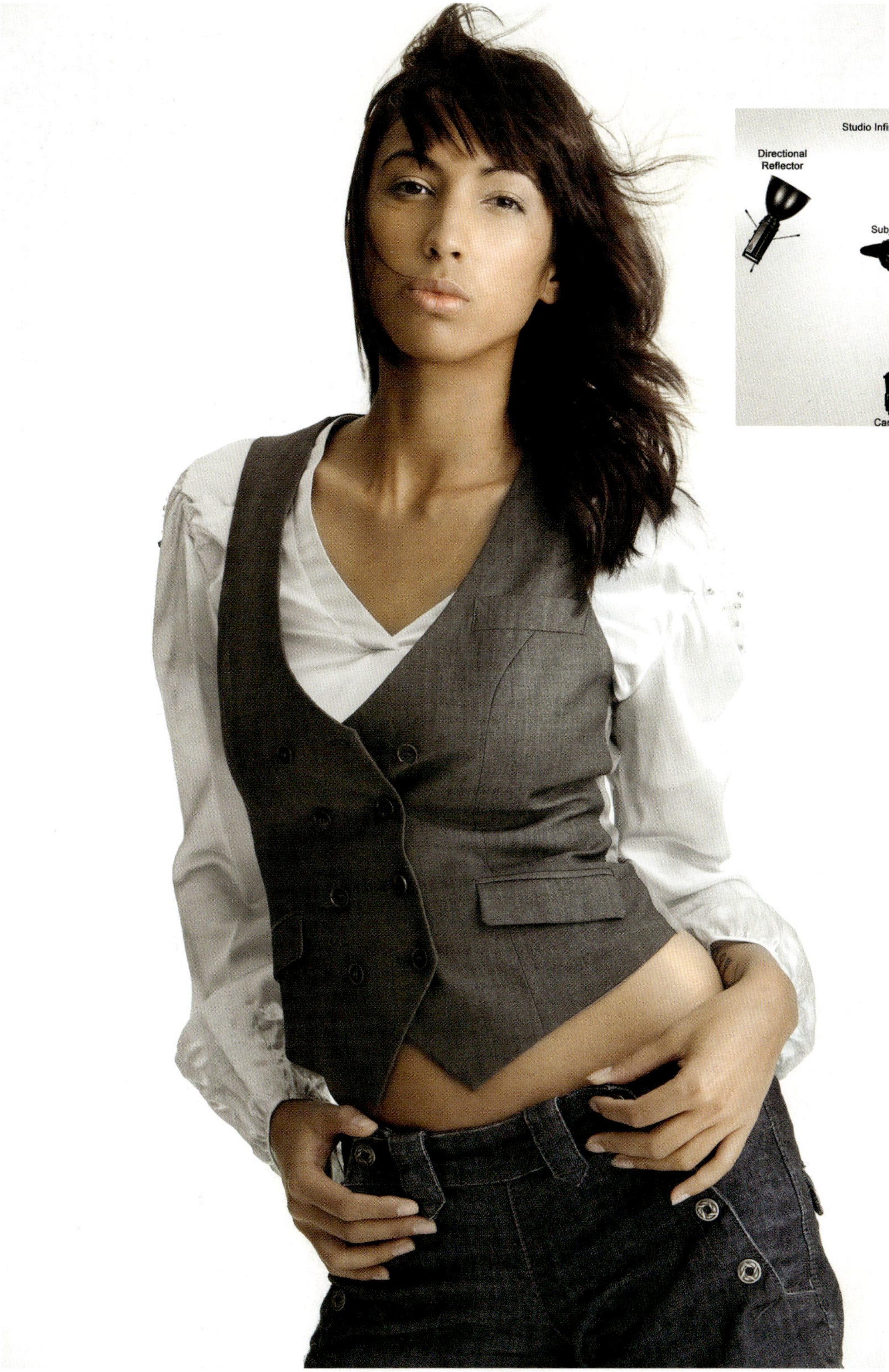

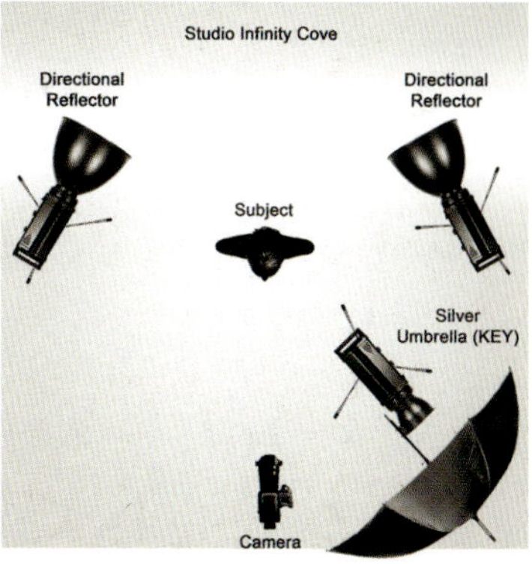
Studio Infinity Cove
Directional Reflector
Directional Reflector
Subject
Silver Umbrella (KEY)
Camera

Three Light Setup 4

Getting up close to your subject can really help give an image a different perspective. Instead of using a more familiar studio focal length of 80–100mm, you may find that zooming out to a slightly wider angle can make an interesting alternative and allow you to get in closer and higher, squeezing more into the frame. Zooming out just a little can make a big difference.

What works in this image [Fig. 3.4] is the angle, crop and contrast. The slightly wider angle of 64mm has enabled getting in closer and slightly above the model, which brings the top of the arms and collarbone into the frame. However, the majority of the frame is filled by the model's face, drawing the viewer's attention to the interesting eye make-up. The dark eyes work nicely with the low-key background, whilst the highlights produced by the side lights bring shape and definition to the model's face. More interestingly, the key light was actually flagged by me standing in front of the model, thus evenly filling the shadows and making the side lights the main accent. Finally, the framing helps the viewer focus on the face as there are no distractions from hair or clothing.

Getting Started

This shot consists of a standard three light setup that was modified purely due to positioning. The setup and modification are simple yet effective. Begin by setting up your black paper or fabric background. If you are limited with space, you will find that a black velvet background will prove more effective at absorbing light. Once done, position a backless seat or stool approximately two metres from the background. Depending on the angle you intend shooting at, you may find that you need to pull the background down to the floor and under the stool so that you do not get any unwanted background scenery once you start shooting at higher angles.

For your key light, attach a medium-sized silver reflective umbrella to a standard reflector; fit it to your studio head and position this directly above the camera. A good starting point for the height of the umbrella is approximately two metres from the ground and approximately four metres in front of the stool. This will allow enough distance for the light to spread and not to be completely blocked by your body. Meter this to *f*11.

Now you need to set up your side lights. Begin by erecting two stripboxes, fixing them to two studio lights, and then place a light either side of the model, approximately one metre behind the stool. Now turn the stripboxes back towards where the model will sit. Meter the two side lights evenly to approximately *f*8.0. If you don't have stripboxes it is possible to clip black fabric or thick black card to a standard softbox to create a strip effect. Failing this, you can always use standard reflectors and honeycomb grids.

SETTINGS AND EQUIPMENT

Camera Settings

Aperture: *f*9.0
Shutter: 1/160sec
ISO: 100
Focal Length: 64mm

Lighting Equipment Required

- Three flash heads.
- Silver umbrella or large beauty dish.
- Two stripboxes or two reflectors with honeycomb grids.
- Black seamless background paper or black fabric.
- Three standard lighting stands.
- Silver bounce reflector.
- Flash meter.
- Radio trigger or sync lead.

Position your model and, without standing in front of the light, take a test shot. You should find that the umbrella lights the face, whilst the two stripboxes highlight the sides of the cheeks. Once you are satisfied with the positioning of your lighting, you can now consider zooming out and getting closer, flagging the key light with your body. You will now find that your shots are underexposed, as you are blocking out the key light. The simple solution is to stop up by approximately one stop to compensate. To help lift the shadows, use a silver bounce reflector at about knee height. Not only does this lift the shadows, but it also creates a small catchlight in the model's eye. The great thing is that you can now return to a more typical shooting position by simply stepping away from the model and stopping back down to *f*11. You get two uses out of a single setup.

Common Issues

LIGHT SPILLING ONTO BACKGROUND

- Ensure that you have positioned your side lights so that they are pointing away from the background and towards the model.
- Stripboxes and honeycomb grids will help control the light more than a large softbox.
- Alternatively, check the softboxes for leaking light.
- It is also possible to flag the side lights and move them further from the background, to reduce the amount of spill light.

STANDARD SETUP TOO FLAT

- Adjusting the height of the umbrella will help; raise the umbrella to increase the downwards shadows or lower the umbrella to decrease them and make the face look flatter.

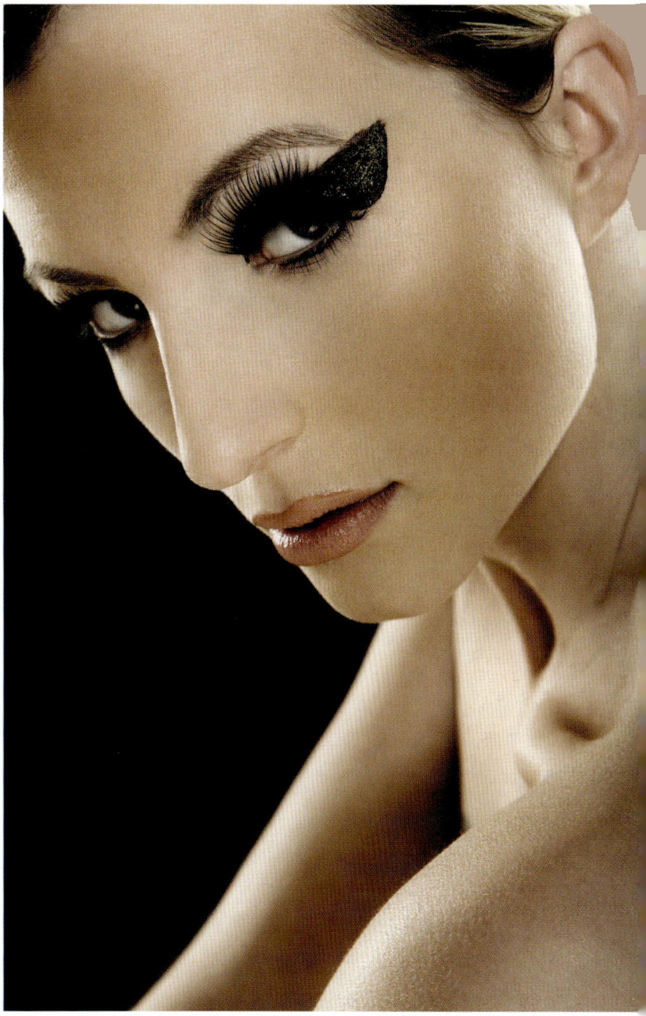

▲ Fig. 3.4
Image © Christian Hough. Model: Jaala Pickering.

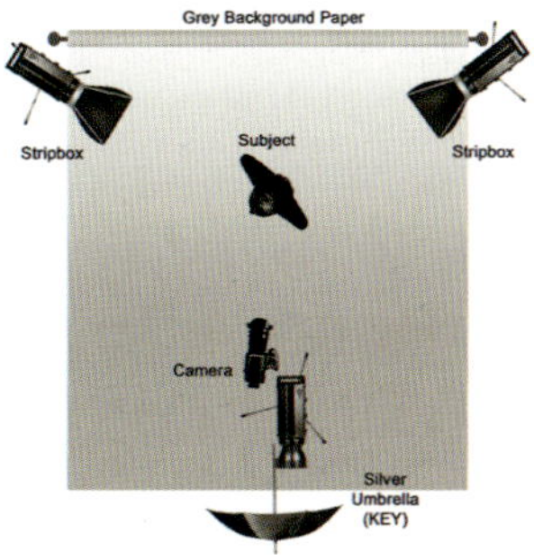

▲ Original setup.

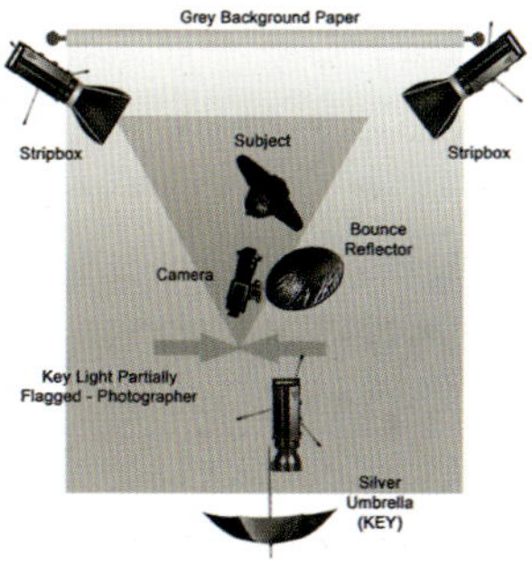

▲ Flagging light with body.

Three Light Setup 5

Babies and children can be a delight to photograph, and there are times when virtually every picture you take will please a loving parent! However, they can also be some of the most challenging subjects and occasionally need lots of patience, so it pays to keep the lighting simple and flexible. Using broad light sources is the key to success, enabling you to concentrate on positioning and shooting, without the additional worry of the light.

You may find that babies around the six months mark can be particularly challenging. Every child develops at their own rate, so assumptions cannot be made as to whether they can support themselves or sit upright unaided. You may need to use something to assist the child, such as a baby poser, covered with fabric or a throw. What makes this shot [Fig. 3.5] is the clothing and the baby's expression. A denim jacket and a pair of pink sunglasses give the child a funky appearance, made all the more apt by the cheeky expression. The high-key background and white fur throw help soften the image and allow the baby to be the main focus point.

Getting Started

Begin by setting up your white background. Any white background can be used – paper, fabric or even a wall. Position a low and broad table approximately two metres in front of your background and then position the baby poser on top. I have used a very low and wide table, as it lifts the baby high enough to be photographed, but is also more than wide enough to stop the baby from toppling over the edge. You can use any material you wish to cover the baby poser; however, it is preferable and more acceptable to use 'soft' material and throws.

Once in position, attach a small softbox or semi-directional reflector to a studio light and position this to the side of the table, pointing it towards your background. Place it approximately half a metre closer to the background than the baby poser, and meter it between *f*11 and *f*16. Remember the more reflective your background, the less power it will need to blow the highlights.

For your key and fill lights, set up two lights onto stands and attach a silver reflective umbrella to each of them. If you don't have silver umbrellas, then shoot-through umbrellas or softboxes will perform just as well. Position one of these umbrellas approximately 45 degrees off-axis and approximately one metre higher than the head of the baby. This will be your key light, so meter this to *f*11. Now place your fill light on the opposite side of the key light and closer to the camera axis. Meter the fill light between *f*5.6 and *f*8.0. Try not to produce too many hard shadows as babies' and children's faces are very soft and therefore suit softer images. If you have an older child who is moving around more, then you may wish to move the umbrellas further apart so that you cover a broader area with light.

Once your subject is in place, take a test shot and ensure that the background light is lighting the wall directly behind. Keep your key and fill light around two metres away from the subject, to ensure that you retain a catchlight in the eye; this can often be a problem when subjects are positioned low to the ground.

Finally, always ensure that you have a responsible parent or guardian with any child. Studios are dangerous places with hot lights, electric cables and delicate equipment. Be sure to fully brief the parent or guardian about all the hazards and what you expect from them, ensuring that they remain close to the child at all times. For very young children, it is advisable for at least one parent to be just out of frame and ready to control the child between shots.

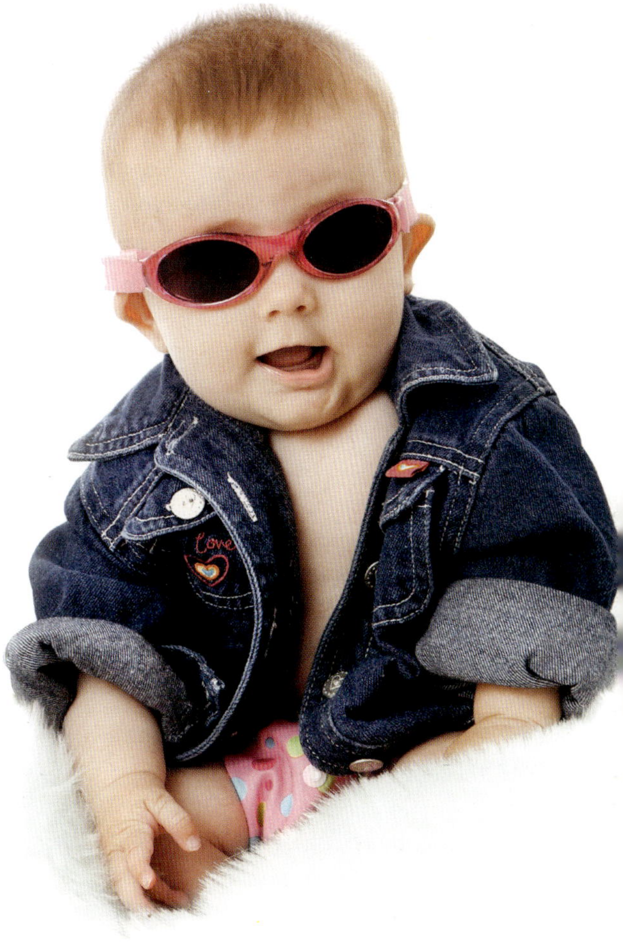

▶ Fig. 3.5
Image © Christian Hough. Model: Tabetha Wydymus.

Common Issues

WASHED-OUT IMAGE

If you are shooting in a confined space you may be experiencing bleed from the background.

- Begin by reducing the power of the background light, as you may find that the umbrella is partially lighting the background.
- Secondly, try turning off the fill light and using a reflector or polyboard instead, as there may be sufficient light from the key light to adequately fill the shadows.

NO CATCHLIGHT.

- Begin by either raising the subject or lowering the lights.
- If you are still unable to obtain a catchlight, try moving your key and fill light further back to reduce the angle between them and the subject.

SETTINGS AND EQUIPMENT

Camera Settings

Aperture: $f11$
Shutter: 1/125sec
ISO: 100
Focal Length: 120mm

Lighting Equipment Required

- Three flash heads.
- Two silver reflective umbrellas or medium-sized softboxes.
- Once small softbox or semi-directional reflector.
- White seamless background.
- Three standard lighting stands.
- Table, baby poser and throw/fabric cover.
- Flash meter.
- Radio trigger or sync lead.

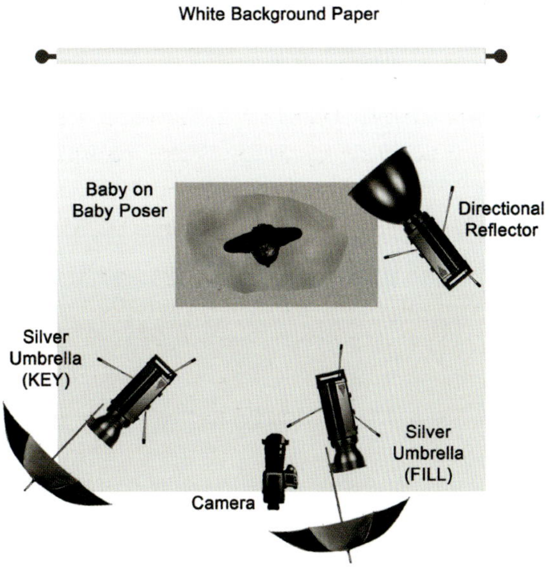

Three Light Set Up 6

Simple movements and small adjustments to your lights can make a huge difference to the mood of your photograph. In this example [Fig. 3.6], the lighting has been kept direct and the background subtle, placing more emphasis on contrast on the subject, rather than contrast against the background. The face has been short lit and the second light tightly controlled to bring out the shape of the model's face and body from the side, while retaining more shadow towards the lens of the camera. The simplicity of the background creates a gentle gradient that doesn't distract the viewer.

Getting Started

For this shot to work, it is important to find a smooth white background. A painted white wall, white paper or vinyl will work perfectly and allow the light to drop off smoothly, creating a gentle crease-free gradient. Of course, if you plan on converting the shot to black and white, it is possible to use any light coloured wall. The success of the background will depend on the available space, as the further away the background light is positioned from the wall, the greater the spread of light and the more subtle the gradient. Positioning the background light close to the wall or background paper will increase the angle at which the light needs to be placed and thus the contrast of the gradient.

Begin by attaching a light to a stand at waist height and fit it with a broad directional reflector. Position the light approximately 2–3 metres from the wall. Direct the light back towards the wall and use the modelling facility to ascertain the strength of the gradient. At 90 degrees, the light should be fairly flat on the background, however, as you position the light closer and decrease the angle, the contrast of the gradient will increase. Once you're happy with the effect, meter the background light to approximately *f*5.6 at the central point behind the model.

For the key and side light, it is a good idea to mark a position for your model on the ground and then use this as a reference point for your metering. Begin by positioning the attaching a reflector and honeycomb grid to a single studio light and placing this to the right side of the model. Position it approximately 1 metre higher than the model. This will be the key light so with your model in position, move the light around her until you achieve the familiar Rembrandt/short lighting pattern on the face and meter to *f*11. Providing you keep the light the same distance from the model, it will be possible to move it around and shape the face, without the need to re-meter continuously.

Finally, attach a second honeycomb grid and reflector to a second studio light and position this to the left of the model. This will be used to light the shoulder and the hair. Position the light slightly behind the model and approximately 1 metre higher. The strength of this light will ultimately depend on the colour of the hair and skin of the model and you will find that darker hair and matt skin will need a little more power than fair hair and shiny skin, so meter between *f*5.6 and *f*11, making adjustments as necessary.

SETTINGS AND EQUIPMENT

Camera Settings

Aperture: *f*11
Shutter: 1/250sec
ISO:100
Focal Length 82mm

Lighting Equipment Required

- Three flash heads.
- Two reflectors and honeycomb grids.
- Once broad directional reflector.
- White background (wall, paper, vinyl).
- Flash meter.
- Radio trigger or sync lead.

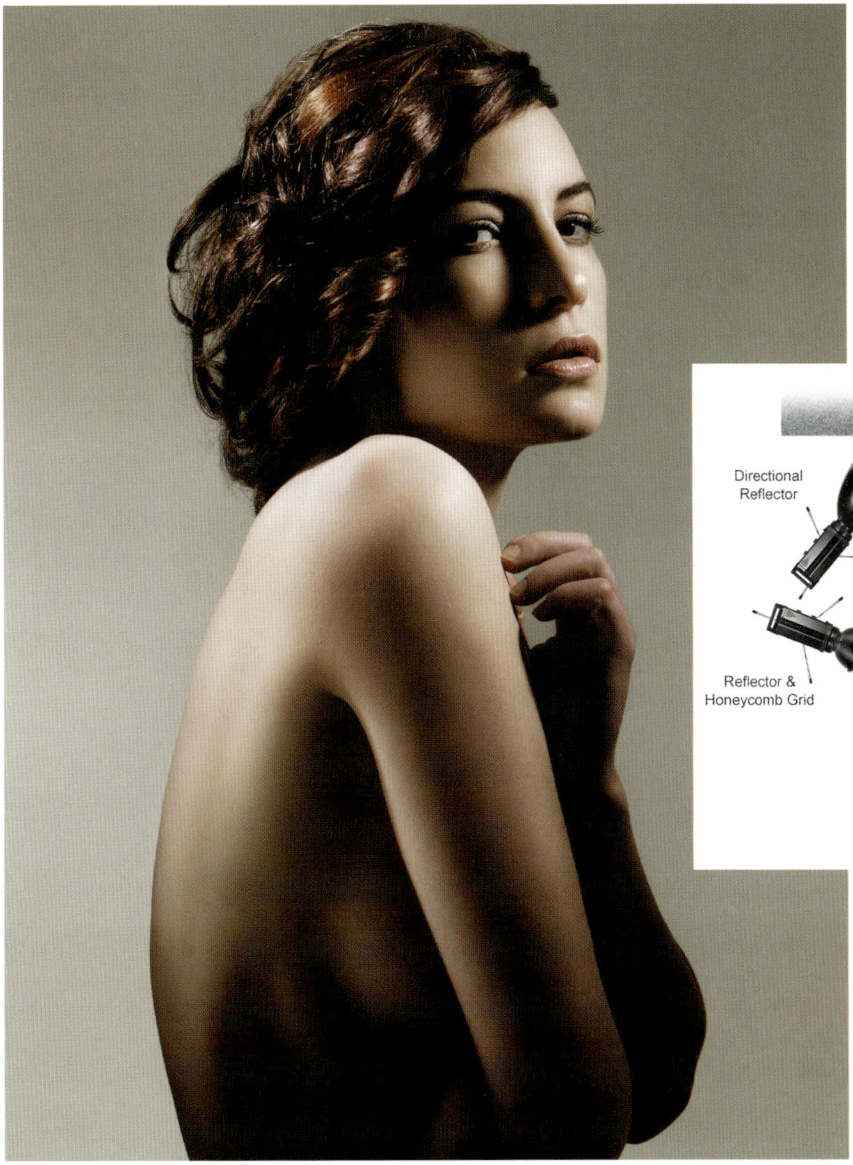

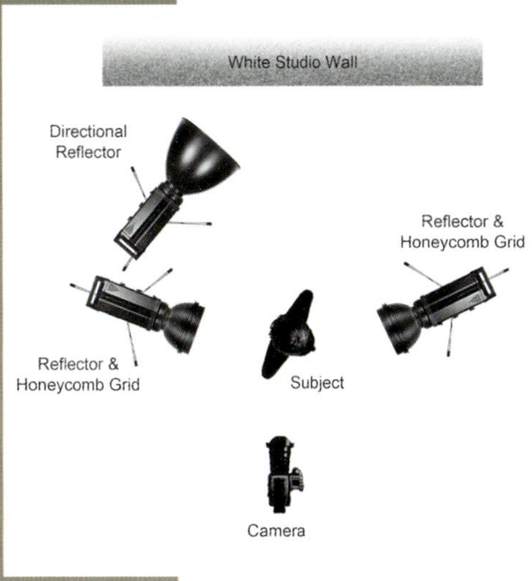

Fig. 3.6
Image © Christian Hough.
Model: Kayt Webster Brown.

Common Issues

SHADOWS TOO DARK

If you find that there is too much contrast, then use a reflector or white polyboard to help bounce the light and lift some of the shadow detail. Position the reflectors close to the camera axis. More than one reflector can be used if necessary.

GRADIENT TOO STRONG

Begin by adjusting the angle of the background light. The more 'square on' to the background the light, the less contrast the gradient will have. It is also worthwhile experimenting with different reflectors. Broad directional reflectors will increase the contrast over a smaller distance and vice versa. Finally, you can always use a reflector on the opposite side to the background light to help reduce the overall contrast.

FOUR AND FIVE HEAD LIGHTING TECHNIQUES

As you increase the number of lights you allow for more flexibility, but it can also mean more work and the need for additional control. However, it is of course possible to use all of the techniques that we have applied with the one, two and three head setups in a single shot, making the most of the shape, tone and texture of any subject.

One of the key principles of studio photography is to understand when to use more light. Quite often, inexperienced photographers will throw as much light as possible at a subject, without any cognizance of why they are lighting the subject and the particular aspects of the subject they need to draw out of the photograph. Remember that 'less is often more'.

Before you progress, think about the various aspects of additional lighting, such as side lighting, rim lighting, hair lights, gels and fill lighting. Which of these techniques will your subject and photograph benefit from? Try and picture the finished result and discard any lights and techniques that are not suitable.

Four Light Setup 1

Beauty images can require a different approach to portraits. For the most part, they concentrate on the shape and expression of the face and eyes. The majority of beauty images are used editorially and commercially, usually in conjunction with cosmetic products. In a similar vein, this shot [Fig. 3.6] was created to focus the viewer's attention on the eyes and the cheekbones. To draw out the shape, the four heads have been used to light the face evenly on each side, making it symmetrical. The background has then been gelled red, to enhance the wintery/ Christmas theme.

Getting Started

Begin by setting up your background and attaching a three-metre roll of grey background paper. A darker shade of grey will work better as it deepens the colour from the gel, whereas lighter shades have a tendency to make the colours look too pale and watery. Once your background is in place, set up your background light, attaching a set of barn doors. On the front of the barn doors, clip a red gel. Position the light so that it is lighting the background. The 'doors' can be adjusted so that they flag the light, which is particularly useful for preventing unwanted red spill light reaching the back of the model. By spreading the doors, you are effectively allowing the light to spread outwards and cover a greater area. Use the modelling facility on the studio head to ascertain where on the background the light is falling and then adjust the barn doors to control the light. Meter this between *f*8.0 and *f*16. You will find that different shades of background paper require different amounts of light.

SETTINGS AND EQUIPMENT

Camera Settings

Aperture: *f*13
Shutter: 1/125sec
ISO: 100
Focal Length: 200mm

Lighting Equipment Required

- Four flash heads.
- Barn doors and coloured gel.
- Three honeycomb grids (at least two the same).
- Grey seamless background paper.
- Boom arm/stand.
- Flash meter.
- Radio trigger or sync lead.

▶ Fig. 3.7
Image © Christian Hough. Model: Christine Hogan.

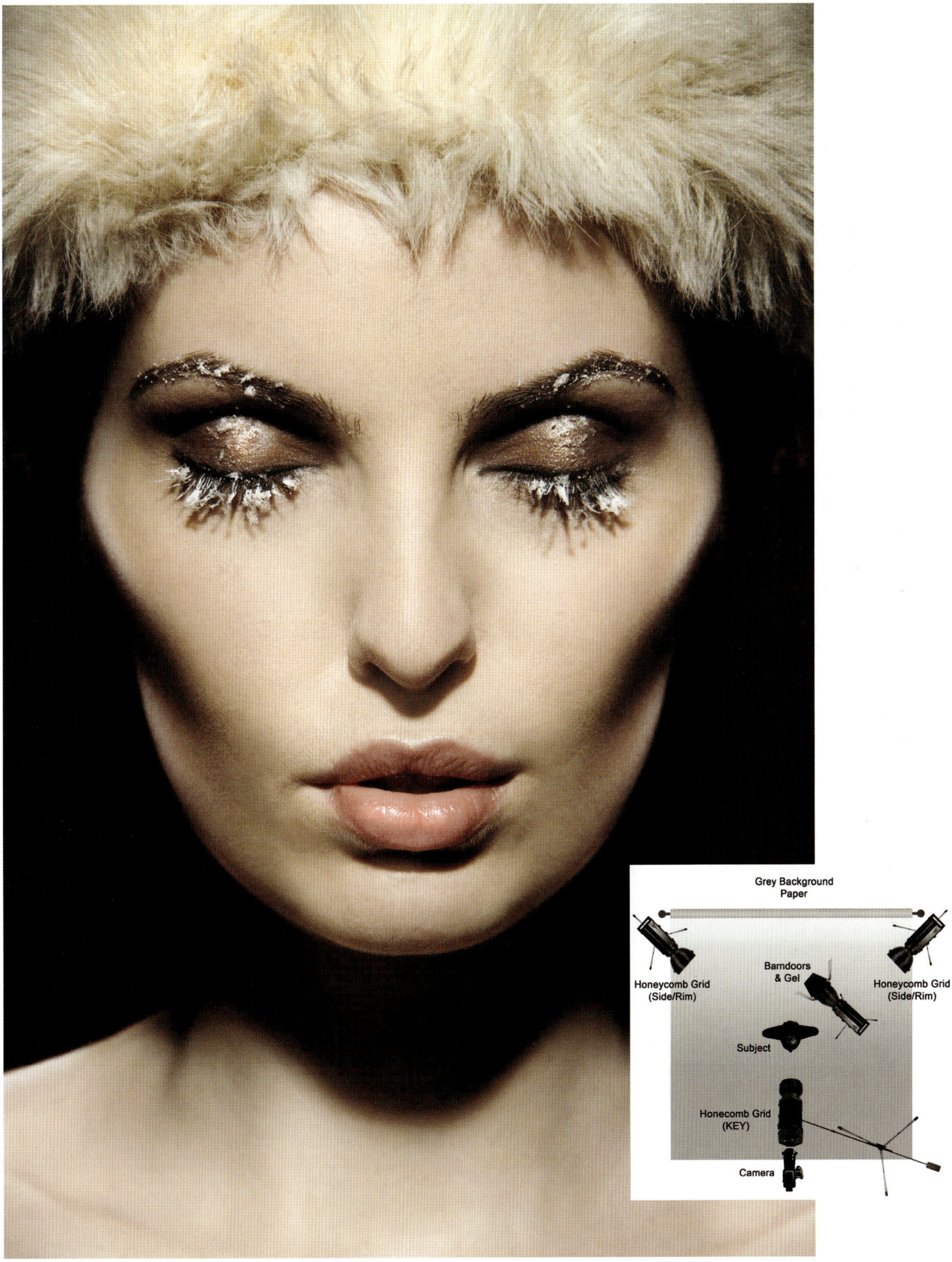
Grey Background Paper
Honeycomb Grid (Side/Rim)
Barndoors & Gel
Honeycomb Grid (Side/Rim)
Subject
Honecomb Grid (KEY)
Camera

For your key light, fix a reflector and honeycomb grid to your studio head and then attach this to a boom arm. Mark a place for your model at least two metres from the background and then ask them to stand in position temporarily. Place your key light approximately two metres back and position it so that the light is central to the model's face, casting the shadows directly downwards. You will find that the further back and lower down you position the key light, the shallower the shadows will become and the flatter the face will look. Moving the light closer and higher will force you to increase the downwards angle of the light, which will make the shadows longer. Ideally the light needs to be between one and two metres higher than the model, although this will depend on the type of honeycomb grid you are using. Meter your key light to *f*11. This is effectively known as butterfly lighting.

It is of course possible to use any light as your key light; however, maintaining an evenly gelled background requires control over your lighting and some separation between the subject and the background. If you were to use an umbrella or beauty dish as your key light, you may find that it will throw unwanted light onto the background, decreasing the intensity of the coloured gel.

The next step is to set up two side lights. Fit two heads with reflectors and the same sized honeycomb grids and then position one on each side of the background paper. Move each light backwards so that it is almost level with the background support, and with your model in place adjust them so they are picking up the cheeks on each side. Meter each head evenly between *f*5.6 and *f*8.0. You may find that light shiny skin requires less light than darker matt skin.

Honeycomb grids make the light much more directional, so your model will have less latitude for movement before they move out of the light. Keep the modelling facility on whilst you are shooting, so that you can see where the light is falling.

Common Issues

PALE-COLOURED BACKGROUND

- Try using a darker grey background (18% grey is ideal); light shades do not give enough depth to the colour.
- Ensure that spill light is not falling onto the background from the key light or side lights as this will wash the colour out.

INCONSISTENT EXPOSURE

If you are using a very tight honeycomb grid then it will create a very narrow light source; you will find that small movements by the model will move them out of the light.

- Start by marking a position for your model to stand, to provide a reference, or try using a broader honeycomb grid to spread the light more.

Four Light Setup 2

If you wish to introduce more movement into your image, yet retain a similar lighting setup, you will need to use a broader reflector. This shot retains the grey background without the use of a gel, but progresses from a butterfly style lighting technique into a clamshell lighting technique. For the most part everything else remains in the same place, and it is more a case of repositioning the background light around to the front and changing a couple of reflectors.

Here [Fig 3.8], the model is wearing black, which absorbs light. Whilst there are only four lights in use, the key light has now been fitted with a silver reflective umbrella, which helps light more of the model and partially lights the dark grey background. A fill light has then been positioned to the floor to lift the shadows (creating the clamshell), drawing out some of the texture of the clothing and the colour of the red accessories. The black and grey create enough separation to illustrate the shape of the model, whilst the two side lights add to the separation on the exposed parts of the model's arms and face.

Getting Started

Begin by suspending your grey background paper and draw out a good length train underneath the model. If you are only intending to shoot half-length, then it may be possible to pull the paper only to the ground to prevent it becoming soiled unnecessarily. Mark a position for your model to stand no less than two metres from the background.

Set up your key light, attach it to a boom arm and then fit it with a silver reflective umbrella. If you do not have an umbrella, then a medium-sized octabox or large beauty dish will also work; however, you may find that a beauty dish is much less suitable for full-length photographs due to the sudden light fall-off on the edges and hardening of the shadows at a distance. Position the boom arm so that it is central to the model and camera, and between one and two metres higher than the model. Remember, the further back and lower down you position the key light, the shallower the shadows will become and the flatter the photograph will look. Moving the light closer and higher will force you to increase the downwards angle of the light, which will make the shadows longer. Once in position, meter the key light to *f*11.

For your fill light, attach a studio head to a floor stand and fit it with a standard reflector or small softbox. Position this light approximately two metres in front of the model and direct it upwards towards the model's torso/face. Meter the light to approximately *f*5.6. Depending on the reflector you are using, you may find that you need to increase or reduce the power to get the fill light at a level you are comfortable with.

The next step is to set up two side lights to create the rim light effect. Fit two heads with stripboxes or small softboxes and then position one on each side of the background paper. Move each light backwards, so that it is almost level with the background support, and with your model in place, adjust them so they are picking up each side of the model. Meter each head evenly between *f*5.6 and *f*8.0. Care needs to be taken to ensure that you do not direct the light from the side lights down the lens of the camera, especially if you are using a standard softbox. Studio polyboards and black fabric make ideal flags to counteract this problem. It is also possible to use broader honeycomb grids in place of strip lights if they can be placed far enough away to achieve enough spread to cover the length of the model.

Common Issues

BACKGROUND SHADOWS

- Begin by moving your subject further from the background.
- Secondly, raise your key light to throw more of the shadows downwards.
- Finally decrease the angle and power of the floor light to ensure that it is not casting unwanted shadows upwards onto the background.

FLAT IMAGE

The higher and closer the key light, the longer the shadows will be.

- Begin by raising the key light to create longer shadows.
- Secondly, reduce the power of the fill light to deepen the shadows, creating more contrast.

LENS FLARE

It is important to control the light coming from the side lights.

- Stripboxes will help to cover the full length of the model whilst controlling the sideways spread of light.
- It is possible to use softboxes and flag both the camera and the background from unwanted spill.
- Finally, using a longer lens and lens hood will also help alleviate lens flare.

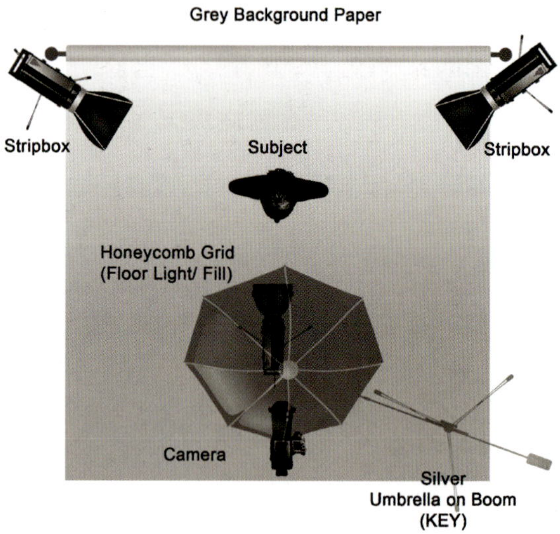

SETTINGS AND EQUIPMENT

Camera Settings

Aperture: *f*11
Shutter: 1/125sec
ISO:100
Focal Length 110mm

Lighting Equipment Required

- Four flash heads.
- Silver reflective umbrella.
- Two stripboxes.
- Standard reflector.
- Grey seamless background paper.
- Boom arm/stand.
- Floor stand.
- Flash meter.
- Radio trigger or sync lead.

▶ Fig. 3.8
Image © Christian Hough. Model: Freya Berry.

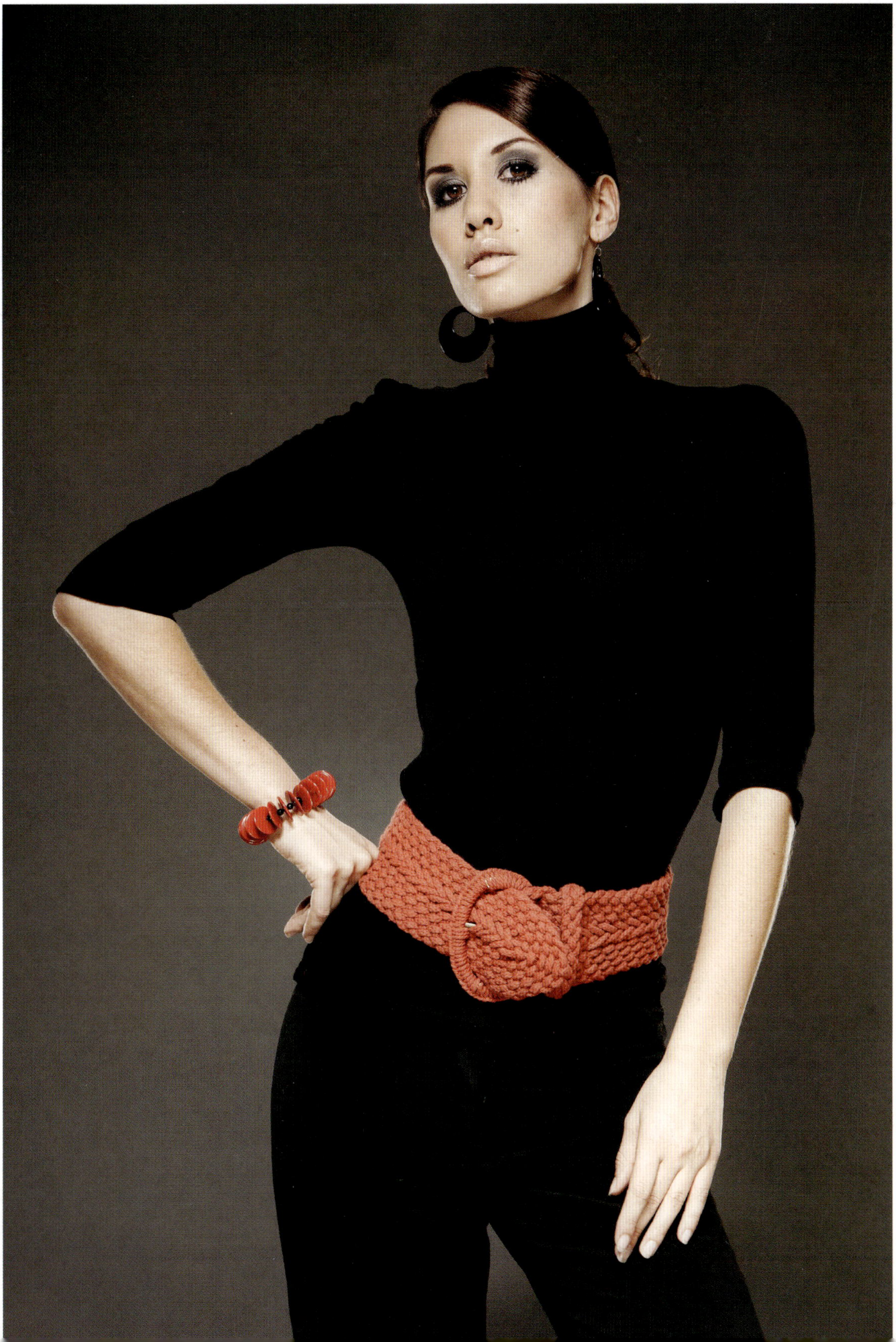

Four Light Setup 3

Getting in at different angles can help to give an image a more interesting perspective. In this example [Fig. 3.9], using a wide-angle lens for a portrait and getting in above the saxophonist has accentuated the size of the saxophone and, his head, and enabled him to peer over his glasses at the camera, all this whilst fitting the shot into the frame. This approach wouldn't necessarily work for every subject, but the change of perspective is both quirky and refreshing. The lighting in itself is nothing complicated, using a key and fill light with a high-key background; however, just a little more thought was required to the positioning of the background lighting to light the floor immediately underneath the subject as well as the background.

Getting Started

Start by setting up your white paper/fabric background and pulling a train of paper/fabric underneath the intended position of your subject. This will allow you to experiment with different angles and focal lengths whilst reducing the risk of getting unwanted background scenery in your photograph. Once done, position a stool on the floor for your subject. Now set up your key light and fill light. Umbrellas or medium-sized softboxes are both ideal as they need to cover most of the subject, plus it isn't always necessary to worry about the spill onto the background from your main lighting when shooting on a high-key background.

Attach your softbox or umbrella and then position your key light approximately 45 degrees off-axis to camera left, raising it approximately a metre higher than your subject. Meter the key light between *f*11 and *f*16 (depending how much depth of field you prefer at different angles). Attach your second softbox or umbrella to the fill light and position this between 20 and 45 degrees to camera right. Raise the fill light to the same height (or higher) as the key light and meter to *f*5.6.

For your background lights, attach two directional reflectors or small softboxes to each light and then position them on each side and slightly behind the subject so they are lighting the background. Meter these jointly to around *f*16. It is possible that you can reduce the power; however, this will depend on the power, proximity and positioning of the key and fill lights in relation to the background.

This setup will allow you to shoot from a standard and slightly elevated frontal angle at typical focal lengths. Once you move closer to your subject and shoot from an elevated position and wider angle you will need to make a couple of small adjustments to the background lighting. Firstly compose and frame your subject and whilst looking through the camera lens check to see that background scenery is visible. Adjust the angle of the left background light so that it is lighting the background directly behind the subject. Now rotate the right-hand background light and change the angle, pointing it downwards so that it lights the floor immediately underneath and behind the subject. Depending on the distances involved, you may need to decrease the power of this light. As you continue to shoot and move around your subject, check the background scenery

SETTINGS AND EQUIPMENT

Camera Settings

Aperture: *f*11
Shutter: 1/160sec
ISO: 100
Focal Length: 20mm

Lighting Equipment Required

- Four flash heads.
- Two medium-sized softboxes.
- Two directional reflectors.
- White seamless background paper or fabric backdrop.
- Flash meter.
- Radio trigger or sync lead.

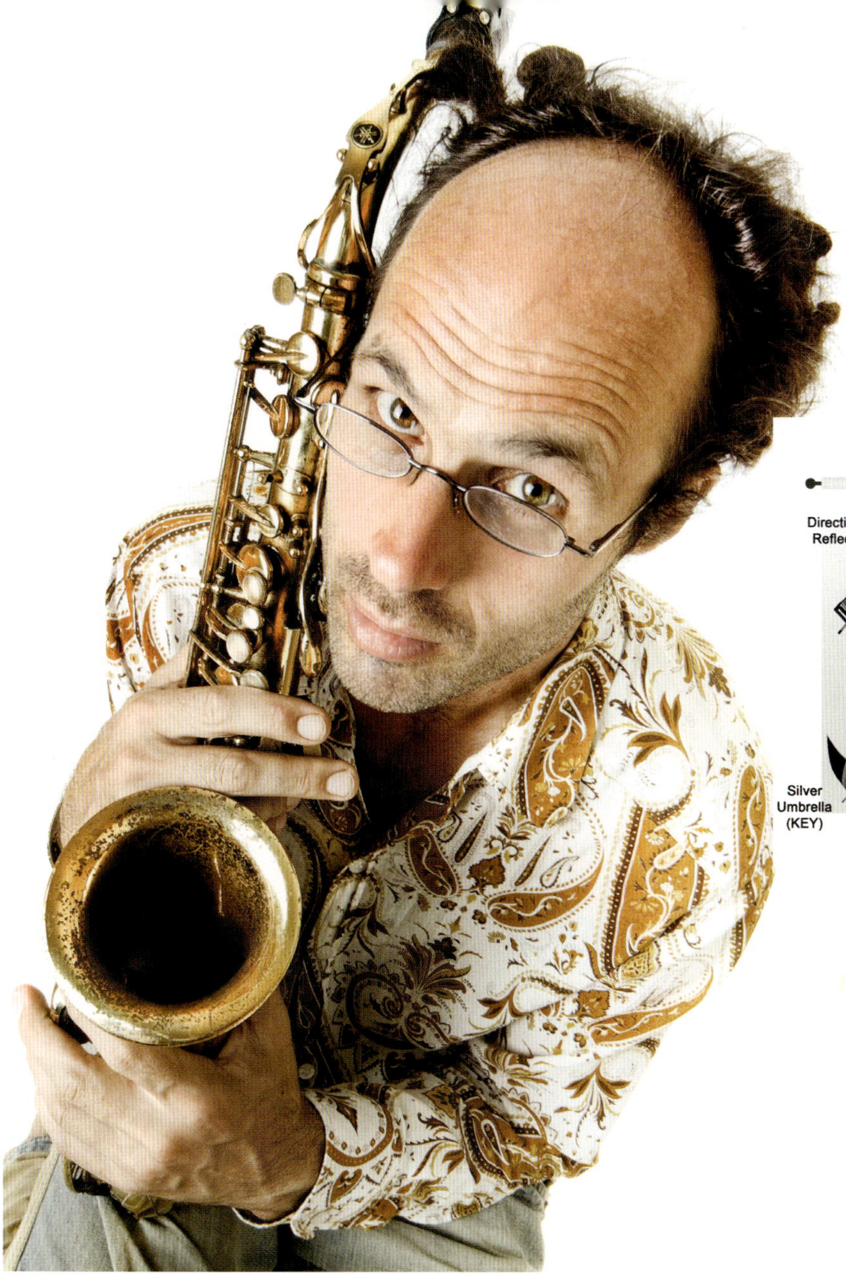

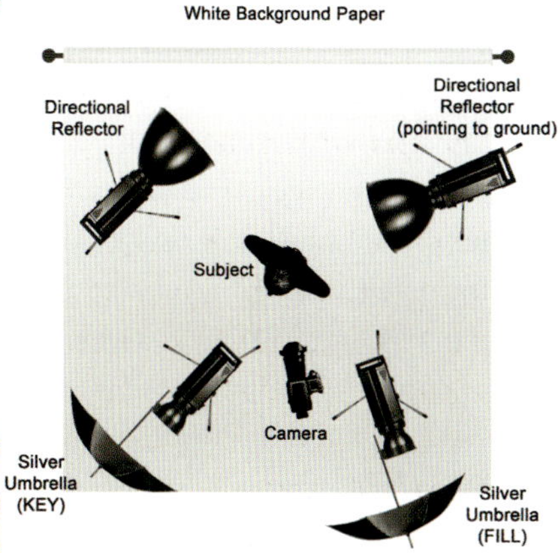

Fig. 3.9
Image ©Christian Hough.
Model: Gavin Randle.

and readjust the position of the background lighting if necessary.

Common Issues

HAZY IMAGE

Begin by increasing the distance between the subject and background and if necessary reducing the power of the background lighting. Quite often haze is attributed to excessive light bouncing off the background.

YELLOWING OF BACKGROUND

It is common for fabric backgrounds to quickly grey and yellow in areas where the light falls off or is underexposed, especially if it becomes creased.

- If you are using a fabric background, you may require more power to light it.
- Try using a flat and smooth background, such as paper or vinyl.

Four Light Setup 4

Studio glamour photography is and will always remain popular with many photographers. It is, of course, quite a particular market, yet its popularity remains as strong today as it did many years ago. Glamour photography is synonymous with female models and a male readership; however, there is an ever-growing female audience, so male glamour models have become more common over the years. The concept behind the glamour shot is fairly simple and that is to push the boundaries of what is acceptable to the widest possible audience. This normally involves the minimal use of clothing, maximum exposure of skin and usually involves underwear and other sexually provocative items!

From a lighting point of view, glamour is usually fairly straightforward as the main emphasis is on the model and not so much the mood and the lighting. You will often find that direct light sources can work well with glamour as they create strong shadows that emphasize shape and create more specular highlights, especially if the skin of the model has been lightly oiled; however, a lot will depend on the physique of the model, and a particularly voluptuous model may require flatter and more diffused light. Finally, the use of underwear will help prop the shot as it helps create 'the tease'. It shouldn't be too explicit, as it is not about what is visible, but about firing the imagination of the viewer!

Getting Started

In the shot [Fig. 3.10] we have used a simple high key background. As we have seen in other examples, there are several ways in which you can set-up a high key background. In this shot, I have used an infinity cove in a studio; however, paper, vinyl, fabric backgrounds or even a white wall will also work just as well.

Begin by setting up your white background and then attach two studio heads to two stands, positioning one on each side of the background. Fit each of the heads with a broad directional reflector and move them approximately 2–3 metres away from the background, aiming them so that they create a broad spread of light onto the white background. Now mark a position on the ground for your model, approximately 1–2 metres in front of the background lighting. Before you progress any further, it is a good idea to use the modelling facility on the background lights ensure that no light is spilling onto the model and adjust if necessary. Meter the lights between *f*11 and *f*22, depending on the reflectivity of the background surface. Remember, the more reflective the surface is, the less power it will need to light!

Once you are happy with the background lighting, it is time to progress to lighting the model and setting up the key light. In this shot, I have used a simple butterfly lighting technique to cast the shadows downwards and allow the model to move around relatively freely. This also maintains a constant broad lighting pattern on the face, regardless of which way the model is facing. Begin by setting up a single head onto a boom arm and position it approximately 2 metres higher than the model and 2 metres in front. It is a good idea to position your model and move the light so that it adequately lights the head and body. The choice of reflector for the key light is quite personal and you can literally use anything from a wide angle reflector to a softbox. In this shot, I have used a medium sized softbox without the front diffuser, so that the shadows retain a little more definition. You will find that the lower down and further back from the model you position the key light, the narrower the shadows and the flatter the light will be. Once you're happy with the position of the key light, meter between *f*11 and *f*16, depending on the depth of field required.

It is quite possible to shoot with only a single light and the broader the light modifier or reflector, the less need there will be for any fill light. However, you may find that using a single light causes the light to fall off fairly quickly, leaving the lower half of the body darker than the top half. Alternatively it may create too many shadows, making the light less flattering. You will find that glamour models tend to be curvaceous if women or very muscular if men. Whereas strong shadows are good for drawing out muscle tone and definition, they are not always flattering for the curvaceous woman. In this situation, it is a good idea to use a fill light to lift the shadows and make the image flatter.

To set-up your fill light, begin by attaching a studio light to a floor stand and positioning it approximately 2 metres in front of the model. The choice of reflector is again a personal thing. In this example I have chosen to use a bare wide angled reflector; however, it is possible to use a small softbox. Remember, if you are shooting full length, you will find that a large reflector on the floor stand may obscure the feet and you will have to adjust your angle of shooting and focal length to compensate. Meter your fill light between ƒ8.0 and ƒ11, depending on how much fill you require for the shadows.

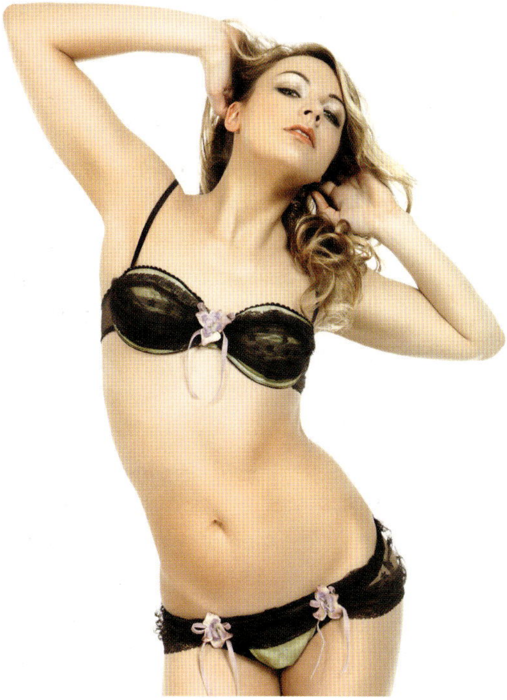

▲ Fig. 3.10
Image © Christian Hough.

Common Issues

SHADOWS CAST UPWARDS

This is caused by the fill light positioned on the floor.

Begin by decreasing adjusting the key/fill light power ratio, by reducing the power output of the fill light.

If you are still seeing some upward shadow definition, move the fill light further away from the model to decrease the length of the shadow or use a more diffused modifier.

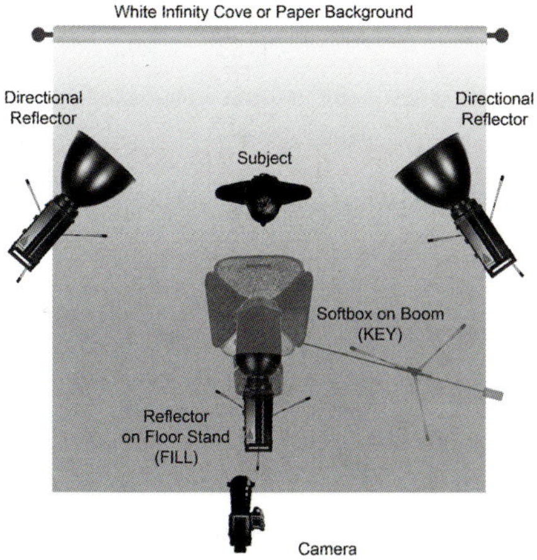

SETTINGS AND EQUIPMENT

Camera settings

Aperture: ƒ11
Shutter: 1/200sec
ISO:100
Focal Length 90mm

Lighting Equipment Required

- Four flash heads.
- Two medium sized soft boxes or broad reflectors (key/fill).
- Two directional reflectors or small softboxes (background).
- Infinity cover or white background.
- Boom stand.
- Floor stand.
- Flash meter.
- Radio trigger or sync lead.

Five Light Setup 1

It is time to draw together some of the techniques you have learned so far and apply them to master a basic five light setup. The idea [Fig. 3.11] is to accentuate the shape of the model, create separation from the background, whilst drawing out the necessary detail and texture of the clothing.

The lighting has been deliberately set up to allow the model to move relatively freely along a two metre parallel, enabling her to create different poses in different outfits. It is very similar to the previous image, with the addition of a hairlight to add more detail and contrast to the model's hair, whilst also creating more separation from the background. More, it is very quick and easy from a photographer's point of view, as once you have set up, there is very little in the way of adjustments that are required, allowing you to concentrate on the shoot and the model.

Getting Started

Start by suspending your grey background paper and draw out a good length train underneath the model. Dark grey paper works best as black creates too much contrast, whilst a lighter grey advances the background too much, making the photograph look too flat. Once done, mark a position for your model to stand no less than two metres from the background.

If you have a boom stand, then set up a hair light to that it is central to the model and positioned above and behind. Direct the light to the top and back of the head so that it only lights the hair and doesn't spill onto the face. It is possible to use a small softbox, strip light or even a honeycomb grid for this. If you do not have a second boom stand to hand, then attach you hair light to a regular stand and position it behind and above your background. You will need to fit a honeycomb grid to control the light and reduce the risk of flare. The hair light in this position will also need to be placed very high, so it may not be possible to achieve this effect in a room/studio

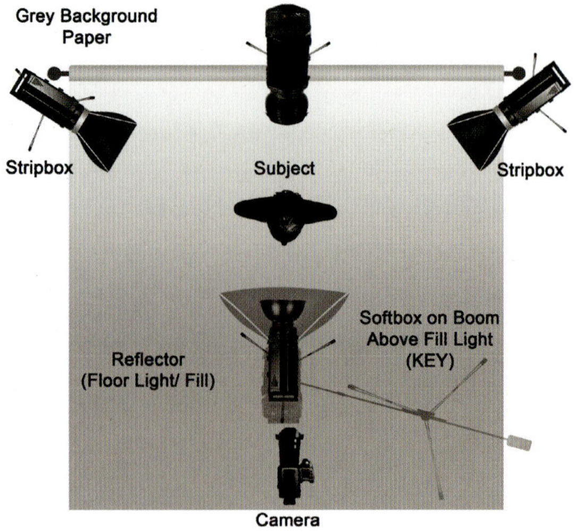

▲ Original.

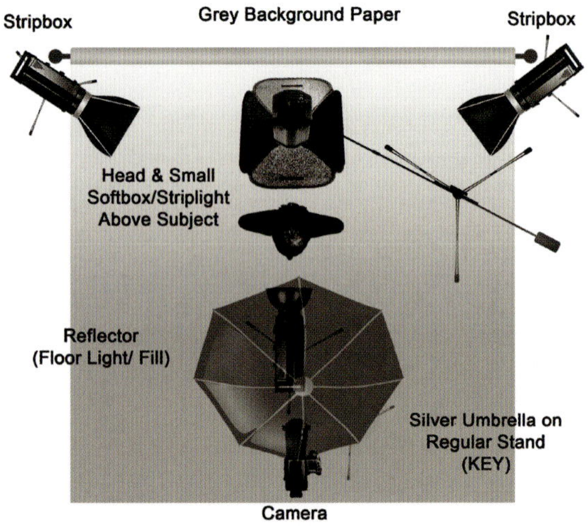

▲ Alternative.

▶ Fig. 3.11
Image © Christian Hough. Model: Jaala Pickering.

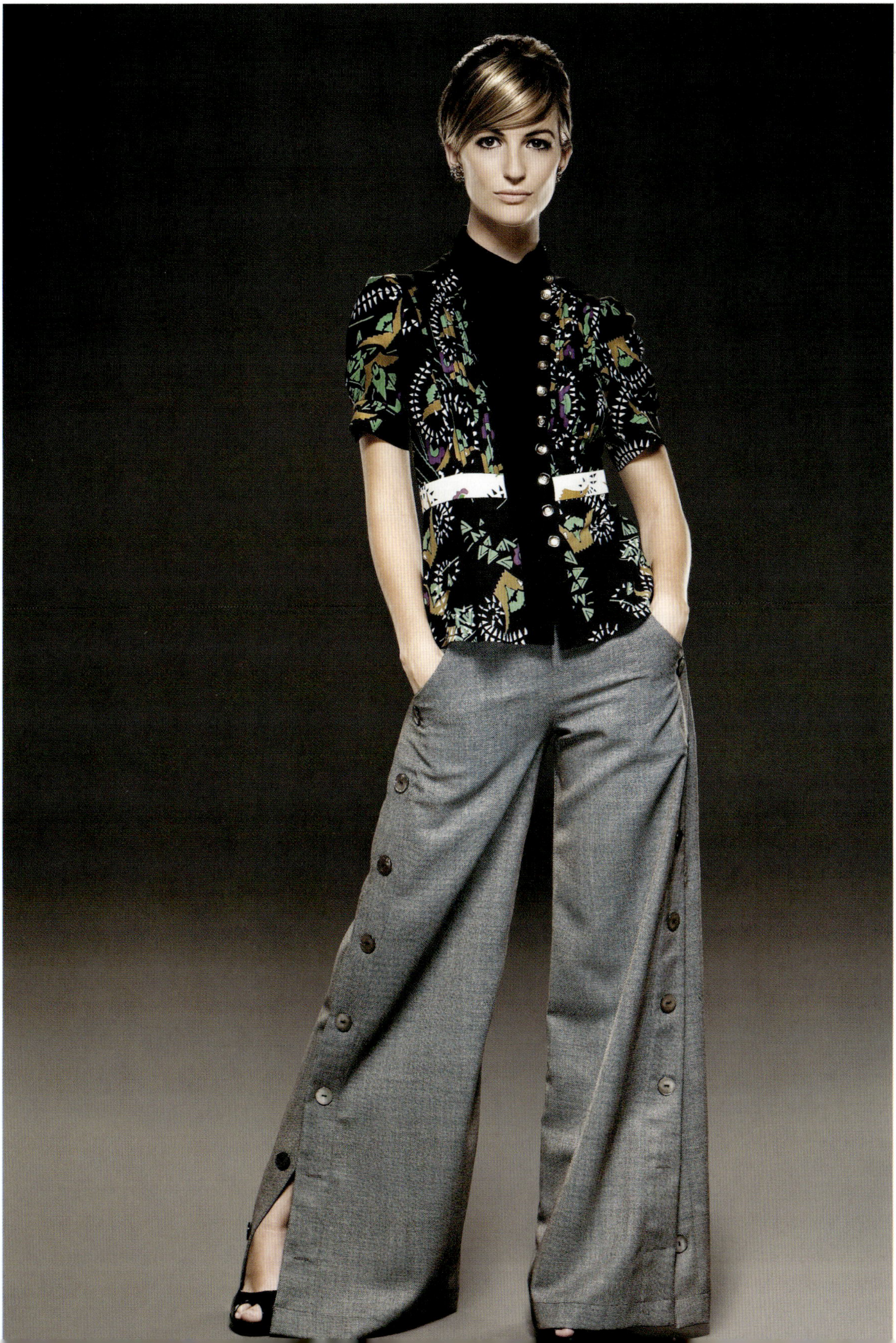

with low ceilings. Meter to approximately *f*8.0.

As for your key light, attach it to a boom arm and fit it with a medium-sized softbox. If you do not have a softbox a medium-sized silver umbrella will also work. Position the boom arm so that is central to the model and camera and between one and two metres higher than the model. Remember, the further back and lower down you position the key light, the shallower the shadows will become and the flatter the photograph will look. Moving the light closer and higher will force you to increase the downwards angle of the light, which will make the shadows longer, but also decrease the amount of light hitting the background. Once in position, meter the key light to *f*11.

For your fill light, attach a studio head to a floor stand and fit it with a small softbox or standard reflector. If you need to control the spread on the fill light, fit it with a honeycomb grid. Position this light approximately two metres in front of the model and direct it upwards to towards the model's torso/face. Meter the light to approximately *f*5.6. Depending on the reflector you are using, you may find that you need to increase or reduce the power to get the fill light at a level you are comfortable with.

The next step is to set up two side lights to create the rim light effect. Fit two heads with stripboxes and then position one on each side of the background paper. Move each light backwards, so that it is almost level with the background and, with your model in place, adjust them so they are picking up each side of the model, including the face. Meter each head evenly between *f*5.6 and *f*8.0. Care needs to be taken to ensure that you do not direct the light from the side lights down the lens of the camera, especially if you are planning on using a standard softbox. Studio polyboards and black fabric make ideal flags to counteract this problem and will also help prevent spill light from the side lights hitting the background. It is also possible to use broader honeycomb grids in place of strip lights if they can be placed far enough away to achieve enough spread to cover the length of the model.

Finally, it is possible to substitute the boom arm for the hair light and instead attach the key light to a regular stand, positioning as close to the camera axis as possible. This will give you more flexibility as to where you position the key light and reduce the possibility of lens flare.

SETTINGS AND EQUIPMENT

Camera Settings

Aperture: *f*11
Shutter: 1/125sec
ISO: 100
Focal Length: 83mm

Lighting Equipment Required

- Five flash heads.
- Medium softbox or silver reflective umbrella.
- Two stripboxes.
- Reflector and honeycomb grid.
- Small softbox or standard reflector.
- Grey seamless background paper.
- One/two boom arms (two boom arms preferable).
- Floor stand.
- Flash meter.
- Radio trigger or sync lead.

Common Issues

BACKGROUND SHADOWS

- Begin by moving your subject further from the background.
- Secondly, raise your key light to throw more of the shadows downwards.
- Finally decrease the angle and power of the floor light to ensure that it is not casting unwanted shadows upwards onto the background.
- Also consider flagging your side lights.

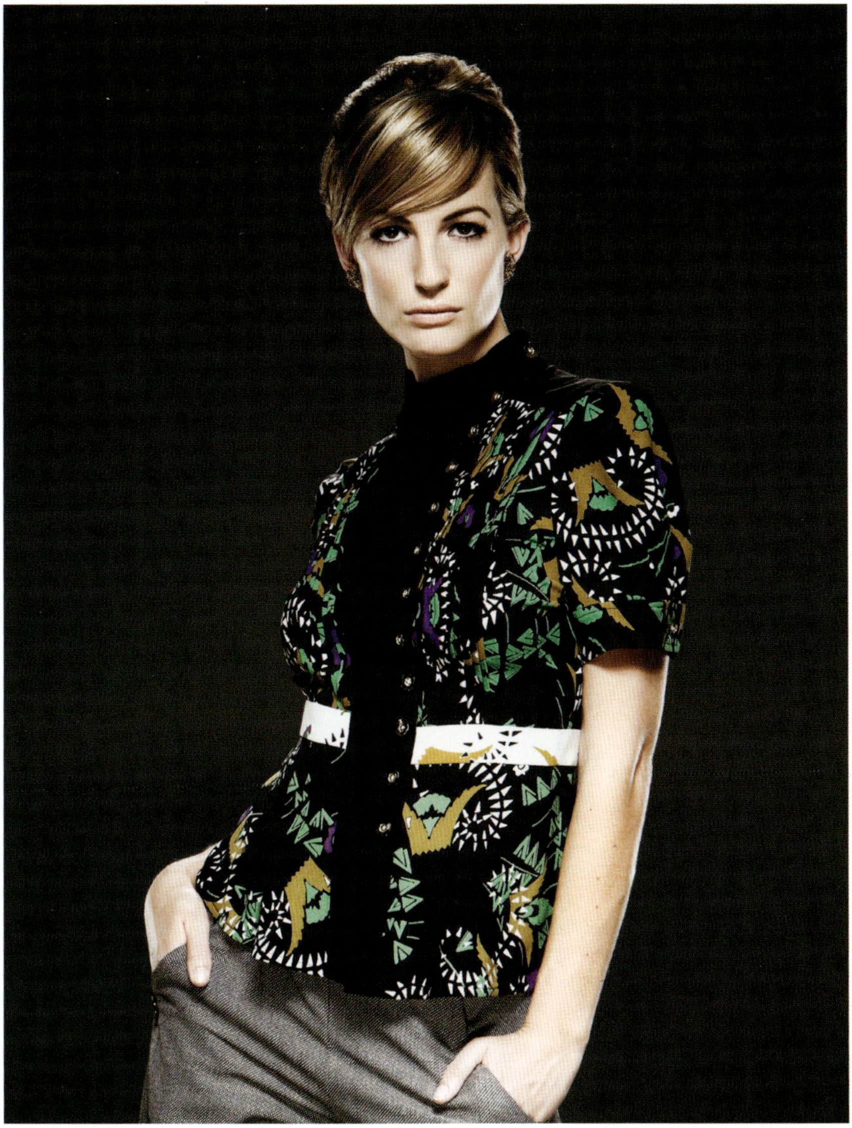

Fig. 3.12
Image © Christian Hough.
Model: Jaala Pickering.

FLAT IMAGE

The higher and closer the key light, the longer the shadows will be.

- Begin by raising the key light to create longer shadows.
- Secondly, reduce the power of the fill light to deepen the shadows, creating more contrast.

LENS FLARE

It is important to control the light coming from the hair light and the side lights.

- Stripboxes will help to cover the full length of the model whilst controlling the sideways spread of light.
- It is possible to use softboxes and flag both the camera and the background from unwanted spill.
- Finally, using a longer lens and lens hood will also help alleviate lens flare.

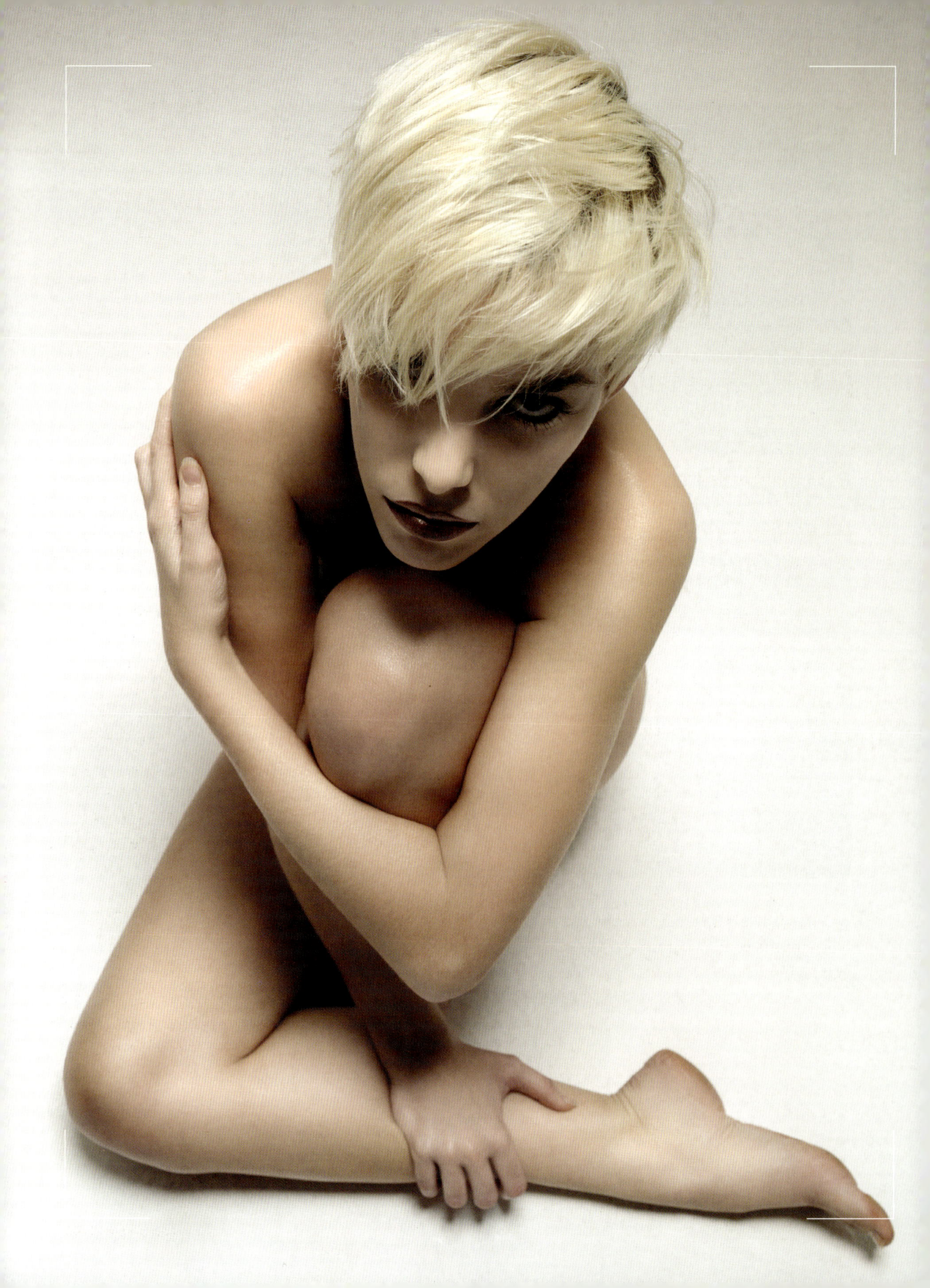

Chapter 4

Artistic Nude

Shooting any form of nude photography needs tact, skill and a good understanding of light. The beauty of fine art nude photography is that it does not rely on the usual props of fashion and is therefore timeless. The idea is to bring out the shape and form of the subject and the subtle textures of the skin and not to seek maximum exposure of flesh.

Fine art nude should not be confused with glamour photography, which seeks to be deliberately explicit and arousing. However, on occasion it is worthwhile challenging established concepts, and I often deliberately blur boundaries, creating something that is evocative yet possesses artistic merit – more of a fashion nude. In art it sometimes pays to challenge established concepts and create a stir. While the balance of art and taste is entirely down to individual perspectives, remember that if you are considering shooting for sales then you will need to consider the global market and what is acceptable within different countries and communities. Make your work too explicit and you may well limit your market.

From a lighting perspective, art nude needs a combination of consideration and control and you will find that less is definitely more. Controlling the light and your exposure is paramount to your success, and it will help you to draw together a moodboard beforehand, to help you play with your lighting and poses.

PLANNING

Most models will be willing to attend some form of a fashion or beauty shoot, providing it is beneficial to their portfolio. However art nude requires a different sort of model, and the subject should be approached with tact and diplomacy. The majority of nude models will be experienced models in their own right and will therefore require a photographer to have a good portfolio of work to prove that they are a serious photographer and proficient with a camera. Unfortunately, there are many stereotypes that you have to overcome, especially if you are male, the most common being a 'GWC' (Guy With Camera), which is normally a photographer who has no artistic intent. Your portfolio is paramount in overcoming this stereotype, even if you have never shot a nude photograph in your life. A portfolio of well-lit and cutting-edge fashion photographs will demonstrate that you are serious about your work, whereas a portfolio of swimwear and glamour photographs may well typecast you, before you have even started.

Start by drawing together an achievable moodboard of images that you have found to be inspirational. Keep the moodboard realistic. I say achievable, because it is important to deliver the results, otherwise you will only disappoint the model as well as yourself. There is no point having images on your moodboard shot in expensive properties in faraway locations, if you are going to be shooting in an inner-city studio. Instead, try and concentrate on one or two themes, focusing on both lighting and

◀ Image © Christian Hough. Model: Pip Hanks.

shape. This will produce a more coherent reference and help you project your ideas towards the right models. The rest is down to you – it is for you to experiment and really consider your lighting.

Security in Numbers

I feel that it is worth a brief mention about the security of both yourself and the model when shooting any form of photography that involves nudity. When people are naked, then you may find yourself in a more tentative position than when they are fully clothed. Therefore, it is absolutely paramount to consider the personal space of your model. There have been a few stories of photographers not respecting this golden rule and they have subsequently found themselves the subject of allegations of assault.

If you are unfamiliar with your subject, then it is recommended that you have a third-party of the same sex as the model present. Not only will this help the model to feel more comfortable, but it will also protect you against any unwanted allegations and guard your professional reputation. Remember, it takes a long time to build a reputation, but only moments to destroy it. When shooting nudes I have worked with only a handful of models on a one-to-one basis, where we have an established professional working relationship. For the most part, I employ the use of a make-up artist or hair stylist as a matter of course. Not only does this improve the finish of the photographs, but it also serves as a completely independent third-party witness.

Ask First

It is important for you to direct your subject in front of the camera and on occasion help them into certain poses. Stick to medical terms and avoid any slang when describing parts of the body. This way you will avoid causing offence. If you are unfamiliar with the medical terms, be sure to familiarize yourself with them first, as it will build confidence and enhance your reputation as being professional. A similar rule applies to touching: do not touch unless you have asked first. There are occasions when you need to move an arm or a leg into position, so if you are unable to direct your model verbally, ask them if it is okay if you move them into position. Touching another person is by its very nature invasive, so be sure to ask first and restrict any contact between you to less intimate parts of the body, such as hand to elbow, head, foot and calf.

Tone and Texture

As would be expected, there is more skin exposed when shooting art nudes. Nobody is perfect, and everybody has birthmarks and blemishes. Regardless of this, it pays to minimize marks in the skin, such as impressions made by clothing or goose bumps, as this will greatly reduce your post-processing time. A cold model normally means goose bumps. Start by ensuring that the studio or room where you are shooting is warm. Remember, the model is constantly moving around shifting lights so will get cold quickly, especially on a cold studio floor. Invest in a medium-sized fan heater.

In the following setups, we will look at several lighting techniques to help you get started and get those creative ideas flowing. In much the same way as the previous chapters, we will begin with a single head and work upwards in complexity, so that you have a solid foundation and understanding as to how to light something and why it is being lit a given way.

ONE HEAD LIGHTING TECHNIQUES

One Light Setup 1

Photographing art nudes has a fairly unique perspective on 'person-based' photography in that it does not have to revolve around the face of the subject but can in fact concentrate on particular areas of the body. These are known as abstracts. Subtle use of light and shadow, plus clever framing, can bring a whole new perspective to a photograph.

In this shot [Fig. 4.1], I deliberately maximized the use of the shadow, concentrating on the outline of the model, to produce a continuous band of light from one side of the frame to the other. The idea behind this was to treat the scene as a landscape, the body of the model providing the undulating curves similar to that of hills. The background has a very subtle gradient, which lifts it from the shadows but still provides enough depth to contrast with the highlighted skin of the model. It is simple but very effective.

Getting Started

Set up a dark grey background paper onto a support system and drag the paper to the ground and outwards, to give yourself a paper train of about four metres or more. It is possible to use a fabric background; however, the gradient on the fabric background is unlikely to be smooth, leaving you with more post-processing work.

Once the paper background is out, attach a single head to a boom stand, together with a stripbox. A stripbox or strip light is most suitable as you need to light the length of the model and avoid lighting too much of the background. Place the boom so that the head remains slightly behind and above the model, but pointing back towards the camera at approximately thirty degrees. The idea is to 'short light' the model's back, leaving the side nearest the camera in the shadows. You may find that you need to adjust this back and forth until the shadows are cast on the nearside of the model. Take extra care when adjusting the position of the boom so as to avoid it falling onto the model. You will find that a boom stand fitted with castors/wheels will facilitate movement and reduce the risk of toppling.

Once in you are set up, meter the light between *f*11 and *f*16, get your model into position and then take a test shot. There should be a constant light down the back that slowly tapers off towards the front. Try shooting at an angle slightly higher, so as to just get both buttocks into the shot, along with the outline of the back.

This setup can be used to capture many different shapes, so experiment by moving between short lighting and rim lighting. It's the simplicity that works.

Common Issues

BACKGROUND TOO LIGHT

- The obvious route is to ensure that you are using a dark grey paper.
- Try to minimize the light falling onto the background from the key light. You can achieve this by using a narrower stripbox, changing the angle of the stripbox so that it points more towards the subject.
- Or try moving your subject further away from the background so as to reduce the amount of spill.

FRONT OF THE MODEL TOO DARK

This may be a matter of the dynamic range of your camera.

- If you need to lift the shadows on the nearside of the subject, try using a long strip of white card placed underneath the camera, so that it reflects some light back onto the subject. A white reflector will produce a more even and subtle result than silver.

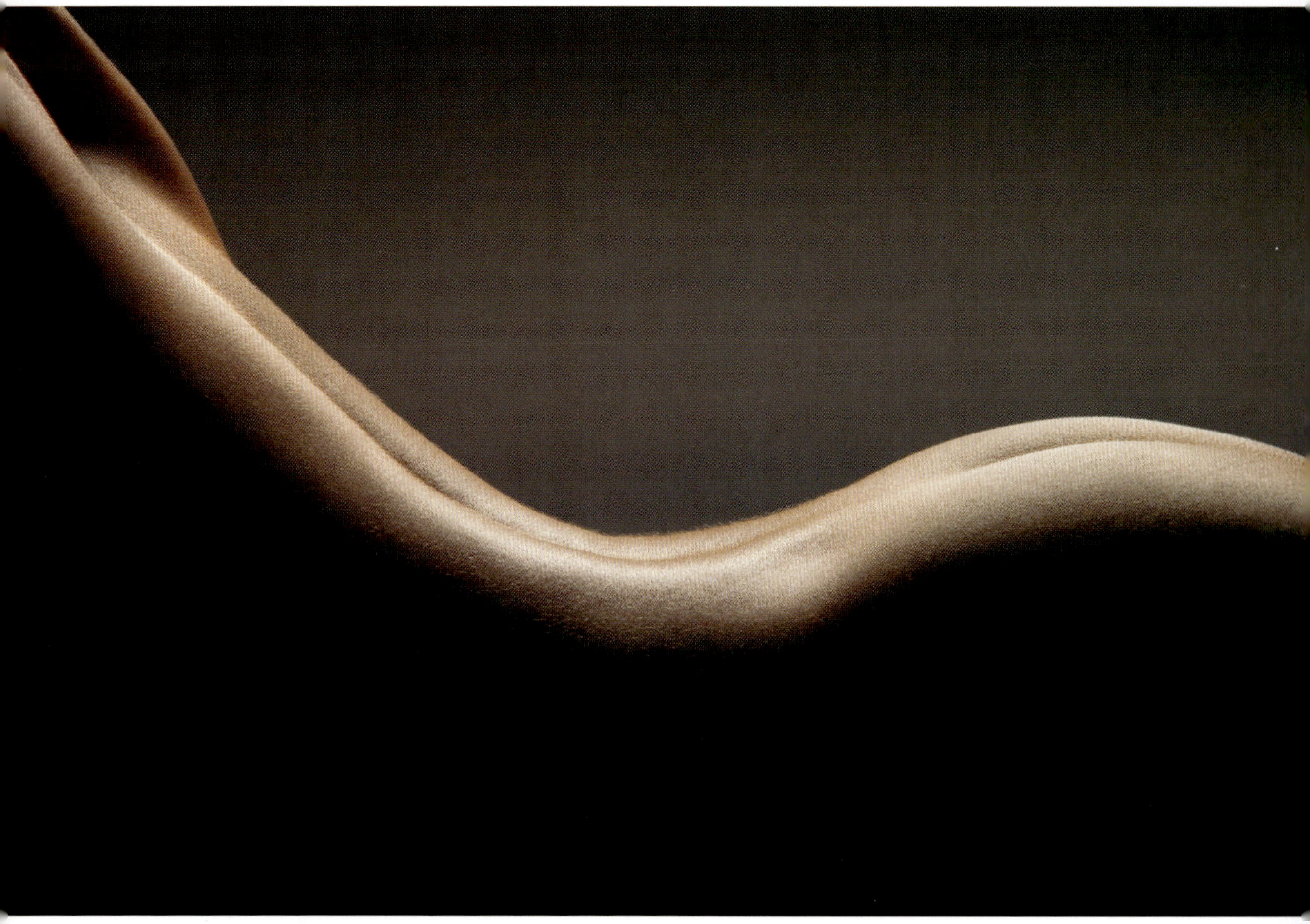

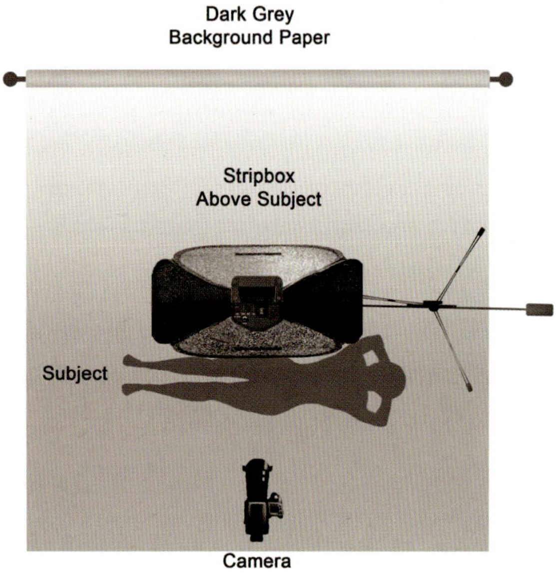

SETTINGS AND EQUIPMENT

Camera Settings

Aperture: ƒ13

Shutter: 1/125sec

ISO: 100

Focal Length: 200mm

Lighting Equipment Required

- One flash head.
- Boom arm and stand.
- Stripbox/strip light.
- Background support and dark grey paper background.
- Flash meter.
- Radio trigger or sync lead.

Fig. 4.1
Image © Christian Hough. Model: Alli Andrews.

One Light Setup 2

There are a lot of things you can do with a single light, and experimenting with different modifiers is one of them. Art nude photography works particularly well in black and white, but it can benefit from hard lighting sources, such as honeycomb grids, snoots and bare reflectors. Like every other photograph, there needs to remain a strong emphasis on shape and form to give the photograph a visual dynamic.

In this shot, there remains a lot of expression in the pose from the model. Getting the model to change the pose with small movement between frames is hugely beneficial and will certainly increase your chances of getting the shots you need. However, a gobo has been added to the front of a spot attachment to create the beautiful dappled effect with the light. It is this contrast between the skin and the filtered light that adds the artistic interest to the image, giving it an additional dimension. It also has the benefit of making the plain black background part of the frame.

What is a Gobo?

A gobo is basically a piece of steel with a pattern cut into it, similar to a stencil. They come with various patterns and sizes and therefore produce a range of different effects, from imitation window light to that of tree branches. Gobos are made by several manufacturers – it is not a case of one size fits all – so be sure to get the right size for your equipment. Finally, it is possible to make your own gobos out of thick card, but remember that studio modelling lights get very hot and may cause your homemade gobo to combust. If you are taking this route, be sure to turn the modelling light off when not in use to reduce the risk of fire.

Getting Started

The best and most effective way to use a gobo is via a focused spotlight. A spotlight will enable you to control the intensity of the shadow edges, allowing you to sharpen and diffuse them very easily. Light is at its most diffuse when closest to the subject, so you will find that simply placing a shaped cut-out in front of a standard reflector will not give you the same results as using a focused spotlight and gobo. A manufactured spotlight or spot attachment has a focusing lens built within, so that it can focus the light behind the gobo to project the cut-out shape.

Using a spotlight with a gobo can easily fool a light meter, as small movements from the hand-held light meter may cause it to move in and out of the light; therefore, it is important to take several meter readings and check the exposure on the back of your camera's LCD or monitor. In a similar fashion to Technique 21, it is the placement of the light and positioning of the model that must be considered. The difference here is that we tend to 'broad light' the model, otherwise the effect of the gobo would almost be lost with short lighting.

Start by setting up a black paper background and dragging a large train of paper to the ground; enough for the model to lie down on and for you to move around comfortably. The black paper will help maintain a more subtle background and keep the viewer's attention on the model. It is possible to use a black cotton fabric background, but you need to bear in mind that it will ruffle, fold and crease with movement. Black velvet absorbs light, so it is not ideal for this setup unless you are deliberately intending to restrict light to the subject only.

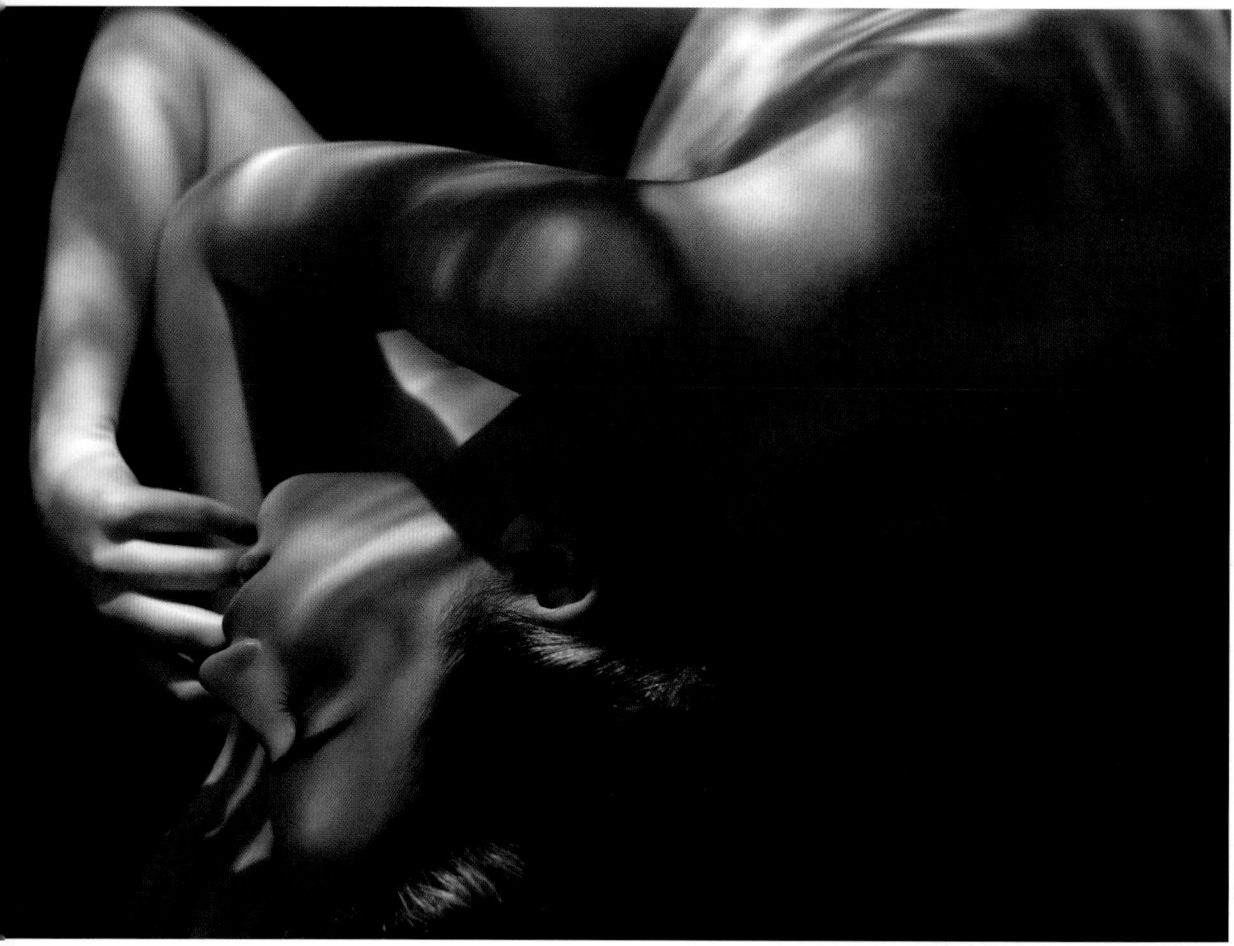

▲ Fig. 4.2
Image © Christian Hough.Model: Lydia Turner.

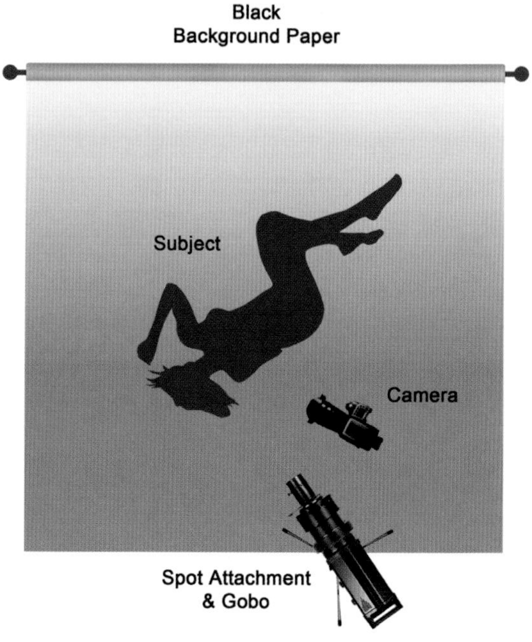

Once the background is ready, place the head onto a regular stand and fix your spot attachment and gobo to the head. There are no rules as to where you position this light, but try to avoid placing it too close to the camera axis, otherwise you will not be successful in bringing out the shape of the model. A good place to start is at about 45 degrees, making small adjustments to the height and angle when your model is in position. Meter this light several times, both in the shadow and light areas to get a rough reading, but be sure to double check your exposure on your camera's LCD or histogram, ensuring that you refrain from blowing any of the highlights. Once you have positioned and metered the light, you are ready to shoot. It really is that simple. The key to success is experimenting with different poses, several gobos and lots of lighting positions to find out what produces the most visually interesting result.

SETTINGS AND EQUIPMENT

Camera Settings

Aperture: ƒ4.8
Shutter: 1/180sec
ISO: 100
Focal Length: 100mm

Lighting Equipment Required

- One flash head.
- Boom arm and stand.
- Stripbox/strip light.
- Background support and dark grey paper background.
- Flash meter.
- Radio trigger or sync lead.

Common Issues

TOO MUCH CONTRAST

Dynamic Range (DR) is a still a challenge for many digital systems.

- If you are not using medium format with around twelve stops of clean and noise-free DR, you may need to lift the shadow detail by way of a white card bounce reflector. This will help you claw back this detail in post-processing, without drawing out too many unwanted digital artefacts.
- With this in mind, RAW shooting is recommended. Expose for the highlights and use the white bounce to lift the shadow detail a little.

SHADOWS LONGER FROM THE GOBO

- The more obtuse the angle of the light to the subject, the longer the shadows will be, similar to those of the late afternoon sun. This can mean that the shadows get longer.

TWO HEAD LIGHTING TECHNIQUES

Two Light Setup 1

There are many different props that may be utilized with art nudes, giving the model something to interact with and offering an additional visual dimension to the photograph. Some photographers use textures, others abstract objects and some colours. Water on the other hand not only props the model but also brings with it a feeling of motion. Product shots splashing water are always appealing as they produce shapes that we are not used to seeing with the naked eye. These effects are even more compelling when mixed with other photographic genres such as art nude.

This photograph was shot as a series mixing the motion of water with art nude photography. The hard lighting and high-contrast of black and white tones catches the viewer's attention and has more impact than the same photo in colour. The water droplets have been lit from behind to ensure that they stand proud of the dark background, whereas the model has been lit with a butterfly lighting pattern to throw the shadows downwards and add more drama to the lighting.

Health and Safety

It is essential to concentrate on health and safety when mixing water with studio lighting and electricity. Studio lights consume an enormous amount of electricity, so having them in close proximity to water increases the potential for an accident; therefore, extra precautions are needed.

Firstly, if your lights are connected to the mains supply (AC) it is important to have them connected through a circuit breaker, which will instantaneously isolate the power supply in the event of an accident. You will find that most modern extension leads will have some form of circuit breaking facility or emergency cut-out. Secondly, it is advisable to position the heads a good distance from your subject and away from any water, ensuring that leads are taped to the ground and that stands are weighted down. This reduces the risk of any studio heads and stands being accidentally pulled over by loose cables or being knocked by assistants and models. Finally, when you are shooting and the model is in place, be sure that you restrict access around the set, ensuring that there is a clear path in and out.

Electricity is your main concern, but it is important to think about the water and its delivery. Attaching a hose to a high-pressure tap is not always recommended, unless the pressure can be adequately controlled. When forced through a hose high-pressure water systems can create a fine mist of cold water droplets, which could cause your hot lights to explode if they come into contact with each other. A hand-controlled gravity-fed system is much more controllable. Ensure that you test the water delivery thoroughly prior to shooting and that

SETTINGS AND EQUIPMENT

Camera Settings

Aperture: *f*11
Shutter: 1/200sec
ISO: 100
Focal Length: 105mm

Lighting Equipment Required

- Two flash heads.
- One boom arm and one straight stand.
- Single reflector and wide honeycomb grid for key light.
- Semi-directional reflector and/or honeycomb grid for backlight.
- Background support and black fabric.
- Water delivery, towels and large paddling pool.
- Flash meter.
- Radio trigger or sync lead.

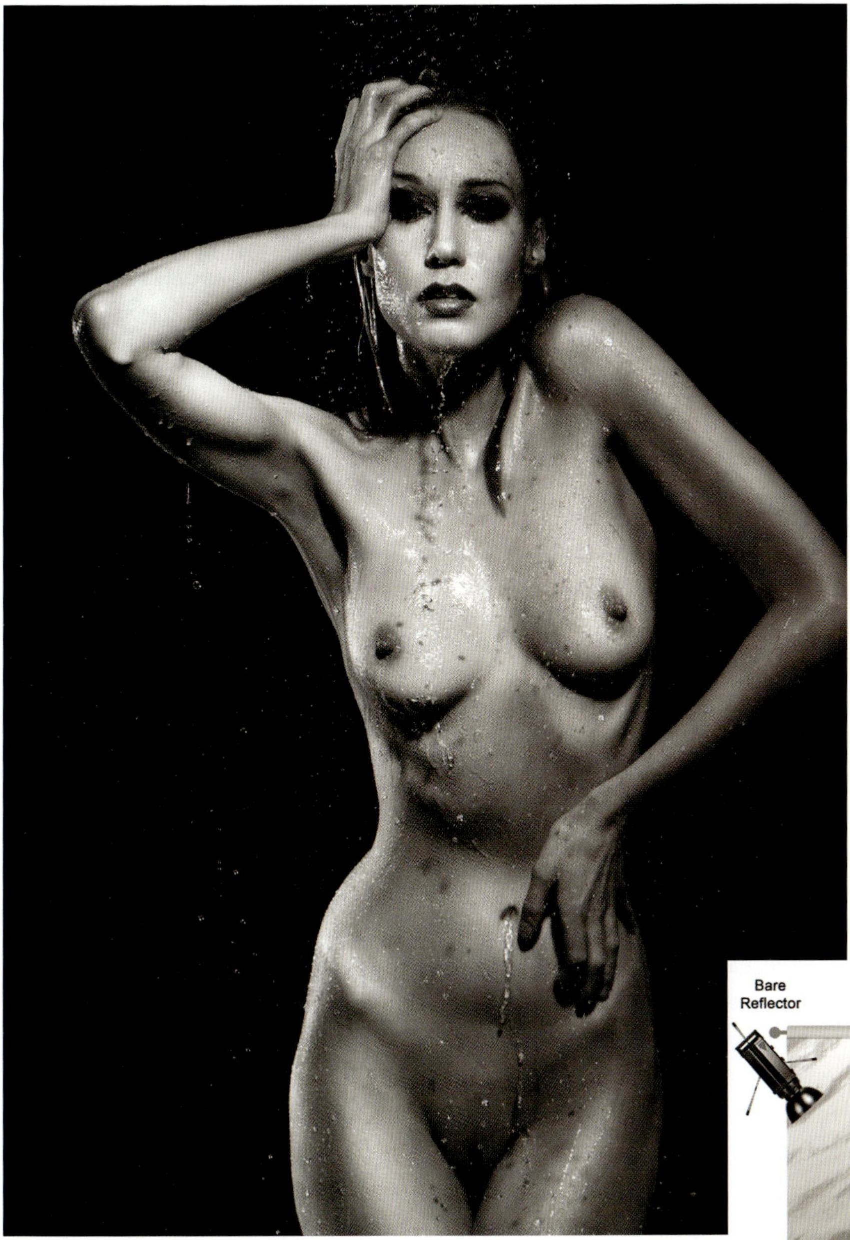

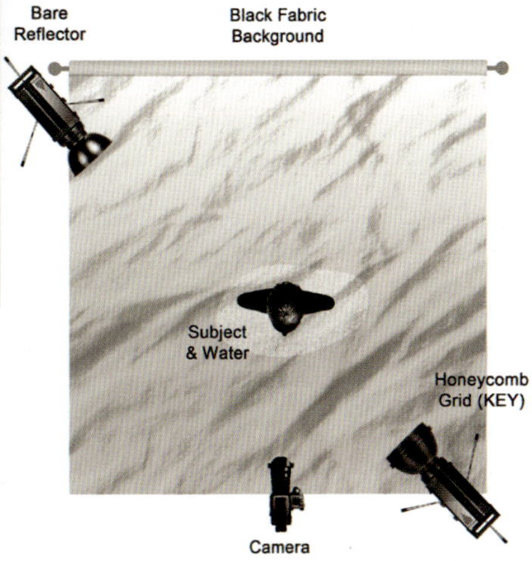

Fig. 4.3
Image © Christian Hough.
Model: Iveta Niklova.

you have some way of collecting the spilled water. A large paddling pool and plenty of towels will help you collect the water and soak up any unwanted spillages, reduced the chance of slipping.

Ideally, make use of a battery generator system to power your heads. This will reduce the risks dramatically. Switch modelling lights off when not in use to reduce heat and do not take *any* unnecessary risks. Remember, control the water, control the electricity and keep the two well apart from each other.

Getting Started

Start by setting up your dark background. Rather than use paper, use black fabric, preferably velvet. Once wet, paper curls and warps, whereas a fabric background will help soak up any spillages and dry out afterwards allowing it to be reused. It is of course possible to use paper, but you may want to consider increasing the distance of your subject from the background to avoid spoiling the paper.

Once you have erected your black background, mark a spot for your subject to stand and place a single onto a boom stand central to your subject, so that it casts the shadows downwards. Position the boom approximately one to two metres higher than the subject and a good distance away so it will not be splashed with any water, and fit a standard reflector with a large honeycomb grid, to help you control the light. It is possible to use broader reflectors; however, these may spill onto your background, leaving you with more post-processing. Meter this light between *f*11 and *f*16.

Now place a second light onto a stand and position this approximately four to five metres away behind the subject and at an angle of 45 degrees. This head will help light the side of the model, creating separation from the background, and also light the water droplets from behind. Fit this head with a semi-directional bare reflector and use the modelling facility on the head to ascertain where the light is falling. Meter the light between *f*8 and *f*11.

Once you have set up and paid particular attention to the health and safety of your subject, your assistants as well as yourself and your set, it is time to get your assistant to supply the water. Start slowly and control the delivery. It is equally important to consider the comfort of your subject. Cold water will quickly chill the model, causing them to shiver and the skin to react with goose bumps, so use warm water and ensure the studio is warm. Achieving the desired effect will take a little practice and time to perfect, so take regular breaks, clean up spillages and continuously empty any collected water from the studio.

Common Issues

UNABLE TO ADEQUATELY LIGHT WATER FROM BACKGROUND

The choice of reflector from the background light will influence the way in which the water is lit.

- If you are using a large reflector, you may find that you light too much of the subject, whereas a narrower reflector with a honeycomb grid may control the light too much, not allowing enough spread to light all of the water.
- Experiment with reflectors or by moving the light further or closer to the subject to increase or decrease the spread of light accordingly.

SIDE LIGHT TOO BRIGHT

- This is a simple case of reducing the power. Remember, wet surfaces are more reflective and will therefore be more specular. The power required will depend on many factors, which include the skin type of your model, the angle of the backlight and the reflector used.

THREE LIGHT SETUPS

Three Light Setup 1

Abstract shots can make an interesting study. It is not always necessary to photograph the face when shooting fine art nude. The expression of the face adds a lot to the mood of a photograph, and removing this allows the viewer to concentrate more on the shape and tone. It does become more important to sculpt the body with light, however, as without the face your photograph is at risk of becoming very flat.

This shot [Fig. 4.4] is simple in terms of lighting and relies more on shape and angles to add interest. The shot has deliberately been framed from corner to corner to fill as much as the frame as possible whilst the model arched her back, creating a curved shape that accentuated the ribs and chest bones. It is the softer lighting that allows it to work in colour against the high-key background.

Getting Started

Begin by setting up a white paper roll onto a background support and pulling a long train of paper to the ground. Ensure that you have enough paper for the model to manoeuvre and for you to move around comfortably. Once done, set up a single head with a broad directional reflector to light the background. You can position this on either side of the paper, but as you are shooting on the floor of the studio, it is more beneficial to direct this more towards the lower part of the background or the curve in the train. Mark a position for your model approximately three metres in front of the background.

Now set up two more studio heads and stands, fitting these with white reflective umbrellas. As we are shooting on the floor of the studio, it is important to provide enough light to illuminate the floor surrounding the model. Position the umbrellas on either side of the paper/model, ensuring that they are bouncing light back towards the ground. Using the traditional key light/fill light setup, meter one of your lights as the key to approximately *f*11, and the second as the fill light between *f*5.6 and *f*8.0. There are no hard and fast rules between the lighting ratios and you may find that under certain circumstances you will need less/more fill light, so be prepared to check your results and adjust the power of the fill light accordingly. Remember, too much fill light will make the light very flat, whereas too little will add more contrast.

Once you have positioned and metered your main lights, it is time to make the final adjustments to your background light. Start by metering this to a similar setting to your key light, around *f*11. The idea is not to completely blow the highlights behind the subject, but to lift the shade of the paper to a similar level to that in the foreground. This effect can be achieved by bouncing light off the background paper, or by using a reflector to direct the light towards the background. Either way, you may find that as you move around your subject, your camera's angle on the background may change, necessitating small changes in the position of the background lighting. For greater flexibility, it is of course feasible to use two background lights to cover a broader area.

The key here is to get in close and concentrate on the angles and positioning of the model. Don't be afraid to move around and shoot from different positions and heights. Make use of a zoom lens to accentuate and distort angles to create a unique perspective – after all, the key to this type of art nude is experimenting with shapes.

Common Issues

TOO MUCH LIGHT FROM THE BACKGROUND

Light reflecting from the background back onto the subject is known as 'bleed'. In certain circumstances, such as this example, bleed can be useful in drawing out some shape.

- Consider moving your subject further from the background.
- Or try decreasing the power of your background lighting.

PAPER AROUND SUBJECT UNDEREXPOSED

- Umbrellas are used here to cover a broad area, which includes the subject and the surrounding white paper background. It is possible to use other modifiers and reflectors that may do a similar job, but with varying degrees of efficiency.
- If you are using a smaller modifier, such as a softbox, consider placing it further away or higher up to increase the spread of light. Remember, the further away the light source, the greater the spread, but the more defined and longer the shadows.

SETTINGS AND EQUIPMENT

Camera Settings

Aperture: *f*11
Shutter: 1/125sec
ISO: 100
Focal Length: 50mm

Lighting Equipment Required

- Three flash heads.
- Three lighting stands.
- Broad directional reflector for background.
- Two white reflective umbrellas or large softboxes.
- Background support and white background paper.
- Flash meter.
- Radio trigger or sync lead.

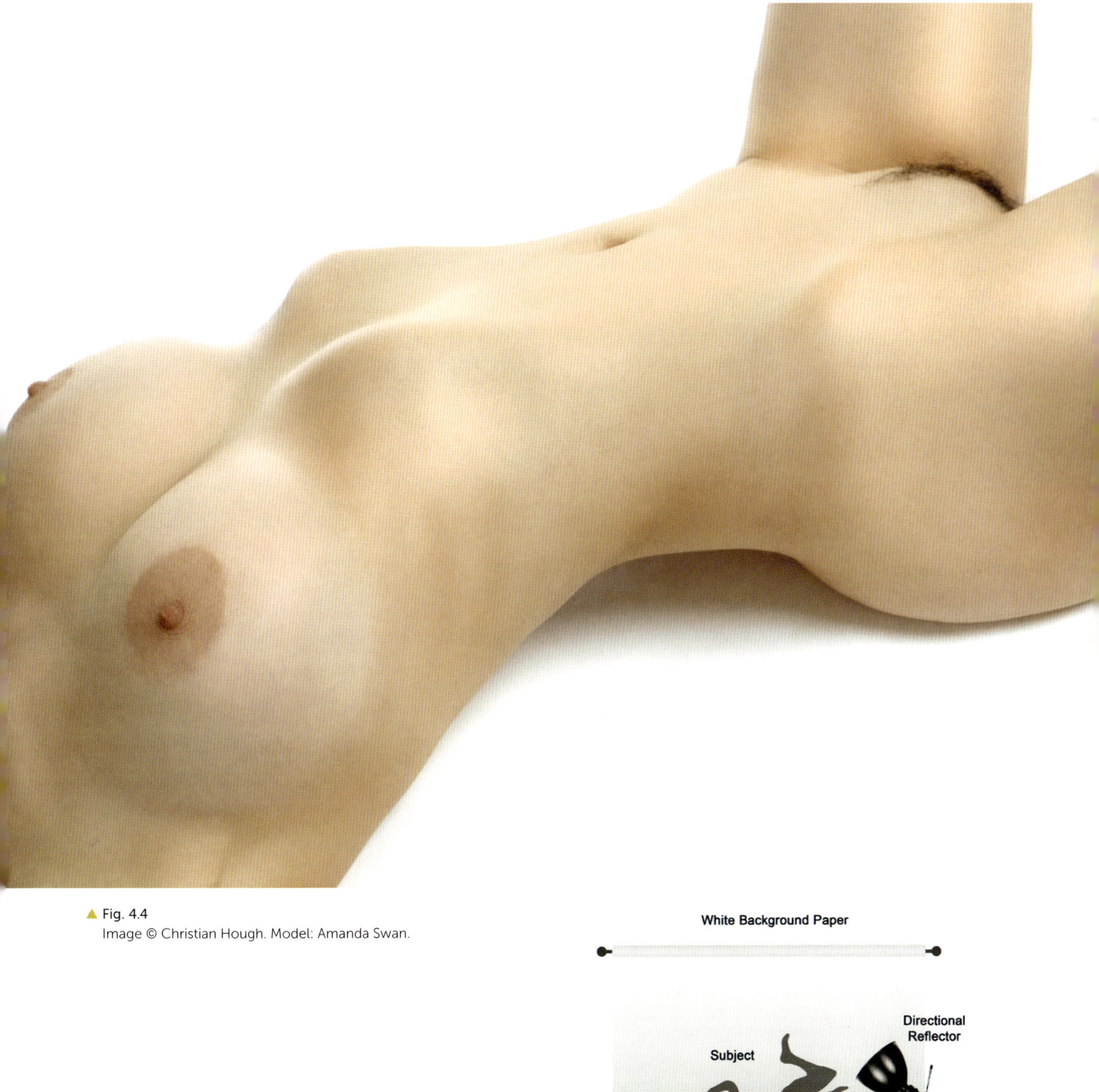

▲ Fig. 4.4
Image © Christian Hough. Model: Amanda Swan.

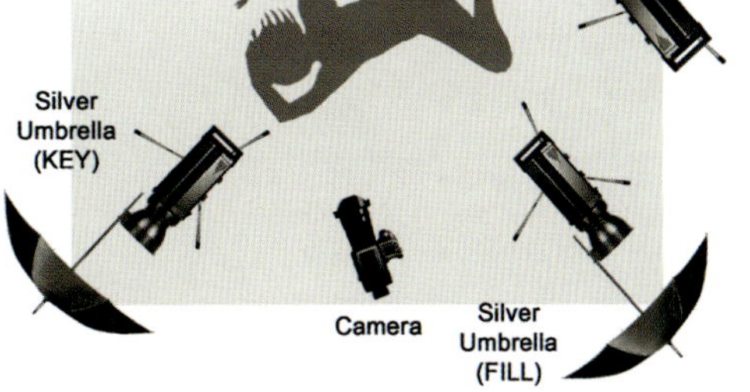

Three Light Setup 2

Shooting nudes does not always have to be about body sculptures, but can also have a fashionable angle. Sometimes, small additions to the photograph can make a very big difference, such as small items of underwear, jewellery and even hair. It can be the combination of shapes and textures that really add interest to an image.

In this shot [Fig. 4.5], I have made use of some designer underwear and a very unusual shaped wig to give the image a more fashionable edge. The underwear is unusual and helps break up the body line around the waist of the model, whilst the wig completely changes the shape of the head, removing eye contact and making the main focus of the photograph the lips, with the side profile drawing out the shape of the body and the outstretched arms filling the frame. As in a lot of artistic nude photographs, there is as much emphasis placed upon the shadows as there is on the light, and it is this consideration that makes the shot work. The background has deliberately been lit so that it is lighter at the bottom of the frame and dark at the top, whereas the model has been lit the opposite way, so that she is lighter at the top of the frame. This retains separation from the background, but not in a way that it becomes overly distracting. In fact, it is so subtle, that not a lot of people even notice.

Getting Started

Start by setting up a dark grey background paper on your background support. Using a dark grey will give you more flexibility and control over the background light, especially if you are working within a confined space. It is still possible to use a background of any colour you are going to convert to black and white; however, depending on the method you use, it is possible that a coloured background may later affect your black and white conversion process.

Once you have set up your background, you need to position two heads on lighting stands on each side of the background. If possible, position the heads about three metres back and fit them with broad directional reflectors. The reflectors fitted to the background lights should be broad enough to allow an even coverage across the background, without creating distracting hot spots. Meter the heads to around *f*4.0 and point them downwards towards the curve in the paper. The idea here is that you are lighting the lower half of the background paper, creating a natural vignette.

Now mark a position for your model and for your key light. Set up a single flash head fitted with a beauty dish. A beauty dish can throw light over a broad area and create a fairly harsh shadow on the background if used too closely. To combat this, you will need a fair amount of separation between the model and the background. To begin with, the beauty dish is best placed about a metre higher than the

SETTINGS AND EQUIPMENT

Camera Settings

Aperture: *f*11
Shutter: 1/125sec
ISO: 100
Focal Length: 110mm

Lighting Equipment Required

- Three flash heads.
- Three lighting stands.
- Two broad directional reflectors for background.
- Single medium-sized beauty dish for key light.
- Background support and dark grey background paper.
- Flash meter.
- Radio trigger or sync lead.

▶ Fig. 4.5
Image © Christian Hough. Model: Gemma Nichols.

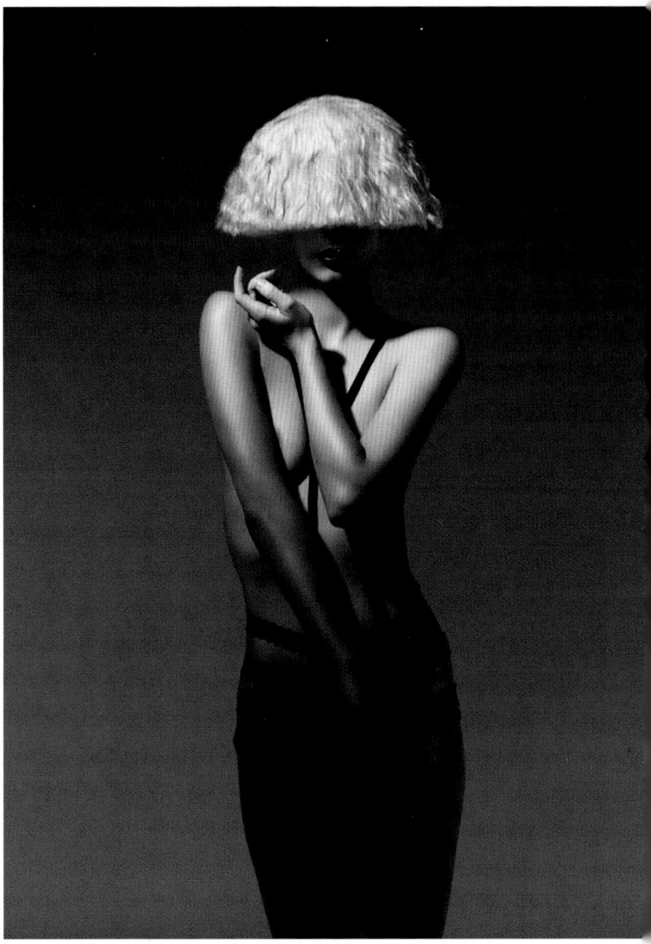

model and approximately 45 degrees off the camera axis. Meter this to approximately *f*11. On the opposite side to the key light, position a black polyboard to help darken the shadows. You will find that if you are using a similar shaped wig or hat, then you will need to adjust the height and positioning of the key light so that it still lights part of the face, the side of the breast and the top of the arms. Don't be afraid to adjust the lights as small movements can make a big difference and save many hours of post-processing.

Common Issues

SPILL LIGHT ON BACKGROUND

If you are using a large beauty dish or softbox on your key light, you may find that this spills onto the background.

- Start by adjusting the angle of the key light
- Or by moving your model and light further from the background.
- If space is a limitation, try fitting the beauty dish with a honeycomb grid or using a smaller reflector also fitted with a honeycomb.

HOTSPOTS ON BACKGROUND

The key to lighting a background properly is using the right shapers and making the most of the space available. The further the background lights are from the background paper, the broader and flatter the coverage. Position them too close and you will get 'hot' areas on the background and uneven coverage.

- If you are struggling for space, try utilizing small 60x60cm/60x80cm softboxes as opposed to standard reflectors. These will assist in controlling the light, but also create a broader spread and more even coverage.

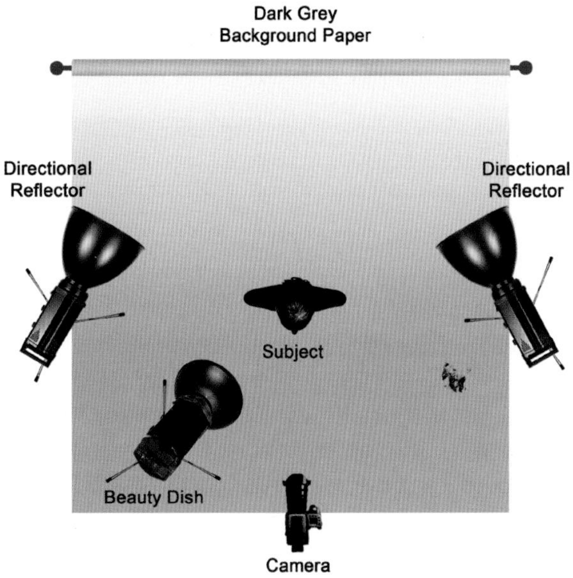

Three Light Setup 3

If you are interested in taking more of a glamorous approach, but would like to retain an editorial feel, then it is possible to make use of a ringflash. Ringflash has long been associated with fashion photography, creating a very flat and stark light, with the characteristic shadow around the edge of the subject. It is quick and simple lighting, allowing you to maximize time on shooting and posing as opposed to lighting.

Building upon the principle of mixing garments with nudity, I have concentrated less on the lighting in this photograph [Fig. 4.2] and more on the expression and eroticism of the model. The idea behind the photograph is that it looks as if she has been caught unaware, adding a semi-voyeuristic feel to the shot. The photograph is meant to have a raw paparazzi feel to it, but not appear as 'traditional glamour'.

Getting Started

Ringflash is very unforgiving light. It is by its very nature harsh and unflattering to the majority of subjects, but used correctly, can give a photograph a strong editorial feel. It is simple to use, but needs to be applied in the right circumstances to look good. The telltale sign of ringflash is a narrow continuous shadow around the subject and very flat lighting, with no directional shadows on the face. You should find that the ringflash comes with both a reflector and a diffuser. Adding the reflector will project more of the light forwards, improving the shadow around the subject. There is also a bracket that will attach to the tripod mount underneath the camera, fixing the camera to the same axis and the ringflash.

Start by fixing your camera to the bracket and positioning the camera's lens through the centre of the ringflash. Now meter the ringflash to approximately *f*11 and begin shooting. It really is that simple! Try to introduce some dynamic into your shots, so don't be afraid to move around and shoot, getting your model to make interesting shapes and poses. Just remember to remain roughly the same distance from the subject as when you metered, otherwise you will achieve inconsistent exposures.

Common Issues

RED EYE

Red eye is common with ringflash, simply because it is directional on-axis flash bouncing off the back of the retina.

- If you are using a generator-based ringflash, be sure to use the modelling facility to reduce the effects of red eye by closing down the iris.
- If you are using a monobloc adapter, such as the Ringlite Adapter, it may be beneficial to increase the ambient light.
- Use the modelling facility of a second studio head to increase the ambient light, but reduce the flash power to its minimum to prevent unwanted flash.

SETTINGS AND EQUIPMENT

Camera Settings

Aperture: *f*10
Shutter: 1/125sec
ISO: 100
Focal Length: 146mm

Lighting Equipment Required

- Ringflash and generator.
- Studio wall.
- Flash meter.
- Radio trigger or sync lead.

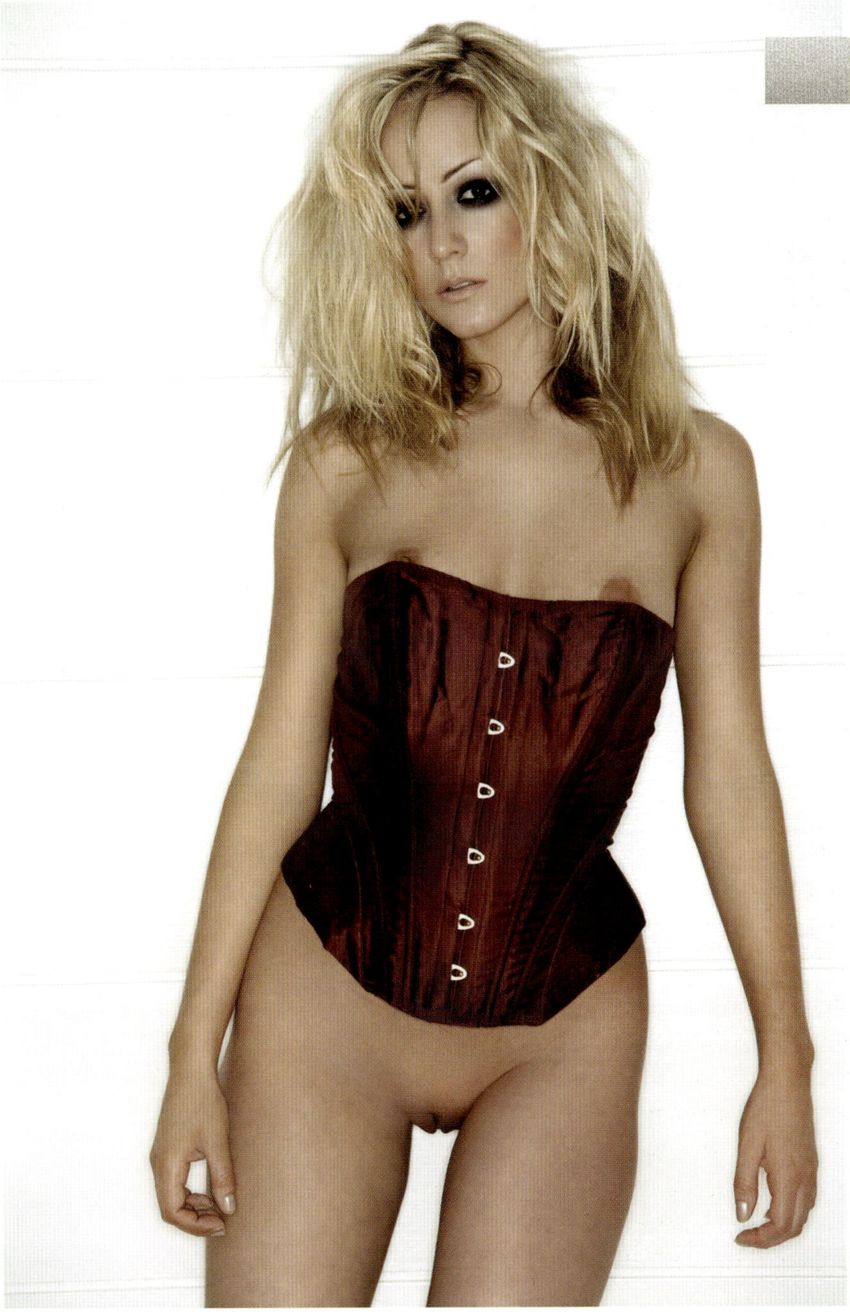

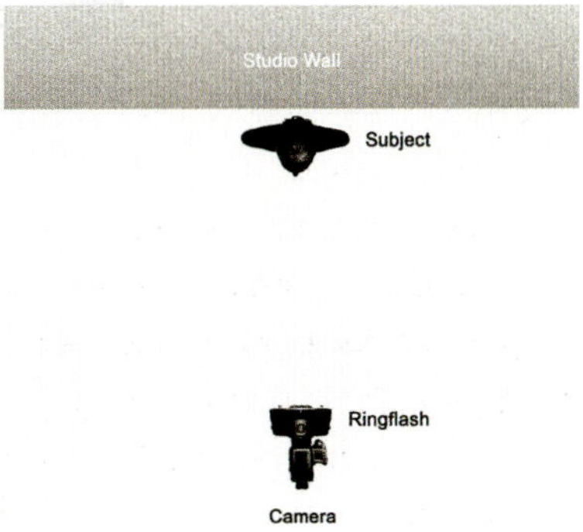

Fig. 4.6
Image © Christian Hough.
Model: Kerri Guiney-Donnelly.

NO SHADOWS

- If a reflector came with your ringflash, then you may find it beneficial to attach this, as it will project more light forwards and increase the shadow.
- Standing your model against a white reflective studio wall will automatically reflect light and reduce the shadows.
- Black polyboards can also help increase shadow depth.

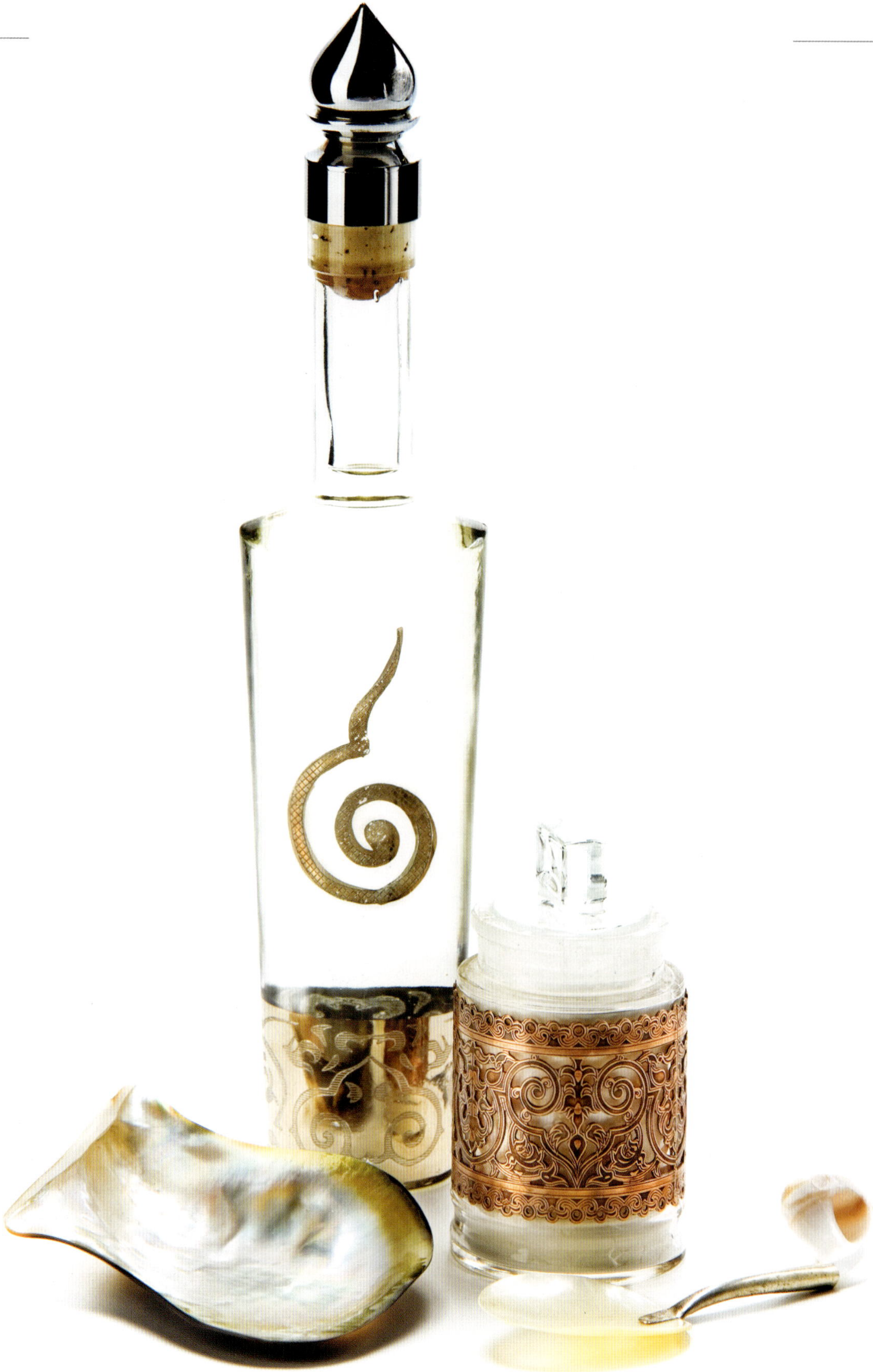

Chapter 5

Still Life Photography

There is a popular misconception that shooting products is a simple job, whereas it is in fact the complete opposite. I have spoken to and written about many product photographers, and their experience shows there is an immense amount of time and skill that goes into setting up each shot. A lot, of course, depends on the end use of each shot, so products placed onto a white background for e-commerce take less technical knowledge and time than those produced for major manufacturers and luxury brands. However, each shot still needs time and consideration, even for mass marketing and retail, and spending time getting the lighting and angles right will save you hours of tedious post-processing work later on. The less time spent behind the computer, the better!

CONSIDERATIONS

Backgrounds

It sounds like common sense, but the background scenery behind the product can be as important as the product itself. In the same way as commercial fashion and beauty, products sell a lifestyle and usually have a brand identity. The props and background help set the scene, generate the identity and place it within the right market, but at the end of the day it is meeting the expectations of the consumer that really counts.

E-commerce

Photographs on the internet allow the long-distance consumer to see what they are buying. E-commerce is essentially the nitty-gritty of still life photography and the photographs need to be clean, bright and without distractions. This calls for a simple background, and by far the most popular choice for this is white, followed by grey and black. Using a plain background allows designers to easily cut out the product and use it elsewhere. It is of course always possible to use other colours – after all there are no rules. However, this choice will ultimately depend on the finish and colour of the product, or even the design of the website or catalogue. It is important to remember that brighter colours are more distracting, and they can occasionally result in colour casts, so they tend to be used less frequently for e-commerce and catalogue shots.

Lifestyle

Every product has a target audience and this audience will have a particular lifestyle. Setting the scene for this by placing the product within a properly designed set can work wonders. Many sets found in the glossy magazines have had large budgets and props specifically bought in; however, lifestyle can also be showcased by simply propping the product with a few carefully placed items. If you search around, you can find a range of items to prop your products, such as flowers, pebbles and even liquids. As for backgrounds, a little imagination can be equally as creative, with photographers using everything from fabrics or wallpaper to raw materials such as concrete and steel in their backgrounds.

Static or Dynamic

Part of placing the product and creating the lifestyle is how the product itself is portrayed. Movement or a sense of movement within a product shot can make the scene more dynamic and energetic, whereas static sets will look more classic and subdued. Your choice as to whether you make the set more dynamic or static should really depend on the product you are shooting and the intended audience. For example an invigorating facial wash will work well with a sense of movement, especially water with bright colours. Cold drinks and beers are enhanced by ice and condensation. Classic jewellery on the other hand works better within a more static and often subdued set, so that the viewer can concentrate on the beauty of the jewellery. So it is important to visualize the context – dropping a 24-carat gold and diamond studded ring into water may not appeal to the target market, while a static shot of a shampoo or shower gel may look rather uninspiring and lack-lustre.

USEFUL EQUIPMENT

You might assume that a set of good quality studio lights, a decent camera and a studio table are all you need to capture studio-based still life photographs. There is a lot you can do of course with this basic equipment, but most professional product and still life photographers will use a variety of different items and tools to get results. It is not simply a case of placing items onto the table; the skill comes in positioning them exactly where you want them, at the right height and the right angles. This will not only ensure that the light is right and consistent, but will potentially save you hours of Photoshop. You still need Photoshop, but with the right techniques you can reduce the time you spend behind the computer.

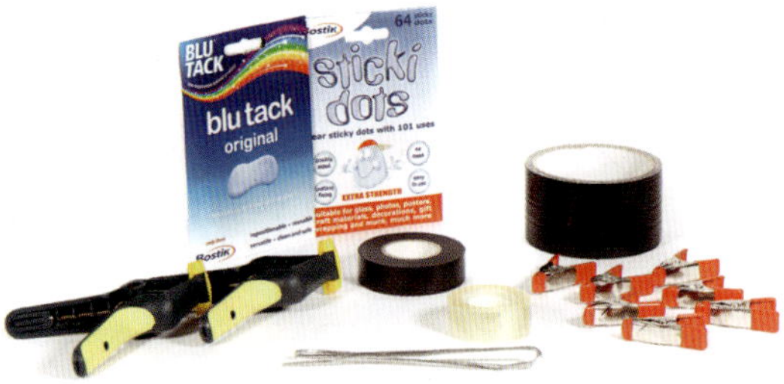

▲ Fig. 5.1
Various useful studio accessories.

The good news is that many of these items are fairly cheap and widely available from various stores or photographic retailers.

Common Accessories

Sticky Tape

Tape is useful in many ways, in particular double-sided tape and duck tape. It is ideal for sticking objects together, suspending and stabilizing things. There are other specialized tapes that do not leave any residue, which can also be very useful on reflective surfaces or even assisting to pick up dust.

Brushes

Make-up brushes, cotton buds, paintbrushes or even Pec Pads are extremely useful for dusting and cleaning objects without disturbing your set, especially if you are photographing food.

Anti-Static Spray

Dust is a real problem, and it is not until you get your shoots to the post-processing stage that you realize just how much dust is flying about. It can then take ages for you to heal and clone the specs of dust. However, an anti-static spray can remove the static from the item you are photographing and greatly reduce the amount of dust clinging to it.

Grips, Clips and Pins

Large and small, they are always useful. Bulldog clips are particularly good at gripping things such as paper, wire, mirrors and small reflectors, and they are available in a variety of different sizes. Grips on the other hand will enable you to quickly fasten two items together, such as wire and a stand. If you are photographing clothes, then safety pins and butterfly clips will assist in shaping the clothing and holding the fabric.

Wire and Cable

Strong and stiff wire and cable can help you accurately place items in the frame, whilst minimizing intrusion. They can be quickly edited out in post-processing.

Blu-Tack, Sticky Dots

Blu-Tack or some similar putty/non-permanent adhesive is perfect for holding small items in position, without blocking out the item. It is ideal when used with wire, cable and clips, plus it can help stabilize objects.

Tweezers

If you have large hands or are shooting small items, then a decent pair of tweezers will help you manoeuvre props and products and fine-tune your set with minimal disturbance.

Matting Spray

This spray is ideal if you are photographing very reflective and shiny products. The spray effectively removes the shine.

Water Atomizer/Spray

Water produced as a fine mist using a spray can be used to replicate condensation or add water droplets. Spray is most commonly used for drinks and plants. Remember: it is essential to exercise extreme care and caution when working with water close to electronic items, and especially hot lights.

Glass

If you are planning on photographing items such as drinks, then there are a variety of glass props you can buy, such as glass cubes and glass pellets to replicate ice cubes and crushed ice. These are even more convincing when used in conjunction with sprayed water.

Gloves

Lint-free cotton gloves and Pec Pads are very useful when handling shiny and reflective items, such as steel and glass, to reduce the risk of fingerprints and dust.

Cleaning Products

During a shoot it is inevitable that something will get dirty and need cleaning. Try to stock up on a range of different cleaners and polishes to allow you to clean items without leaving marks.

Black Fabric

If you are shooting within a confined location or cluttered studio, you may find that you get unwanted reflections in your shots. A good work around is to suspend large pieces of black fabric to block off these reflections. Simply clamping the fabric to unused lighting stands can help you flag a large area very quickly.

Vinyl/Polycarbonate Board

Reflective vinyl board is extremely useful for placing items on, creating a mirror-like shadow or reflection. Depending on the thickness of the board, it can be ridged or flexible, so can also be curved and utilized as a background. Solid colours work best, as clear boards create a double reflection. As it is so reflective, it usually requires less light to lift backgrounds and shadows, and more restraint may be needed to retain highlights, especially when using hard light sources.

Cameras and Lenses

You can use any type of camera or lens you wish to shoot still life, but some cameras and lenses work better than others. Traditionally, large-format bellows cameras have been used for still life and products, which allow the lens to be tilted, thus correcting the issues associated with parallax errors. These cameras are speciality items and work on an entirely different format 35mm, plus usually require a digital or film back, further increasing the expense.

It is of course possible to utilize a longer focal length lens on your DSLR. Increasing your focal length to around 120mm and above will ensure that you fit the product you are shooting neatly into the frame, and exclude the unwanted studio interior, whilst minimizing distortion. However, using a standard lens is not suitable for every product and you may be required to correct perspective errors in Photoshop, which will dramatically increase your post-processing time and begin to introduce unwanted artifacts into the photograph.

A little post-processing is not an issue if you are only planning on shooting a few still life shoots, but if you are thinking about shooting still life and products commercially, then it is definitely worth investing in a few pieces of equipment. This does not mean that you have to sell your 35mm DSLR as there are affordable ways in which to quickly transform your DSLR into a highly flexible tilt and shift system that accepts large-format lenses, giving you the best of both worlds. If you wish to use your 35mm or medium-format based system, you may find that many manufacturers produce a tilt and shift lens. These lenses are traditionally more expensive than standard prime lenses, but will help correct some parallax issues.

Light Tent/Lightbox

A light tent is basically a pop-up box covered in a semi-translucent or nylon white fabric. Specifications vary from manufacturer to manufacturer; however, you will generally find that the light tent has a removable panel, slit or hole in at least one side of the box, allowing the camera's lens to be pushed through. The white fabric is used to diffuse the light, in a similar way to a softbox, resulting in soft light whilst reducing unwanted reflections from immediate surroundings. Once erected, a product is positioned within the light tent and then it is lit externally by one or more studio lights. This will to some degree produced a white surround in the finished photograph, allowing the object to be isolated and later cut out if necessary. The larger the light tent, the more lights will be required to obtain a pure high-key background.

Light tents are a cost-effective and space-saving alternative to a product table, as they are highly portable and very cheap. They are ideal for shooting smaller items and are generally used for e-commerce product photography.

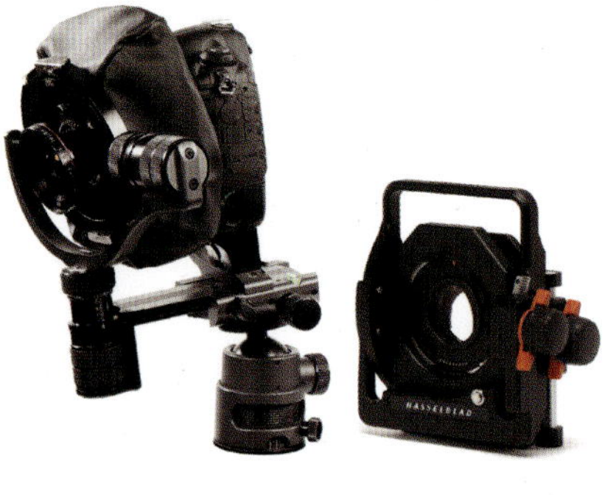

▲ Fig. 5.2
X2-Pro by Cambo, and Tilt and Shift adapter by Hasselblad.

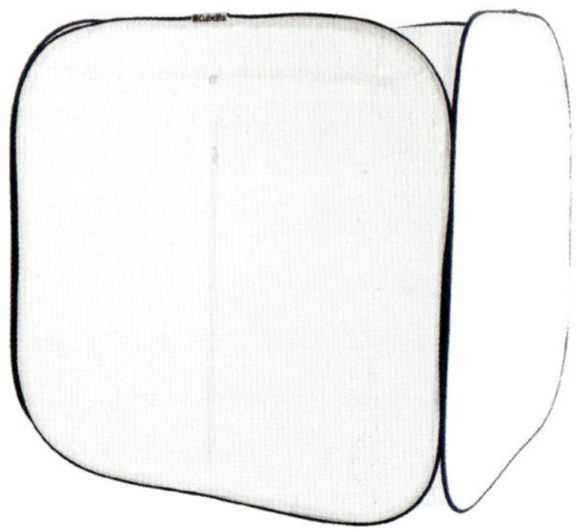

▲ Fig. 5.3
Light tent: Cubelite by Lastolite.

Product Table/Tabletop Studio

Product tables (also known as tabletop studios) are available in several sizes and consist of a semi-translucent piece of Perspex mounted onto a frame, which curves up at the rear of the table to form a seamless background. Products can be placed directly onto the Perspex or otherwise a paper background of your choice can be used and clamped onto the Perspex. The use of Perspex allows you to light products from underneath, whilst some of the larger and more expensive product tables will allow 4ft paper rolls to be mounted and the angle of the background to be raised and lowered. If you are shooting a lot of still life, then a quality table will be a worthwhile investment, offering considerably more flexibility than a light tent.

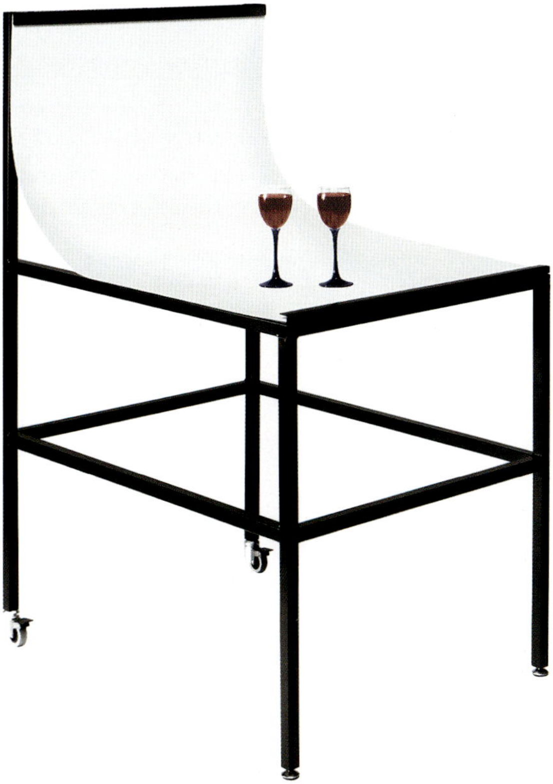

▲ Fig. 5.4
Small product table by Cambo: ideal for still life.

BASIC STILL LIFE TECHNIQUES

A large light tent is perfect for lighting smaller items, helping isolate the subject, create a clean white surround and reducing unwanted reflections. The beauty of the light tent is its simplicity. The light is diffused by the panels of the light tent and then bounces around inside the box, helping to lift both the background and the shadows. It is possible to use only a single light with a light tent; however, the results will vary depending on the size of the box, positioning of the light and the item being photographed.

The following example has been split into three, building up from using a single light, up to three lights, so you should see the subtle difference each head makes to the photograph. For authenticity, I have photographed three everyday items, the very sort of thing you will find for sale on the internet and in the supermarket. Each of the items has a different surface and a different shape. Doing it in this way will help you see how adding more lights will effect the image.

There is no magic formula as to how many lights you should use when shooting with a light tent. A lot can depend on the shade of the background you are using and whether or not you require more or less shadow detail. For example, if you were to use a standard white paper background, you might find that the shadows remain quite dark. Most background papers have a matt finish and are therefore less reflective than a glossy vinyl. If you wish to lift the shadows, then you will need to use either a reflector or a second light. Conversely, if you are using a reflective vinyl background that bounces light everywhere, you will find that the shadows are much lighter, possibly negating the need for a second light.

A lot can also depend on your workflow. It is of course preferable to get the shot as perfect as possible 'in camera', reducing the need for post-processing. However, if you are only photographing a small number of items, it is perfectly acceptable to extract these from the background during post-processing. If you are shooting hundreds of items, then relying on post-processing is the last thing you want to do, as this will dramatically increase your workload and reduce your profit margin. The moral is, don't resort to post-processing unless you really have to. Instead, add additional lights as and when they are needed and light the photograph properly.

Still Life 1

Getting Started

Start by positioning your light tent onto a steady table or flat surface. It is better to place your tent onto a raised surface, as opposed to placing the tent onto the floor, as this will afford you greater flexibility when positioning your lights. Depending on the model of your light tent, remove the front panel between the item and the camera and then fit your chosen background inside the light tent before positioning the item to be photographed.

For your lighting, start by fitting a single head and standard reflector to a light stand, positioning your light to one side of the box and approximately half a metre higher than the item. This will be your key light. Use the modelling facility on the studio light to see where the shadows are falling, and if necessary move the light around the box to control the reflections and shadows. Now meter the light to around *f*11 by placing your light meter inside the light tent, next to the product.

You will find that a longer focal length or tilt and shift lens will work best, helping to reduce lateral and horizontal distortion. To retain the same shooting angle and a degree of consistency between each product, it is advisable to place the camera onto a tripod. This will assist with the accurate positioning of the camera, plus leaving your hands free to fine-tune the positioning of the product. I have suggested metering to *f*11; however, if you are using a very long focal length to photograph a large item, you may find that you require more depth of field and need to meter to *f*16 or even *f*22.

In this example, I stayed with the most common light tent use and utilized a classic white background to help isolate the product. To assist in lifting the white background and softening the shadows, I used a white background with an eggshell finish. This was fixed to the top and rear of the light tent and then pulled to the ground and underneath the product, much in the same way in which you would use a studio paper roll. The eggshell finish is not highly reflective, but is just enough to soften the shadows and lift the background with a single light.

Still Life 2

It goes without saying that adding a second light increases your control over the shadows and will also assist in lightening the background. It is possible (depending on the size of your light tent) to position the second light to light either more of the product or more of the background. In this example I used a fairly large tabletop light tent and concentrated more of the light onto the product, allowing the spill to lift the background.

Getting Started

Fit your second studio light with a standard reflector, place it onto a stand and position it on the opposite side of your key light. This will now be your fill light and used to 'fill in' the shadows. Start by positioning the light at approximately 45 degrees from the camera and meter this to one to two stops lower than the key light. In this example, the key light was metered to *f*11 and the fill light to *f*5.6. If you find that the shadows are still too dark, increase the power of your fill light to lift some of the shadow detail further. If you find that the photograph is looking too washed out, it may be because you are using too much fill light and the image has become flat, in which case you will need to reduce the power of the

▼ Fig. 5.5
Still Life 1
Image © Christian Hough.

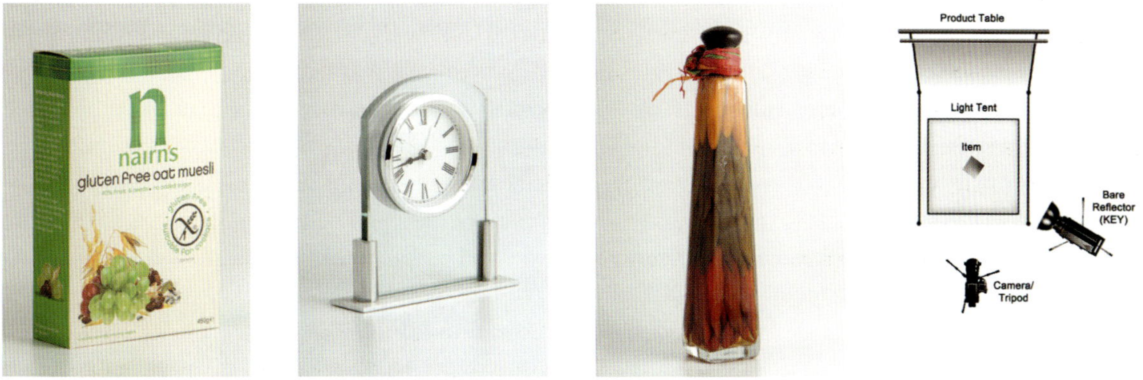

▼ Fig. 5.6
Still Life 2
Image © Christian Hough.

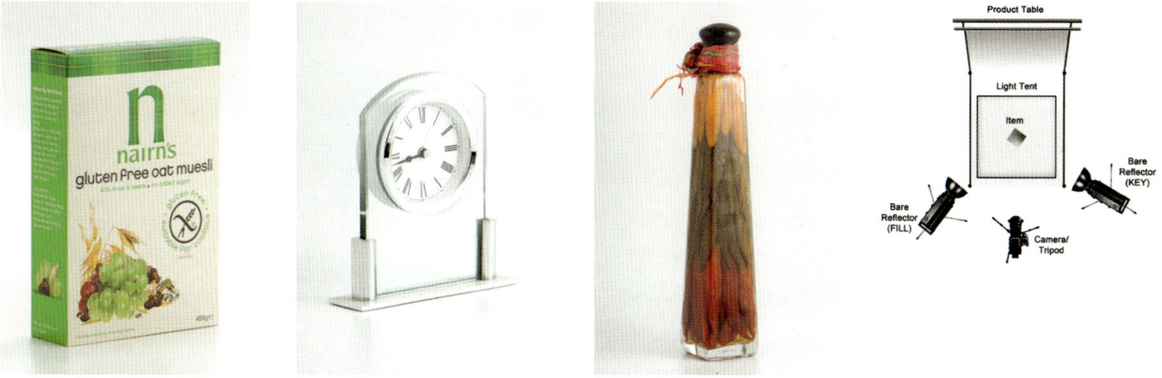

▼ Fig. 5.7
Still Life 3
Image © Christian Hough.

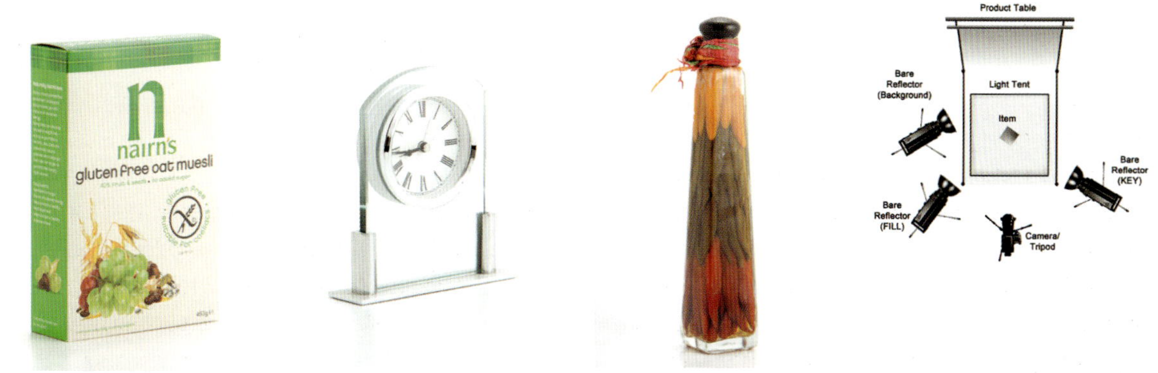

fill light. If the fill light is directed more towards the background, too much power will cause the light to bounce off the background and back into the lens, effectively bleaching the photograph. Don't forget to check the positioning of your fill light to ensure that it is directed towards the opposite side of the shadows and the far side of the product.

Still Life 3

Once you are comfortable with using two lights, you may feel that there is a need to progress to a third light. A third light is not always necessary, especially with smaller light tents. If you are using a medium-sized or larger light tent, it may be necessary to add a third light to partially or completely lift the background, helping to further isolate the subject and to massively reduce your post-processing. If you need a highkey background and are shooting many different products, you may find that using a third light will save you time in the long run.

Getting Started

In this example, the third light was used to partially lift the background. I didn't intend to blow the background detail completely, simply due to the fact that the item I was photographing was transparent, and a white background would have resulted in a white product! The third light was positioned in such a way that it lit the vertical background and the ground immediately behind the product.

Start by fitting a standard reflector to your third studio light and then attach this to a boom arm. Position the light so that it is directly over the light tent and directed downwards towards the background, without spilling onto the product. If you don't have a boom, then use a standard studio stand and instead position the light on either side of the light tent, so that it is lighting the background only. The only caveat is that positioning a single light to one side may make the background lighting uneven if you intend to retain some of the background detail.

Once your third light has been set up, meter this to approximately *f*11. Use the same meter setting as the key light (or less) if you wish to retain some background detail. If you would prefer to completely blow the background detail, then meter the background to *f*16 or until the highlights are completely burnt out. Care needs to be taken not to blow the highlights on the surfaces or around the edges of the product you are photographing, especially if they are very reflective, such as glass.

Common Issues

LONG DARK SHADOWS

- Begin by raising your key light to shorten and cast the shadows downwards.
- To lift the shadows, use a reflector or white piece of card out of frame, to bounce light back into the shadow areas.
- A more reflective background paper will help lighten the shadows when using a single light.
- Failing this, add a fill light.

SETTINGS AND EQUIPMENT

Camera Settings

Aperture: *f*11.0
Shutter: 1/125sec
ISO: 100
Focal Length: 200mm

Lighting Equipment Required

- One, two or three flash heads with standard reflectors.
- Medium-sized light tent.
- Eggshell white background.
- Flash meter.
- Radio trigger or sync lead to trigger the flash.

CROSS LIGHTING

- Start by adjusting the positioning of your lights. Moving the fill light closer to the camera's axis will help reduce this effect.
- You will also find that a larger contrast ratio between the key and fill light will help (when both the key light and fill light are of similar power cross lighting is more apparent).
- Increasing the height of the lighting will also help to shorten the shadows.

WASHED-OUT IMAGE

This is known as bleed and is caused by too much light bouncing off the background.

- Try decreasing the power on any background lighting.
- If you are at your lowest setting, increase the power of your key light to compensate, and re-meter.

MORE ADVANCED STILL LIFE TECHNIQUES

Still Life 4

Sometimes it is the simplicity of an image that works. In these photographs [Fig. 5.8 and 5.9], more emphasis has been placed onto the shape of the subject matter as opposed to the texture, yet the subject remains instantly recognizable as pears. The framing also contributes towards the image, in that it is unusual to see pears lined up in this manner, whilst the large amount of space at the top of the frame contributes towards the sense of scale.

Firstly, the lighting has been deliberately set up to draw out the outline of the pears and has been tightly controlled to restrict the amount of light hitting the background, whilst creating a circle of light around the base of the pears. Finally, the black and white conversion contributes towards the fine-art feel of the image.

Getting Started

If you have your own product table (tabletop studio) then begin by placing some grey background paper onto the table. If you don't own a product table, then don't worry, as almost any sturdy table will work, providing you find some way of suspending the background paper at one end. A standard background support system will help you achieve this. To secure the paper and make it flat, clamp it to the table in several places.

Once the background paper is suspended, set up a single light onto a boom arm and fit this with a reflector and honeycomb grid. Remember, the tighter the honeycomb, the tighter the light source. Place the pears onto the table and position the key light so that it is now approximately 30-50cms behind the pears. Try and keep the light central to the frame to ensure evenness of cover, otherwise you will find once side of the pears lit and the others in the shade. Once done, meter between *f*8.0 and *f*11.

▲ Fig. 5.8
Without fill light.Image © Christian Hough.

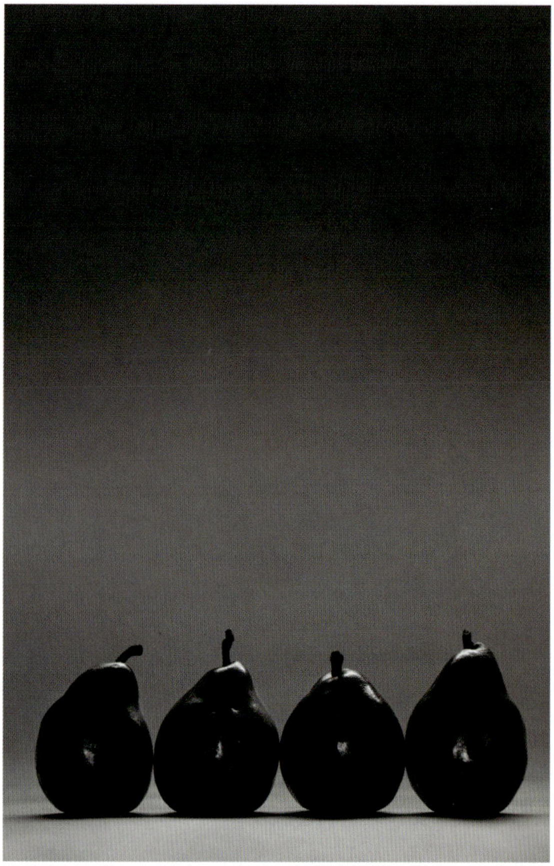

▲ Fig. 5.9
With fill light. Image © Christian Hough.

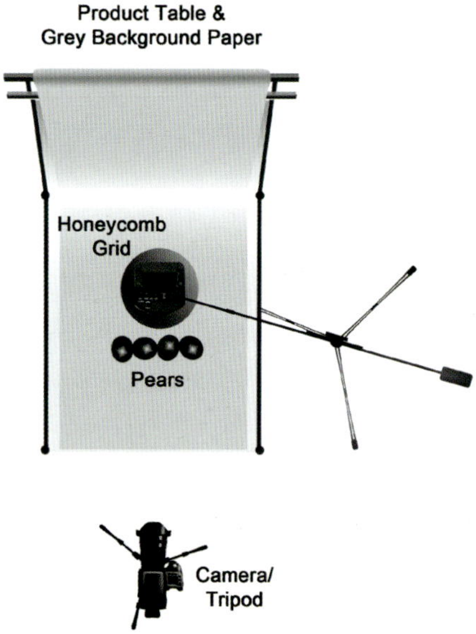

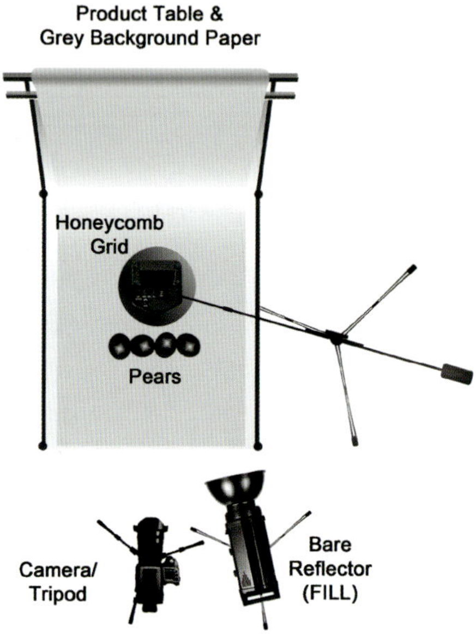

It is recommended that you place your camera onto a tripod. This will help you position the camera at the right angle and ensure that it remains steady when used at a longer focal length.

Remember, all of these distances are approximate and fine adjustments will need to be made based on the size of the honeycomb grid you are using and the distance of the pears from the background. It is important to use the modelling facility on your head to ascertain where the light is falling, continuously moving the light backwards and forwards and adjusting the angle to ensure you are lighting both the top of the pears and the background paper.

If you feel it is necessary, then you can add a fill light to bring out some of the foreground detail. A lot will depend on the type of pears and the finish on their skin. Of course, you can use this setup with any object, not just pears! As you can see from the other two examples, adding a fill light can distract from the shape, creating more of an emphasis on colour and finish as opposed to shape. Adjusting the level of the fill light will increase or decrease the intensity of the colour. In these examples, the fill light was simply placed on the camera axis with a bare reflector. As to which image you prefer is down to personal preference.

Common Issues

UNABLE TO LIGHT BACKGROUND AND PEARS SIMULTANEOUSLY

If you are struggling to achieve this, then it may be that the honeycomb you are using is too tight or that your boom arm isn't high enough to allow the light to spread.

- Try changing the honeycomb and increasing the height of your key light.
- Failing this, move the pears closer to the background.

TOO MUCH LIGHT ON THE BACKGROUND

- Use a tighter honeycomb grid.
- Or lower the stand to decrease the spread of the light.
- Failing this, try moving the pears further away from the background.

TOO LITTLE DETAIL ON FRONT OF PEARS

- Try moving the key light more overhead and adjusting the angle so it gently lights the front of the pears.
- Using a bounce reflector may only provide minimal fill light when used with a honeycomb grid.
- Failing this, set up a second studio head as a fill light.

SETTINGS AND EQUIPMENT

Camera Settings

Aperture: *f*8.0
Shutter: 1/125sec

ISO: 100
Focal Length: 150mm

Lighting Equipment Required

- One or two flash heads.
- Reflectors and honeycomb grid.
- Boom stand/arm.
- Tabletop and background support.
- Grey paper background.
- Tripod.
- Flash meter.
- Radio trigger or sync lead to trigger the flash.

Still Life 5

These shots [Figs 5.10 and 5.11] are similar in approach to the pears, but requires the use of three lights instead of one. It is a further example of how you can photograph an everyday object in an interesting or unusual way. To achieve this, the pebbles were stacked vertically and then lit on each side to bring out their shape with a little bit of texture. The grey background was gently lit to provide an element of separation from the pebbles and reduce the over contrast of the photograph. Finally the black and white conversion has given the photograph more of a fine-art feel.

Getting Started

Begin by setting up your grey background paper onto your product table or tabletop. To ensure the paper remains flat, pull it tight and clamp it at several places down each edge of the table.

Start by marking a place on the background where you intend to place the pebbles. Ensure that you leave 50–100cms of separation between the pebble and the background. Then, on each side of the product table and behind the intended position of the pebbles, place a studio light fitted with a honeycomb grid or a stripbox. Turn each head to face the back of the pebbles and meter between *f*8.0 and *f*11. These will be your side lights/rim lights. Now, set up a third studio light, again with a reflector and honeycomb grid, and fix this to a boom arm. Position the boom arm and light so that they are central to the frame and above the table, either overhead or slightly behind the pebbles. Adjust the angle of the head to that it lights the background and the paper behind the pebbles. This will be your background light. Meter this approximately one stop lower than your side lighting (*f*5.6–*f*8.0).

It is time to stack your pebbles. Ideally, your pebbles will have some flat surfaces to allow them to be stacked. If this is not the case, you can use a couple of household items such as Blu-Tack and Sticky Dots to help secure the pebbles, ensuring that as little (if any) of the adhesive is visible.

Once you have set up and metered all of your lights, take a test shot and fine-tune your composition and lighting. Use a tripod, as this will help you achieve sharp focus and a consistent shooting angle, especially when shooting with longer focal lengths and shallow depth of field.

You may find that you need to adjust the angle and height of the background lighting to adequately cover the background paper. If your background is too dark, simply adjust the power output of the background light a little. Try and ensure that you get both sides of the pebbles evenly lit.

Common Issues

CREASES IN BACKGROUND PAPER

- Begin by trying to increase the tension in the paper to pull out the creases, ensuring that it is clamped tight in several places.
- Alternatively, use a shallower depth of field to blur more of the background.
- Or if possible increase the angle of your lighting to cast shorter shadows.
- Diffused light will also make shadows less apparent.

LENS FLARE

This is commonly caused by light shining into the camera lens.

- If you are using side lighting, adjust the angle of the side lights so that they are not pointing directly towards the camera.
- Or control the spread of the light with honeycomb grids.

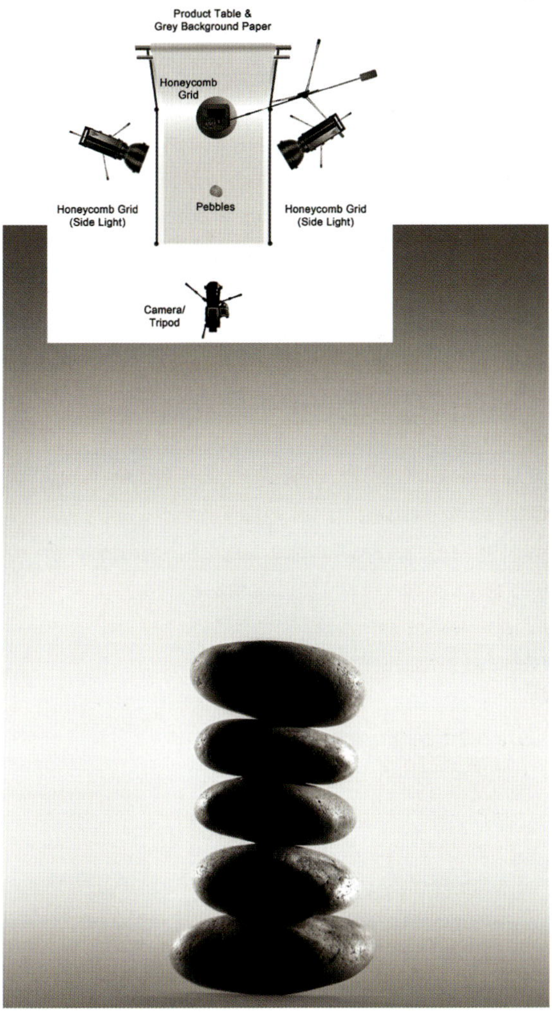

▲ Fig. 5.10
With background light.
Image © Christian Hough.

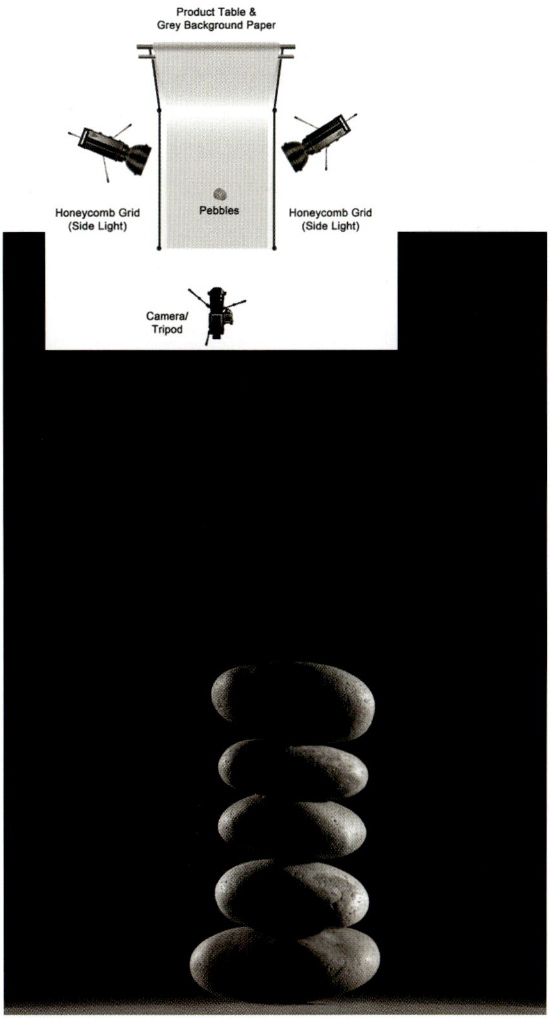

▲ Fig. 5.11
Without background light.
Image © Christian Hough.

SETTINGS AND EQUIPMENT

Camera Settings

Aperture: ƒ8.0
Shutter: 1/125sec
ISO: 100
Focal Length 175mm

Lighting Equipment Required

- Three flash heads with reflectors and honeycomb grids.
- Boom arm/stand.
- Grey paper background.
- Table and background support.
- Tripod.
- Flash meter.
- Radio trigger or sync lead to trigger the flash.

Still Life 6

In still life one key aim is to make everyday objects look interesting. Fruit is always a popular subject as it is often textured, brightly coloured and is something that most people can relate to, and it does not have to be difficult to light. In this example [Fig. 5.12], simplicity is the key and a couple of lemons, limes and kiwi fruits have provided the props. Rather than see the all too familiar 'complete' fruit, the photograph draws attention to the internal structures. The kiwi fruit in particular is interesting, but as a collective they create a colourful wallpaper.

Getting Started

Most shooting tables come with an opaque Perspex tabletop allowing photographers to light the top of the table from underneath. This is very useful when you are intending to lift the immediate background around an object and to create a shoot-through effect as seen in this photograph. If you do not have such a table, then an opaque piece of Perspex supported on both sides will produce similar results.

Begin by placing your studio light onto a floor stand and position it underneath the table or Perspex. Point the light so that it is pointing upwards towards the underside of the Perspex. On this occasion, leave the studio light 'bare bulb' and do not attach a reflector, as when firing in close proximity, a reflector will prove too directional, creating a large central hot spot. Leaving the studio light 'bare bulb' will allow some of the light to diffuse naturally, creating more even lighting.

Once you have set up, meter your light to about *f*11 on the topside of the Perspex. All you have to do now is slice your fruit and place it on top of the table. Your greatest challenge will come with getting above the table so that you can shoot directly down. If you are using a tilt and shift or bellows-based system, you will more easily be able to correct any parallax issues. If you are using a standard lens, then mounting your camera on a boom, tethering it to a laptop and then firing it remotely is a very good alternative and much safer than hanging off a set of stepladders!

Common Issues

WASHED-OUT/OVEREXPOSED IMAGES

- Reduce the power of the light.

PROXIMITY HOT SPOTS

- Try increasing the distance between the light and the Perspex.
- Alternatively try to diffuse the light more.
- Try using a small softbox, but avoid bare reflectors as these will produce hard specular light.

SETTINGS AND EQUIPMENT

Camera Settings

Aperture: *f*13.0
Shutter: 1/125sec
ISO: 100
Focal Length: 110mm

Lighting Equipment Required

- Single studio head 'bare bulb'.
- Product table or opaque Perspex.
- Flash meter.
- Radio trigger or sync lead to trigger the flash.

▶ Fig. 5.12
Image © Christian Hough.

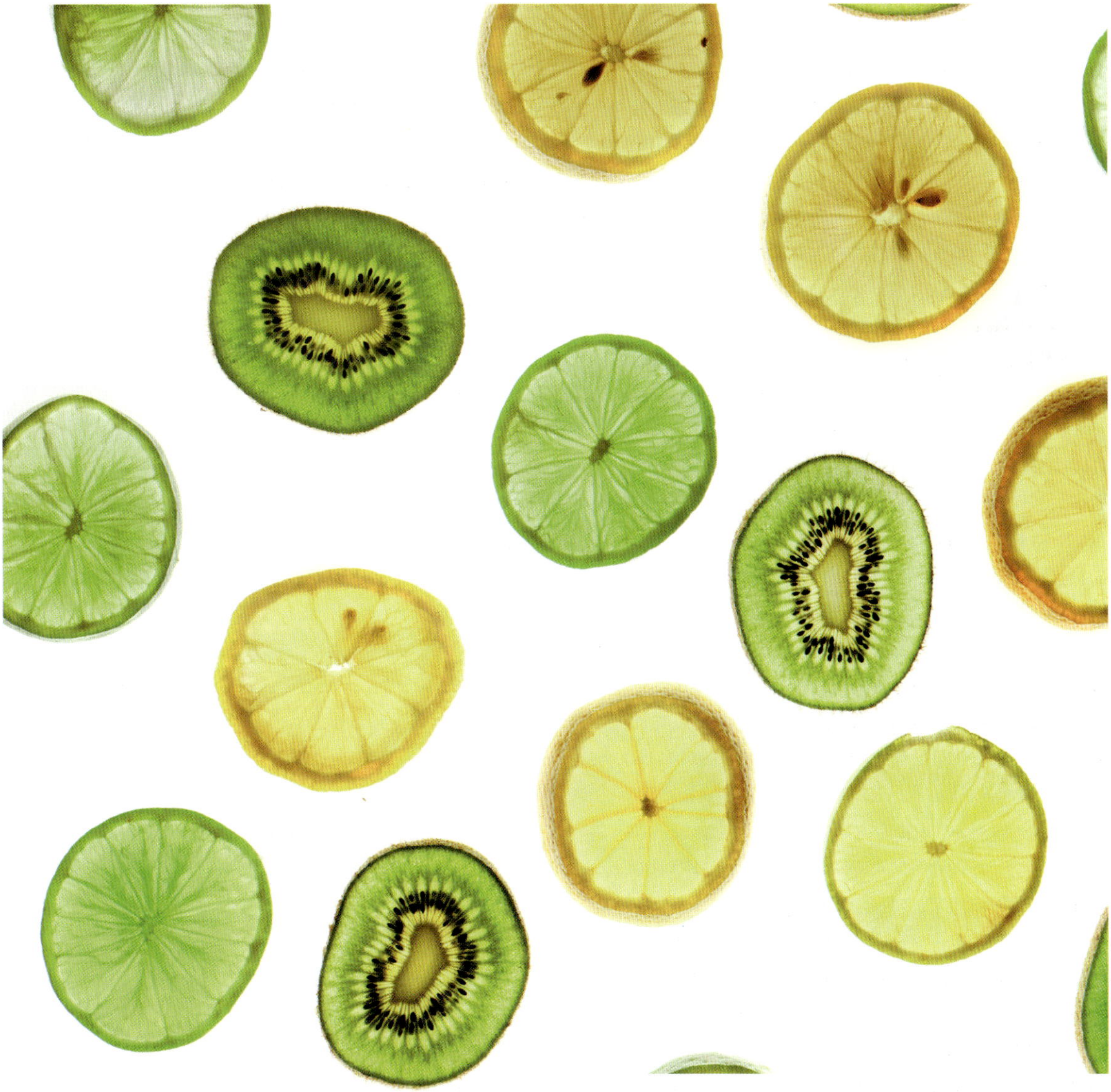

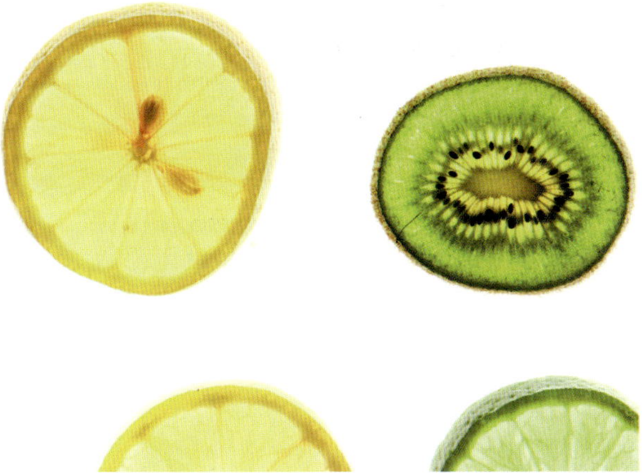

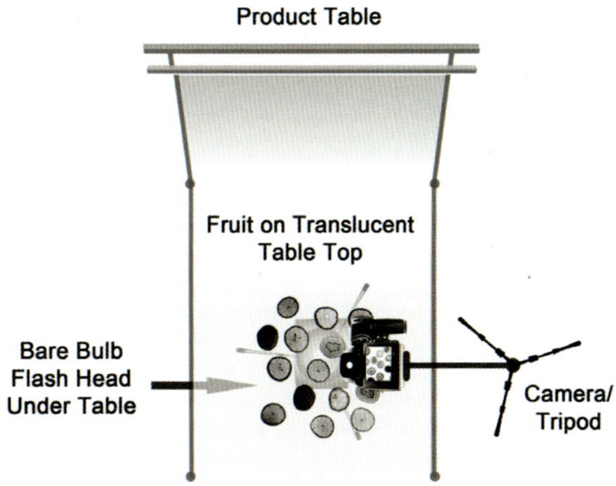
Product Table
Fruit on Translucent Table Top
Bare Bulb Flash Head Under Table
Camera/ Tripod

Still Life 7

Continuing with the theme of fruit and veg, I used the red, yellow (amber) and green peppers to replicate traffic lights (at least in the UK). The concept is simple, yet it is the type of image that you frequently find used in stock photography to illustrate healthy eating [Fig 5.13]. The background has been left grey to draw attention to the colour of the peppers and then spot lit directly behind to create a circular gradient. Finally, the three images were composited together in Photoshop to form the traffic-light effect.

Getting Started

For this shot you will need three studio heads. The lighting concept is similar to that of a portrait, in that you have a key light, side light and background light. Begin by attaching grey background paper to your product table. In the absence of a product table, you can use a standard table and suspend a paper roll from a background support system; once done, be sure to clamp the paper to the table to prevent it from moving.

Before you set up your lighting, it may be a good idea to consider how you are going to position the peppers. In this example, I simply used a very thin 30cm steel pole and pushed it into the bottom of the pepper. I then secured the pole using a large lump of Plasticine (or putty). Whilst you are setting up your lighting, it is a good idea to erect the pole without the pepper as this will give you a better idea where to position your lights. Try and leave around a metre of separation between the pole and the background as this will allow you to light the background properly and minimize any spill light.

For the key light, is it recommended that you use a stripbox or rectangular softbox, as this suits the shape of the pepper and also the light is more diffused and less likely to reflect off the shiny skin. Position the key light to about 45 degrees to camera right. Begin by metering this to *f*11.

For the side light, I deliberately chose a harder light source and used a honeycomb grid attached to a reflector. This created a much hotter reflection on the pepper. Attach your honeycomb grid and reflector and then position your light behind the pole/pepper to camera left. Using the modelling facility on your light, turn it around so that it is lighting the side of the pepper, taking care not to direct it down the camera lens. As the honeycomb grid is a much harder light source, meter this to about *f*5.6. You may find that you need to adjust this later.

Now attach a further reflector and honeycomb grid to your third light and fit this to a boom arm. Position the boom centrally above the paper, turning the light around so that it illuminates the background immediately behind the pepper. This may take a few adjustments, so it is a good idea at this point to mount the camera onto a tripod, place the pepper on the pole and then adjust the background light from the point of view of the camera. Try to

SETTINGS AND EQUIPMENT

Camera Settings

Aperture: *f*11.0
Shutter: 1/125sec
ISO: 100
Focal Length: 110mm

Lighting Equipment Required

- Three flash heads
- Two reflectors and honeycomb grids.
- Stripbox or rectangular softbox.
- Boom arm/stand.
- Grey paper background.
- Putty and pole to mount peppers.
- Table and background support.
- Tripod.
- Flash meter.
- Radio trigger or sync lead to trigger the flash.

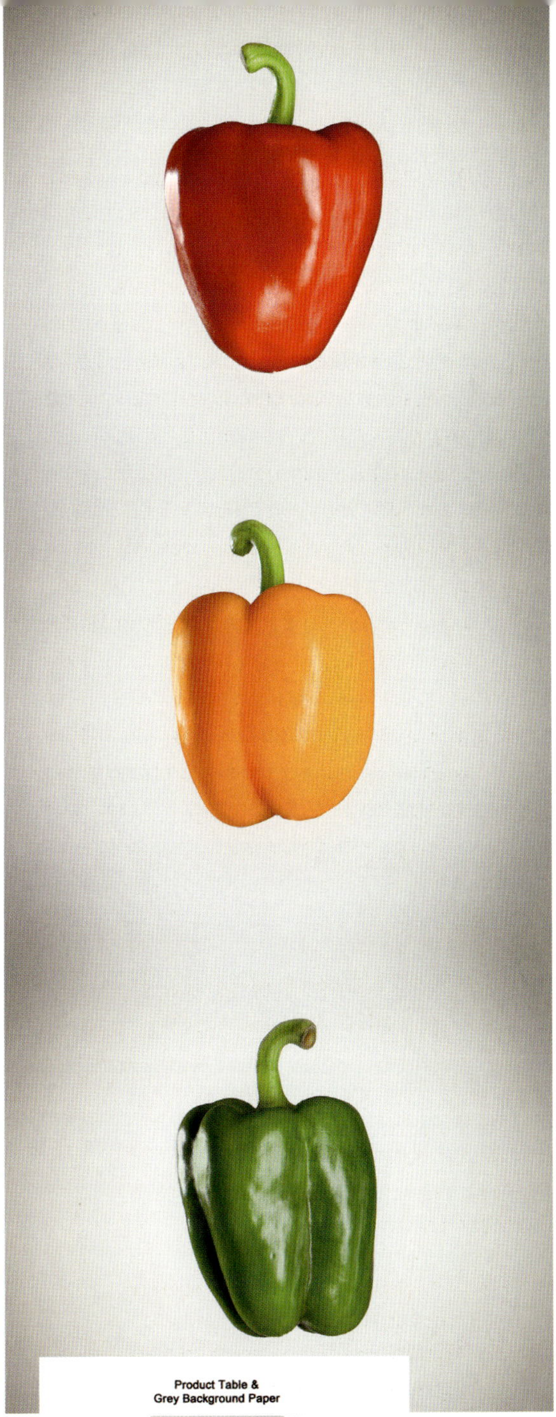

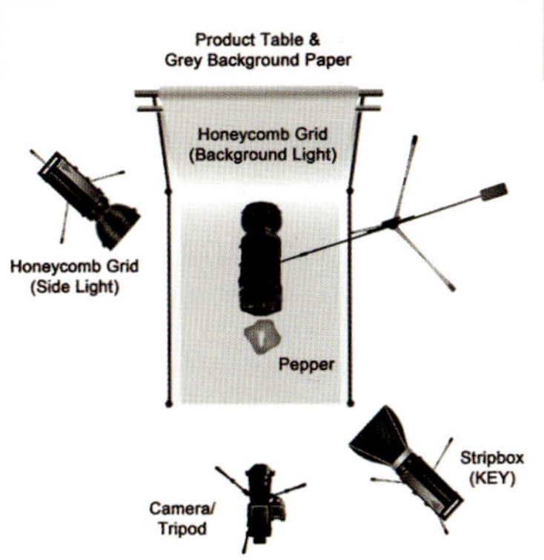

Fig. 5.13
Image © Christian Hough.

get the pepper as central to the background light as possible. The metering of the background light will ultimately depend on the shade of the background paper, but somewhere around *ƒ*5.6 to *ƒ*8.0 is a good start.

When positioning the pepper, be sure to move it around to get the best angle. It is recommended that you position the camera so that it is level to the pepper, with the background light directly behind. Using a tripod ensures that the camera remains at the same angle and focal length for each shot, allowing the peppers to look more consistent when composited together.

Common Issues

BLOWN SIDE LIGHT

Try reducing the power of your side light or moving it further away.

- Alternatively, it is possible to increase the lighting ratio by introducing more power to both the key light and background light and then stopping down on the camera.
- Finally, try diffusing the side light or using a softbox to reduce the power output and soften the light.

BACKGROUND LIGHT

- Try experimenting with different honeycomb grids to see which gives the most suitable effect.
- Moving the background light closer will create a smaller 'spot' effect, but may necessitate inclining the light at a greater angle, resulting in a more oval-shaped spot.
- A snoot may also be used; however, this may result in too much contrast on the background, leaving the outer edges black instead of grey.

Still Life 8

If you are planning on shooting bottles or tall slim cylindrical objects and wish to achieve professional looking results, you will need to use stripboxes or strip lights. A strip light is a tall thin powered flash that can be plugged into a studio generator, where the power can be controlled in the same way as any other generator-based flash. A stripbox is a much cheaper alternative and is essentially a tall thin softbox that attaches to a studio light. In this example, stripboxes were used.

There are several ways in which a bottle can be photographed to bring out different aspects of the bottle and the liquid inside. Many photographers make use of specially designed light tents with strip panels, which have the advantage of being easy to set up and they help to reduce unwanted reflections on the glass. However, in this example, I decided to steer away from the light tent and to use more common studio accessories, concentrating on the shape of the bottle, whilst obtaining an even grey background with minimal reflections, to demonstrate that it is possible to reduce reflections by controlling the light and the surroundings.

The idea and learning point is to accentuate the shape of the bottle, bringing out the contours. As the bottle is highly reflective, it is important to try and retain most of the highlights down the side, as they are intended to be an accent, not the main feature. In this shot [Fig. 5.14], you will find that lighting the bottle is only part of the challenge. It is easy to obtain a high-key background, but more of a challenge to subtly light a dark grey background without creating more unwanted reflections and drawing out the imperfections in the background paper.

The concept used here is fairly straightforward and by no means the only solution when photographing a bottle; however what is important here is the lighting technique and how it may be applied in different situations, without the use of light tents.

It is of course possible to use any reflector or softbox you see fit. However, if you wish to achieve a continuous or semi-continuous highlight down the side of the bottle, you will need to use a strip light or stripbox. This is because a long narrow light creates a long narrow reflection, whereas a normal softbox or reflector would create a round or square reflection. As bottles are generally tall and slim, you will find that a stripbox works best. If you do not have a stripbox, then it may be possible to flag or mask a rectangular softbox by clamping black fabric or thick black card to the front diffuser – not ideal, but it does work!

Alternatively, if you are regularly shooting a number of different bottles on a white background then you may find using a specifically made light tent more suitable. As previously mentioned, there are several light tents available with white diffused strips down each side specifically designed for photographing bottles. These make life a lot easier, although they are limited in space and application.

SETTINGS AND EQUIPMENT

Camera Settings

Aperture: *f*11.0
Shutter: 1/125sec
ISO: 100
Focal Length: 110mm

Lighting Equipment Required

- Four flash heads (possibly five).
- Three stripboxes.
- One standard reflector.
- Boom arm/stand.
- Grey paper background.
- Wine and wine glass.
- Table and background support.
- Tripod.
- Flash meter.
- Radio trigger or sync lead to trigger the flash.

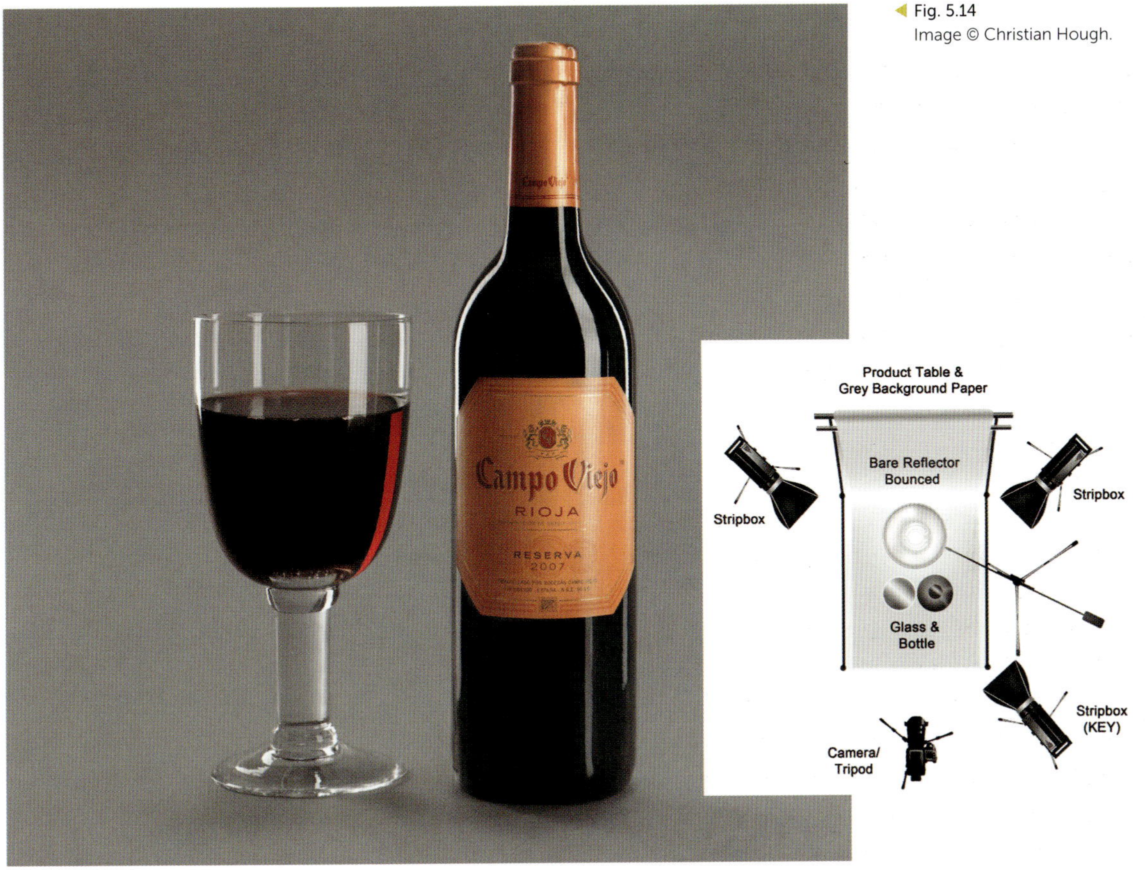

Fig. 5.14
Image © Christian Hough.

Getting Started

For this setup you will need at least four lights. I used four lights; however, you may find that in the absence of a light tent and lots of white reflective surfaces you need more 'fill' on the front of the bottle (depending on the label and bottle), so it is a judgement call as to whether you will find a fifth studio head useful.

Begin by suspending your grey paper background and mark a position for the wine bottle on the paper (to prevent it being accidentally knocked over whilst setting up!). Start by attaching two stripboxes to two studio lights and place them onto stands. Position one of the stripboxes on each side of the table and behind the bottle. Now turn these stripboxes back towards the sides of the bottle. These will create the highlight down each side. The further around to the side the stripboxes are placed, the narrower and less conspicuous the reflections will be. As for metering, a good starting point is to meter them between one to two stops lower than the key light, so that you retain the highlight detail. It is important to keep the metering consistent on each side, so that the bottle is evenly lit.

Now attach a third strip light to another studio head and position this approximately 45 degrees to the camera axis. In this shot, I positioned it to camera right. Use the modelling facility on the light to ascertain where the reflection will be on the bottle in relation to the camera and the label. Occasionally, reflections can prove distracting on very reflective labels, with the reflection partially obscuring the name on the label. Meter the key light to *f*11. If necessary, you can consider using a further strip light around the front of the bottle to lift the shadows and label detail.

Finally, attach a standard reflector onto your fourth studio head and fit them both onto a boom arm. Position the boom centrally over the table and adjust it until it is between the bottle and the background. Now rotate the studio head so that it is pointing directly towards the ceiling (or white bounce reflector). This will bounce diffused light off the ceiling and back towards the table, lighting the background paper without creating unwanted shadows and reflections. The metering of this head will depend entirely on the distance between the table, the ceiling (or white bounce reflector) and the studio light. Aim to fill the unwanted background shadows and adjust as necessary. A meter reading of *f*5.6 at the table would be a good starting point.

Once you have positioned all of your lights, it is safe to place your bottle and glass of wine onto the table. If you are photographing an expensive bottle of wine and would rather not open it for the shot, then it may be worth considering purchasing a second bottle to fill the glass so they may be photographed at the same time. (Try not to spill the wine, as this will warp and pucker the background paper.)

Common Issues

NON-CONTINUOUS REFLECTION

Depending on the shape of the bottle, it may not always be possible to achieve a continuous reflection.

- Begin by raising the side strip lights more and adjusting their angle to point them lightly downwards.
- If necessary, additional stripboxes may be used.
- Ensure that nothing is flagging the bottle, such as the table or background paper.

UNWANTED REFLECTIONS

- Remove as much ambient light as possible and all non-essential nearby objects.
- Use black fabric clamped to stands to flag bouncing light and unwanted spill to further reduce reflections.

UNABLE TO LIGHT BACKGROUND

- Manoeuvre the light on the boom so that it bounces onto the background and the surface of the table.
- High ceilings will require more power.
- Try using a broader reflector and ensure that you are bouncing off a matt ceiling or surface.

Still Life 9

One area of the market that has huge promotional budgets is that of alcoholic drinks. Alcohol has become a lifestyle product, with drinks being marketed at certain age groups and even specific genders. Regardless of markets, one image that is universally popular is that of the ice-cold beer. The idea behind this shot [Fig. 5.15] is to sell the image of a chilled and refreshing bottle of lager. By placing the bottle on ice and lighting the back of the bottle, we are able to capture the beer inside, the colour of the bottle and condensation. At the same time, the bottle and label have been lit from the front to add shape to the bottle and draw attention to the brand name.

Getting Started

First of all, it is necessary to purchase a few props. If you are working within a large freezer, then working with ice is a possibility; however, in a studio with equipment producing lots of additional heat, the ice would begin to melt before you had a chance to photograph anything. Although the ice in the photograph may look real, it is in fact a combination of crushed glass and glass ice-cubes! Imitation ice is widely available on the internet, and you will find that it comes in a variety of different forms, even as semi-melted ice-cubes. Additional effects such as a fine water spray can further enhance both the bottle and the ice, recreating the effect of condensation.

Before you start, it is a good idea to purchase and clean several bottles of beer, then place them in the refrigerator overnight to get them really cold. This will help them naturally condense when it is time to photograph them.

The key to obtaining this effect was by backlighting the opaque top on the product table. Begin by placing your props and spreading the ice over the table, leaving enough depth to support the bottle. Once done, attach a single head to a floor stand and leave it bare bulb. Place the light directly under the table and position it so that it points directly at the underside, shining through the bottle – this is 'backlighting'. If possible avoid using a reflector as this will project the light forwards and will result in a hotspot. Meter the light to approximately *f*8.0 on the top side of the table.

The next step is to fit two stripboxes to two heads, placing one at each side of the table. Adjust the height of the lights so they are approximately one metre higher, then position the stripboxes so they run parallel to the bottle, providing a continuous highlight up each side. Meter the left box as your key light to *f*11 and then the right box as your fill light, between *f*4.0 and *f*5.6. Adjusting the height of the stripboxes will adjust the highlight. The lower down the stripboxes are, the further around to the edge of the bottle the highlight will be, and vice versa.

When you begin to photograph the bottle, it is better to fix your camera to a sturdy and weighted tripod, using a boom from the tripod or a lighting stand in order to position the camera directly over the bottle. If this is feasible, tether the camera to a computer so you may trigger the camera remotely and view the images as they are shot. If you intend to hold the camera and photograph the bottle from above, care must be taken not to overstretch, causing yourself to fall onto the equipment. You may of course shoot the bottle at whatever angle you wish, adjusting the lighting as you go.

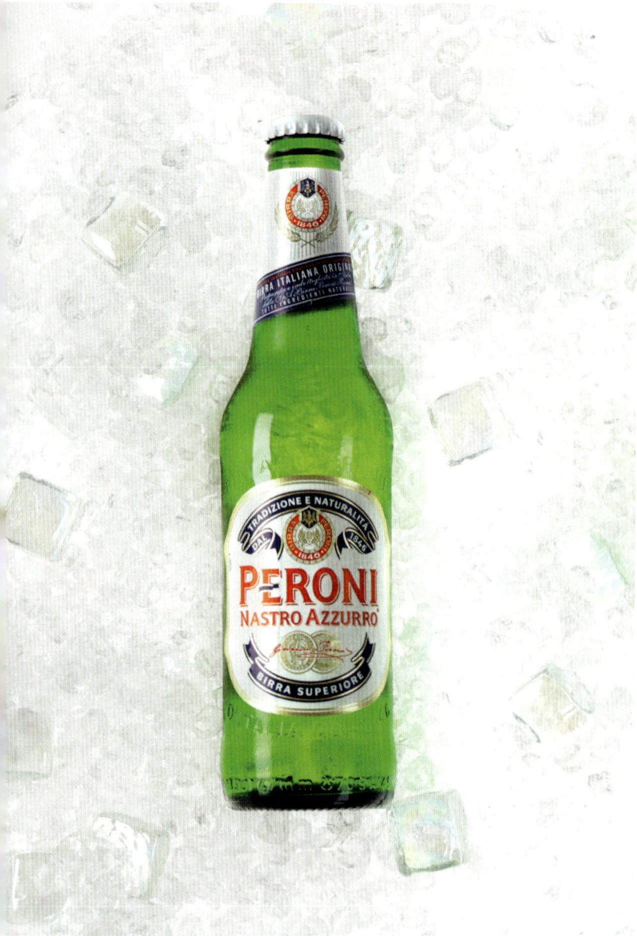

Fig. 5.15
Image © Christian Hough.

Common Issues

IMAGE WASHED OUT

Usually caused by too much power from the back light underneath the table entering the camera lens.

- Reduce the power of the back light.

HOTSPOT

- Avoid using a reflector on the back light.
- If you are still experiencing a central hotspot with a bare-bulb back light, try fitting a softbox and diffusing the light further. More power will be needed to compensate for the softbox.

SETTINGS AND EQUIPMENT

Camera Settings

Aperture: ƒ11.0
Shutter: 1/200sec
ISO: 100
Focal Length: 110mm

Lighting Equipment Required

- Bottle of beer.
- Imitation ice and ice-cubes.
- Water spray/mist spray.
- Three flash heads.
- Two stripboxes.
- Opaque product table or Perspex.
- Weighted or sturdy tripod with boom arm.
- Flash meter.
- Radio trigger or sync lead to trigger the flash.

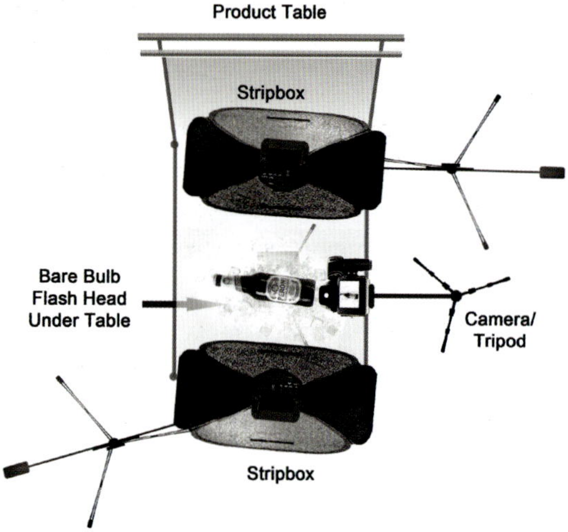

Still Life 10

Recomposing, playing with depth of field and zooming in on particular areas of the set can help give your table top photography a different feel and add to your collection of shots.

Making the most of the limited space available when shooting table top products can at times be difficult. However, considered use of depth of field can really facilitate a sense of scale and distance.

In this shot [Fig 5.19], the long focal length of the lens has assisted with the flattening of the perspective and helped to increase the effect of depth of field. Together with the landscape orientation of the photograph, it enables the two nearest objects to be framed to the left and the positioning of the out of focus products to the right. This helps add to the sense of scale. Some consideration has also been given to the colours, and the darker products positioned closer to the camera and in focus, while the lighter colour products have been placed in the background as their paleness helps them to naturally recesses into the background. The positioning of the taller product close to the middle of the image also helps divide the frame into two.

Finally, a little colour goes a long way! As opposed to making use of a contrasting background such as white, peach background paper has been used to create more of a blend and help draw out the complementing tones, giving the shot more of a brochure appeal.

Getting Started

This set-up can be used with any colour background paper; however, to achieve a similar effect, is worth identifying some paper and products that complement each other.

Begin by fixing the background paper to your product table. It is important to keep this as crease-free and flat as possible, otherwise the creases will cause unwanted shadows. Now position your camera and lens onto a tripod. You will find that a longer focal length lens or tilt and shift system will help you make maximum use of depth of field. Now roughly position your products on the table and check the framing of them in the camera lens. This will give you a rough indication as to where to position the lights.

Start by attaching a stripbox (or slim softbox) to one of the heads and position it at the front of the table to camera left, turning it to face the products nearest the camera. The positioning of the light and size of the modifier will depend entirely on the shape and surface of your product; however, 45 degrees is generally a good place to start. As with all set-ups, small adjustments can be made by using the modelling facility to help you ascertain where the reflections and shadows are falling. Once done, position a white polyboard (or white card reflector) on the opposite corner of the table to help lift the shadows. Meter to around *f*8.0.

The procedure for lighting the furthest products is exactly the same, although this time you will need to place the stripbox/softbox on the right side (or opposite side) of the table at around 20 degrees (more side on). It is possible that you may require a further polyboard (or white reflector) on the opposite side of this light to help lift the shadows. A lot will depend on the size of the product table, the stripbox or softbox used and the distances between the products. It is possible that your key light will sufficiently fill the shadows without the need for a reflector. Meter to around *f*8.0.

It is useful (although not essential) to have two boom arms available for the remaining two lights: one for the background and one to for a bounce fill. For the background light, attach a studio light to a boom and fit it with a reflector and honeycomb grid. Position the boom and light directly over the centre of the table and turn it to face the background. Use the modelling facility to ensure that the background is centrally lit. You only need to add an accent to the background, so keep the power low starting around f4.0 and adjust if necessary. If you do not have a boom for this light, then use a studio stand, position it on the left of the table and aim it towards the background. In this scenario, a carefully positioned stripbox will illuminate the darkest side of the background and create a subtle gradient. Both are nice effects, so there's no wrong or right! Again take a few test shots, adjust the power gradually and see what you're most comfortable with.

Finally, attach a medium to wide angle reflector onto the fourth light. Place the light onto a boom and move it close to the rear of the product table, but central to the frame. Then turn the head around so that it is bouncing light off the ceiling. The idea is to allow the light to bounce and diffuse, gently filling in the darker shadows and any unevenness on the table. Positioning it further back helps prevent light from unintentionally lighting the front of your products, but should instead even out creases and dark shadows. Meter the power at the table and begin low and gradually build up, until you are happy with the filling effect. If necessary, you can place this light behind the product table and instead use your boom arm for the setting up the background light as per the paragraph above.

Of course, a lot of the above will depend on your ceiling! You should find that any white ceiling of approximately 2–3 metres in height should prove suitable. The higher the ceiling, the more power will be required. If your ceiling is very high or not white, it is entirely possible to suspend white polystyrene or paper above the set; alternatively fix it to the ceiling to create a similar effect.

As with anything, it is worth getting a little creative and taking a few abstracts. Simply zoom in and out on particular areas of the set and reframe your subjects to give a different perspective [Fig. 5.20].

Common Issues

LIGHT SPILLING ONTO THE BACKGROUND

Try using stripboxes or smaller softboxes to help control the light.

If you don't have a stripbox, clip pieces of black card or fabric to the front, creating a strip effect.

Move the products further from the background or change the angle of the light so that it no longer illuminates the background.

LOTS OF SHADOWS

Try using more polyboards or white card around the set to help lift the shadows. Silver reflectors are not recommended as they will create reflections on shiny surfaces and the paper.

SETTINGS AND EQUIPMENT

Camera Settings

Aperture: *f*9.0
Shutter: 1/125sec
ISO: 100
Focal Length: 85mm

Lighting Equipment Required

- Four flash heads.
- Two stripboxes (or small softboxes).
- Once reflector and honeycomb (background).
- Once medium to wide angle reflector (fill).
- Coloured background paper.
- Two boom stands or one boom and three standard.
- Product table.
- Flash meter.
- Radio trigger or sync lead.

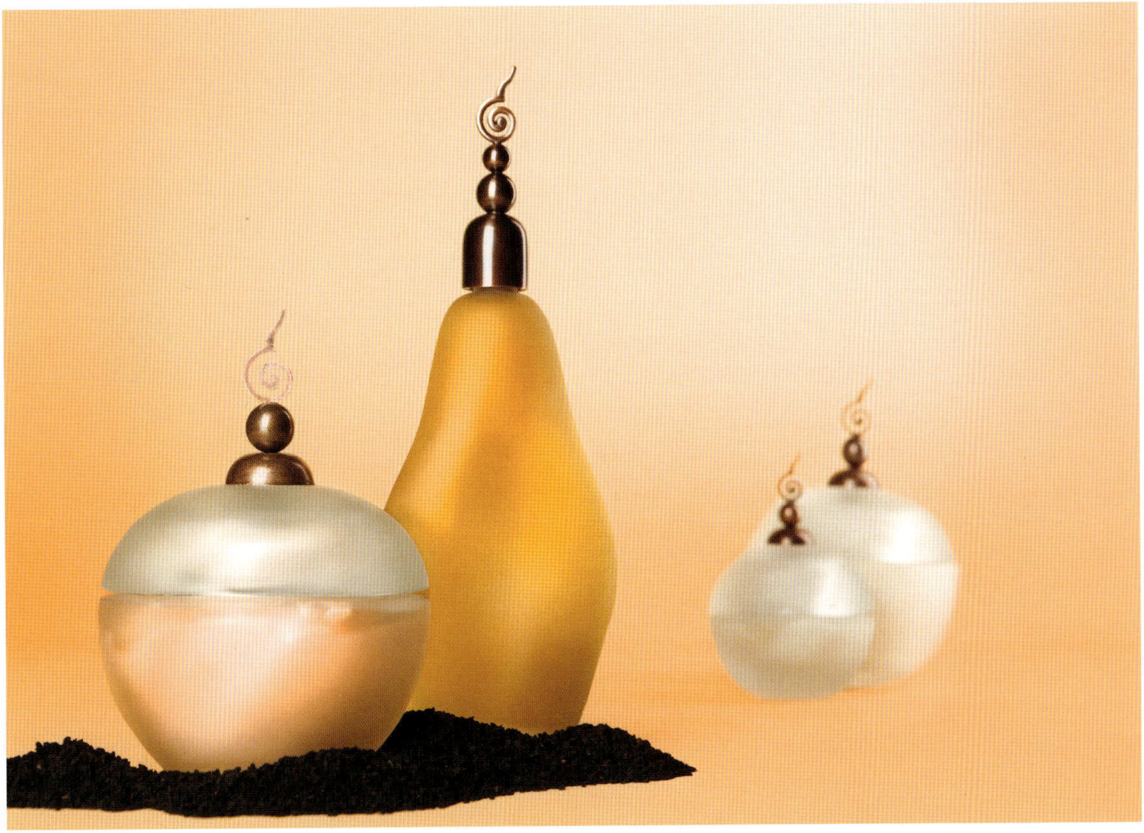

▲ Fig. 5.16
Image © Christian Hough.

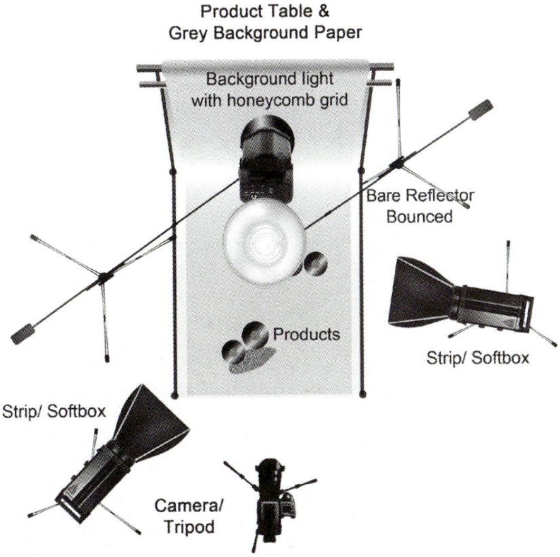

Still Life 11

Some images require more than propping and need to be more dynamic. Sporting goods and bathroom products are good examples, requiring energy and a feeling of invigoration to entice the viewer.

As we have already seen, water is ideal for creating that feeling of movement and energy, plus it is just as suited to products as it is to people. Combining products, props and movement can make a really enticing image as in this example [Fig. 5.17]. Whereas many photographs using water are photographed on a shaded or black background to make it easier to capture the water, this shot remains a little unconventional and was shot on a white background. The white background combined with the bright yellow (or lemon) bottle of shower gel retains an airy fresh feel. To add to the lemon theme, sliced lemon was added to a container of water and then literally poured out over the shower gel, giving the feeling of being drenched in lemons and water.

Finally, in post-processing a blue-coloured filter was very quickly added to the water to give some contrast and variety. You can see both images for comparison.

Getting Started

Begin by erecting your product table, and placing your shower gel onto the surface. To ensure that the bottle remains upright when the water and lemons fall on it, place some Sticky Dots or removable rubber adhesive on the lid of the gel to secure it to the table surface.

Now place a single studio head onto a floor stand and position it under the product table. This will backlight the tabletop and help to reduce the shadows at the base of the shower gel. Leave the light 'bare bulb' to help diffuse the light more, as using a reflector can make the light more directional and cause a white hotspot under the product, resulting in loss of highlight detail. Once in position, meter the light to approximately *f*11. It is also necessary to light the background and produce the high-key effect. For safety, attach a second bare-bulb lamp to a regular lighting stand and position this directly behind the opaque vertical back of the product table, lighting the background. Meter this light to around *f*16. It is of course possible to light the high-key background from the front; however, it is better to keep as many lights as possible away from water splashes.

For the key light, almost any reflector will work. Hard light sources work better with water as they add more contrast and defined shadows. In this example, I used a bare reflector on the key light and positioned it approximately two metres from the table, to reduce any risk of splashback. It is of course possible to use a softbox, as the front diffuser will provide a physical barrier between water splashes and the hot bulb/flash tube. Position the key light approximately 10–30 degrees of camera axis and meter to *f*16. You will find that a greater depth of field will enable you to get more of the splashes and droplets in focus.

In order to assist with the backlighting of the water, set up a fourth head on the left of the table and at 45 degrees to the rear of the bottle, again fitted with a bare reflector. Ensure that it is around two metres from the bottle to reduce any risk of water splashing onto the flash. Meter this light to around *f*16. This is effectively backlighting the water, so be careful not to use too much power as you run the risk of blowing all of the highlight detail in the water.

You would be forgiven for thinking that you have finished setting all your equipment up. However, water reflects light and needs something to create contrast from all of the white background. Place a large piece of black fabric either to one side or to both sides of the table, so that the water picks up the black reflection and increases in contrast.

For health and safety reasons, it is recommended that you use a full-sized large professional product table when working with water, as this will minimize the risk of water splashing onto the hot lights. Ensure that you have at least a dozen large absorbent bath towels, a large absorbent sponge and a bucket

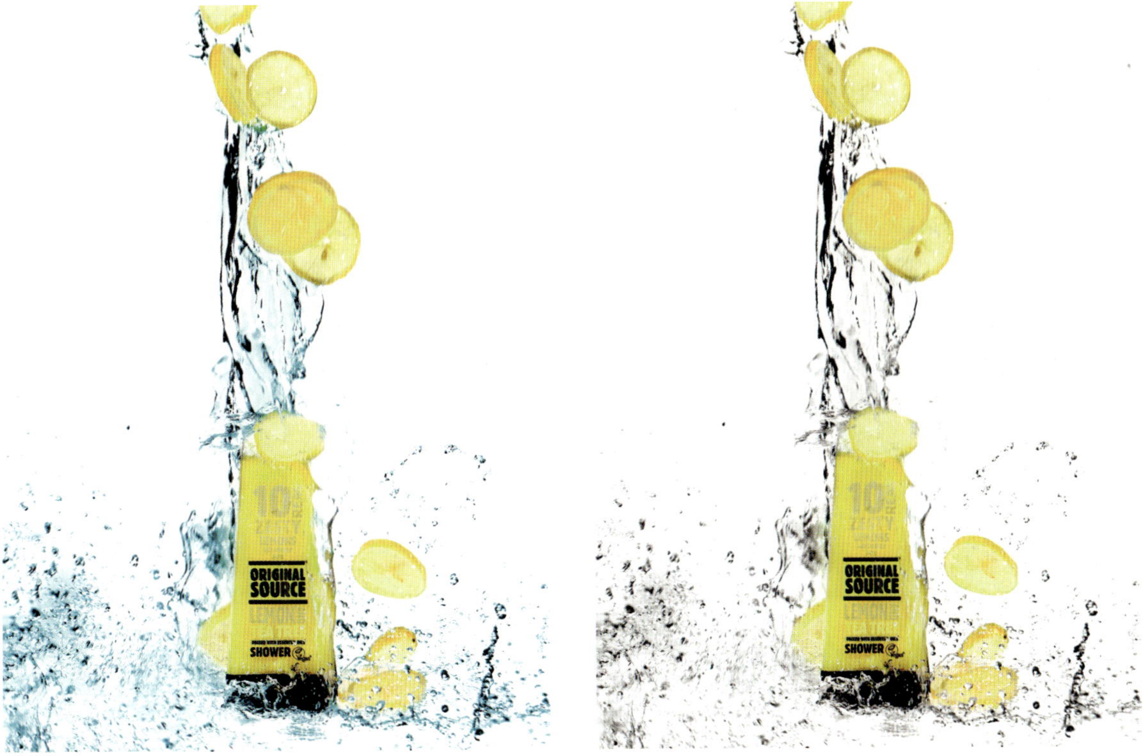

▲ Fig. 5.17
Image © Christian Hough.

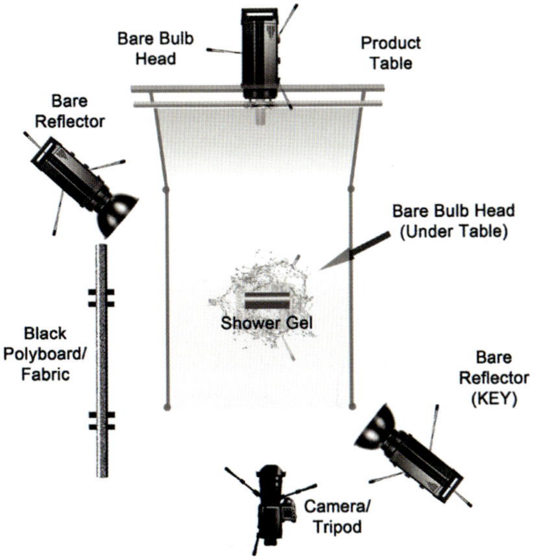

SETTINGS AND EQUIPMENT

Camera Settings

Aperture: ƒ16
Shutter: 1/200sec
ISO: 100
Focal Length: 110mm

Lighting Equipment Required

- Four flash heads.
- Shower gel or shampoo.
- Water and lemons.
- Large absorbent towels, sponge and bucket.
- Floor stand.
- Opaque product table or Perspex.
- Two standard reflectors.
- Sonic or infrared triggering device.
- Flash meter.
- Radio trigger or sync lead to trigger the flash.

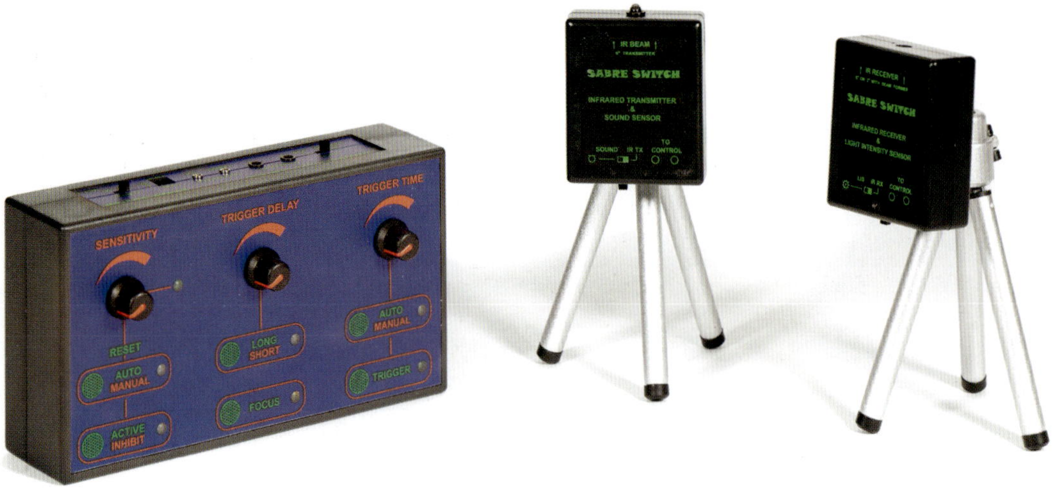

▲ Fig. 5.17
Infrared and sound trigger. Image © Christian Hough.

close to hand. Place the towels all around the edge of the table (over any joins) in order to soak up the water as it is dropped. Use the towels and sponge to immediately mop up spillages, and place soaked towels in the bucket. Electricity and water do not mix and are a lethal combination, so regularly check the towels and replace them as necessary, whilst ensuring all power supplies, plugs, extensions and lights are well out of the way of any splashes, wet towels or potential spillages. Be warned: do not cut corners.

Rather than use a radio trigger by itself, it proves to be more productive to make use of a motion or sonic trigger that fires the shutter the moment the sound or motion triggers the sensor. This in turn fires the shutter on the camera and then triggers the flash via the regular radio triggers. Some of these triggers (such as the model in Fig. 5.17) can be activated sonically or via an infrared beam. The firing of the trigger may be fine-tuned to trigger the camera at exactly the right moment.

SETTINGS AND EQUIPMENT

Camera Settings

Aperture: *f*16
Shutter: 1/180sec
ISO: 100
Focal Length: 110mm

Lighting Equipment Required

- Screwdriver and driver bits.
- Pole and method of support
- Blu-Tack.
- Five flash heads.
- Two softboxes or standard reflectors for background.
- Three reflectors with honeycomb grids for background and product.
- Boom arm/stand.
- Grey background paper.
- Product table or standard table.
- Flash meter.
- Radio trigger or sync lead to trigger the flash.

To capture the water a sonic sensor was used to activate the shutter on the camera at the moment of impact, proving to be far more reliable than simple guesswork and manual timing.

Common Issues

WATER DETAIL BLOWN OUT

If you are overpowering the backlighting, then it is quite possible to blow all the detail in the water, effectively making the water invisible.

- Firstly, ensure you have plenty of black material surrounding the water.
- If this does not prove effective, reduce the power of the backlighting to increase the contrast between the water and the background.

UNABLE TO CONTROL WATER

- Try using a large jug or medium-sized bucket with a spout. The spout will help funnel and direct the water over the shower gel creating more of a concentrated splash.

UNABLE TO FREEZE WATER

- If you are using older or cheaper flash heads, it may be that the flash duration is too long to freeze the water. To ascertain if this is happening, ensure that you are blocking out all natural light and increase the camera's shutter to its maximum sync speed. If the water is still not freezing, then it is likely to be due to your flash heads.

Still Life 12

Occasionally it is the everyday objects that can be the most difficult to photograph in a more interesting or unusual way. In situations like this, lighting remains important, but compositing and editing can help bring an object to life.

In this example [Fig. 5.18] a standard multi-bit screwdriver was photographed along with each individual screwdriver bit. The driver bits and screwdriver were then composited in Photoshop, so that they all appear together. Photographing the screwdriver in this way adds an extra dynamic to the image, clearly illustrating that the driver has multiple capabilities. A medium-grey background was used to contrast against the yellow screwdriver handle yet remain clean enough so not to appear cluttered against the expanded driver bits.

This image is simple in its approach, and there are many professional still life photographers that utilize this effect to its full potential. Yet it illustrates how consistent lighting and Photoshop can be used together to make even the plainest of objects appear more interesting.

Getting Started

Erect your grey paper background and clamp it securely onto your product table. (As with previous examples, a standard table or pasting table is a good second, with the paper suspended using a background support system.) You will find that you need to support the screwdriver and bits in some way; for this I used a very thin pole placed into a lump of Plasticine and then secured the driver using Blu-Tack. Now attach the camera to a tripod and position this at the same height as the driver, fine-tuning the framing before you move on. Doing this will assist you to more accurately position the lighting.

To light the background alone you will need three lights. Fit two of these lights with standard reflectors or small softboxes, position them on either side of the table and face them towards the background, leaving approximately one metre of separation Meter each light evenly to around *f*5.6. This will evenly light the grey background paper. If you are using a light grey paper, you may find that less power is required, but more light will be needed for a darker background. Now mount the third background light onto a boom arm, fit it with a medium-sized honeycomb grid and mount it centrally over the paper. Turn the head around until it is lighting the centre of the background behind the screwdriver, creating a 'spot' effect. Take a test shot with the camera to check the position of the spot effect and then meter to *f*11.

For the key light, fit a standard reflector with a broad honeycomb grid to a regular lighting stand and place it approximately 30–45 degrees to the right of the camera axis. You will find that a honeycomb grid helps prevent light from spilling onto the background and creates harder shadows, accentuating the shape of the driver. If you are using an object with a very reflective surface, you may wish to consider using a more diffused light source such as a softbox, although consideration will need to be given to how this may affect the background. Once you have decided on the modifier for the key light, meter it to *f*16. Using an aperture of *f*16 (or smaller) will help you retain more of the screwdriver in focus, especially if you are shooting close-up at a longer focal length.

Finally, attach a fifth light to a stand and fit this with a reflector and honeycomb grid. Place this light at the side of the table and behind the position of the screwdriver, turning it back 45 degrees to face the back of the screwdriver, whilst ensuring it is not shining directly down the lens of the camera. This fifth head will become the side light and help separate the screwdriver and screw bits from the grey background, whilst accentuating their shape. It is important to keep the side light power low to retain the highlight on any reflective surfaces; therefore it is recommended that you begin with a low power setting, around *f*4.0, slowly increasing the power as required.

Once you have finished setting up and metering, adjust the angle of the screwdriver so it appears to be more three-dimensional, with a clear visual of at least three sides. Once you are satisfied with the shot of the screwdriver, begin to photograph the screwdriver bits one at a time, by attaching them onto the pole with Blu-Tack. A priority task is to ensure that they all remain at the same angle, otherwise you will be unable to maintain the same perspective when compositing them together in Photoshop. It sounds easy, but it takes time and practice. Shooting tethered to a computer is recommended, as this will enable you to quickly view previous images to ensure that the perspective and field of view is not changing between frames. With more time and practice, you will be able to position component parts at different heights and focal planes to reproduce a more accurate perspective.

Common Issues

BACKGROUND UNEVEN

- Ensure that the background lights on each side of the table are fitted with the same modifiers, evenly spaced and evenly powered.
- For a more contrasting gradient, reduce the power on the two exterior background lights and increase the power on the spot.
- For a subtle gradient, increase the power on the two exterior background lights and reduce the power of the honeycomb grid creating the spot effect.

UNABLE TO MAINTAIN PERSPECTIVE

This takes time and patience.

- Ensure that the camera is mounted onto a tripod to maintain a consistent shooting angle.
- If necessary, use an articulated grip to facilitate placing each item in the same position and maintaining the same perspective.
- Small adjustments, such as size, may be made in Photoshop if necessary.

LENS FLARE

- Move the side light to prevent it from shining down the lens of the camera.
- If necessary, utilize a tighter/narrower honeycomb grid to restrict the spread of the light.

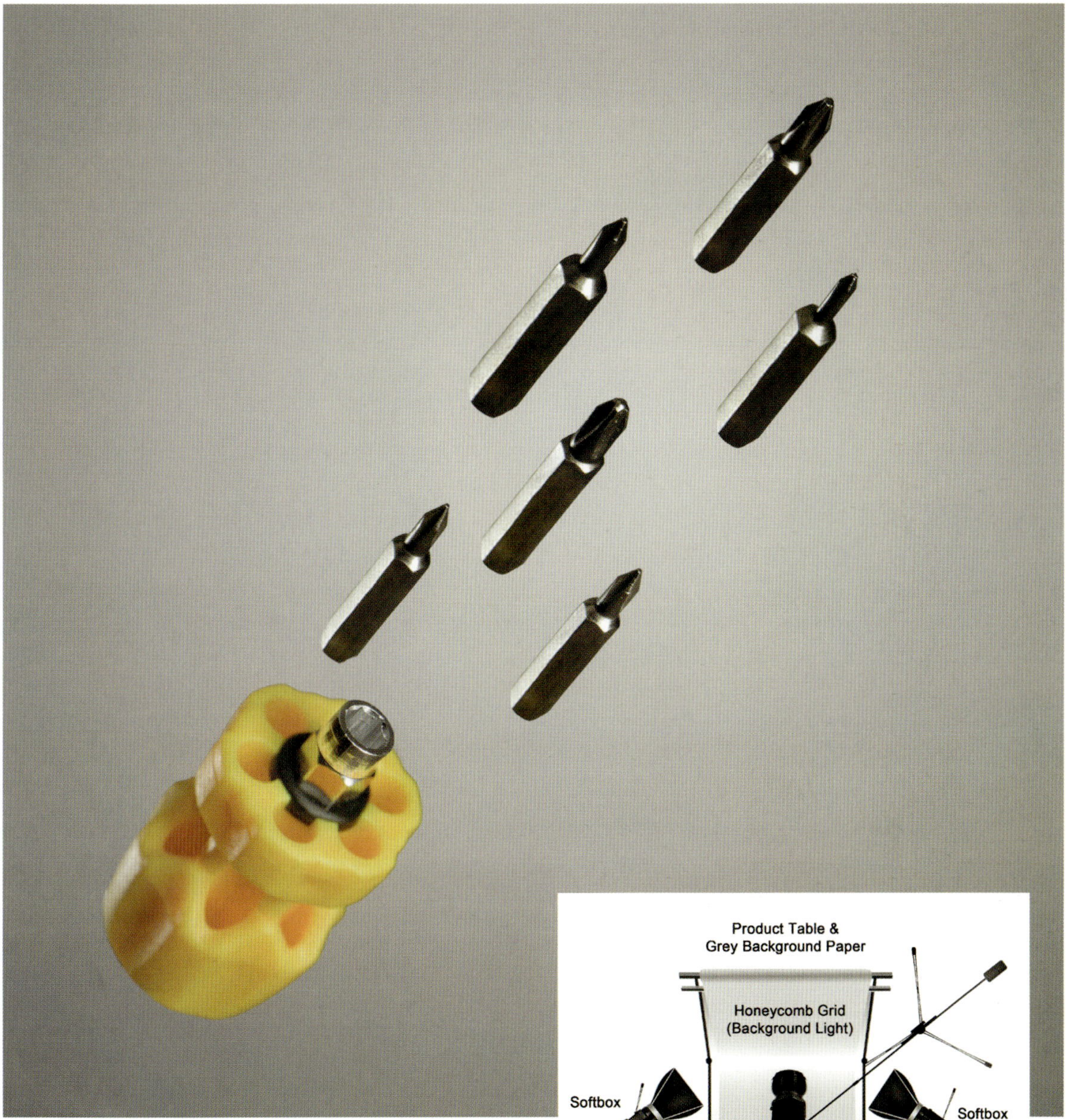

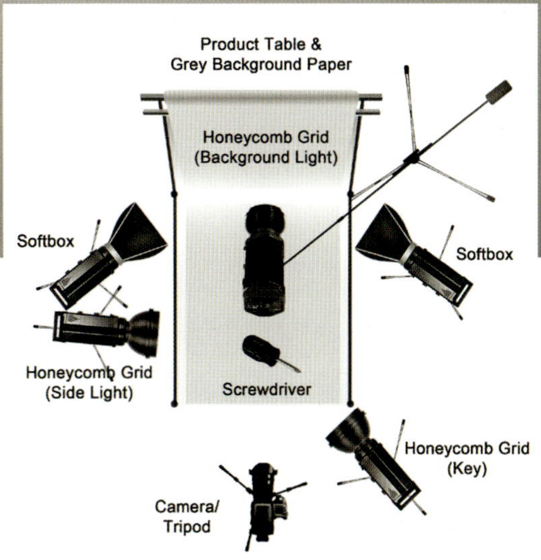

▲ Fig. 5.18
Image © Christian Hough.

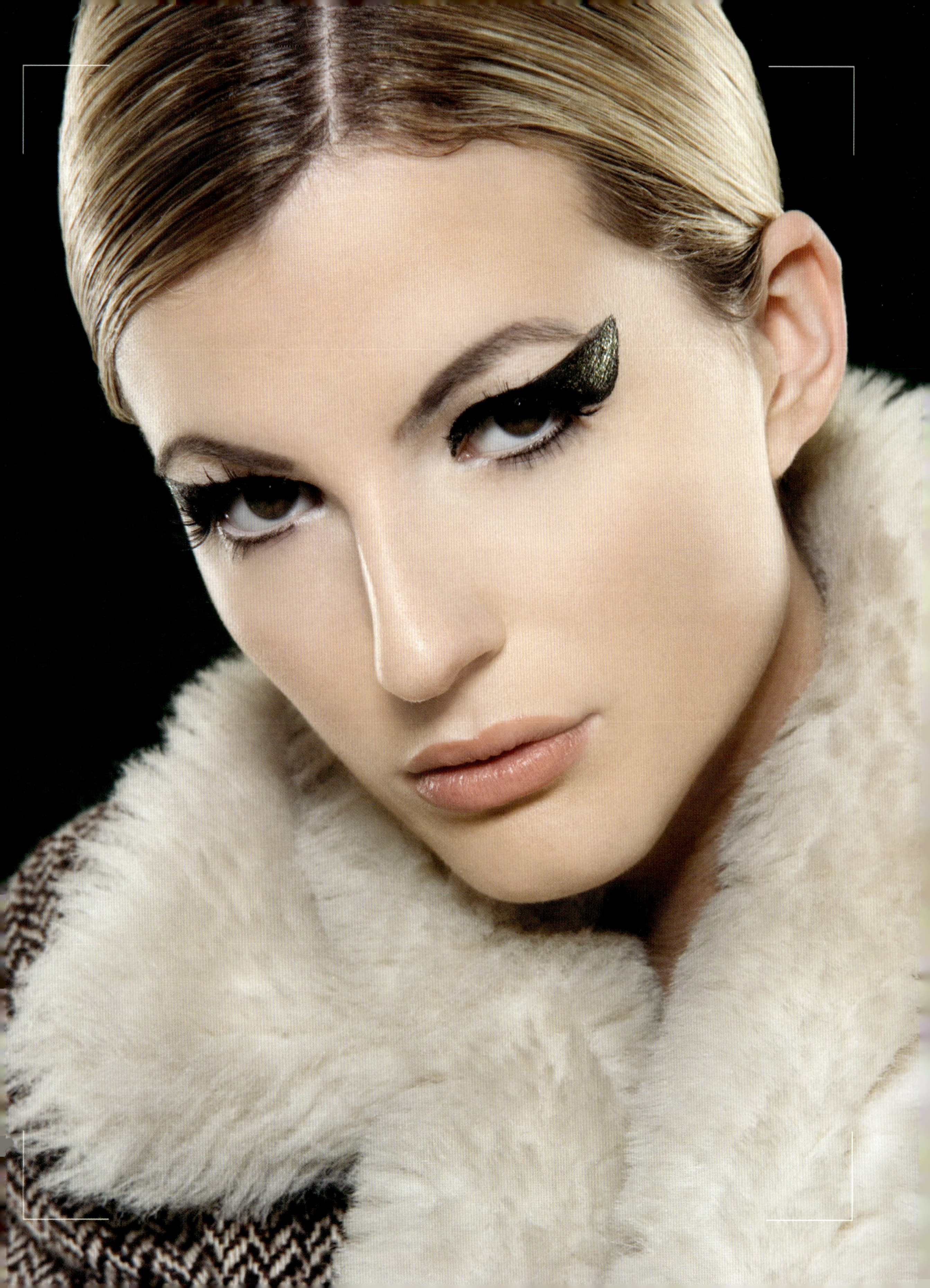

Chapter 6

Basic RAW Processing

The word processing has been associated with photography since its existence. For many years it referred primarily to the processing of exposed film into negatives, which was done in temperature-controlled tanks filled with chemicals to process the film and water to clean it. Once the negative was produced, the photographer used to process the photographs by placing the negatives onto an enlarger, thus exposing light-sensitive paper to the light passing through the negative. The paper was then developed to produce the image, using developer, stop-bath and then a fixer. This was known as print processing. Generally speaking, once the film became a negative the ability to 'edit and retouch' began, with various darkroom techniques such as dodge and burn, although the choice of film and chemicals used to process the film could hugely affect the finished image.

Things have not changed much in the digital age, except that we now work with digital negatives or RAW files. To some degree the task of post-processing images has become hugely more accessible and affordable, if not completely automated on some occasions. As most photographers no longer process film, the term post-processing has generally become accepted as anything that manipulates or changes the RAW file once the shutter has been fired.

Professional and experienced photographers tend not to rely on post-processing techniques to save an image that does not succeed; however, some post-processing is inevitable and to some degree expected in today's market. Whilst I will cover a few RAW processing basics, it is important to bear in mind that the world of post-processing, editing and editing software, such as Adobe Photoshop, are worth an entire book of their own. To this end, this chapter is a very brief and basic insight into how to process your RAW files using the industry standard software, Adobe Camera RAW (ACR).

RAW – THE DIGITAL NEGATIVE

Many people new to the world of digital photography fail to appreciate that their standard compact camera processes photographs in-camera. Any camera that shoots in JPEG or even TIFF format will process the images to some degree and then compress them into one of the recognized file formats.

JPEG may be convenient, allowing you to get many exposures on a single storage card; however, it also massively impacts on flexibility and image quality, introducing unwanted artefacts, colour casts and tonal curves. RAW on the other hand undergoes no or little in-camera processing and needs importing into the camera manufacturer's proprietary software or a recognized RAW converter, such as Adobe Camera Raw, to be processed.

Shooting in RAW allows the photographer to process the images by way of fine-tuning and other adjustments prior to editing. The amount of adjustment that can be made to a digital negative prior to editing is huge, ranging from exposure to vignetting, so it is worth spending a little time exploring the various RAW processors on the market and the effects that you can achieve with them.

OTHER RAW CAPTURE UTILITIES

Note: For simplicity, I am referencing Adobe Camera RAW, as it is the most popular and widely available of RAW capture utilities. However, most major camera manufacturers, plus several third-party software developers, produce their own software to process RAW files. The techniques utilized here may be applied in the majority of RAW capture software; however, the tools and menus will vary.

There are a few useful basic tools and visuals you should be aware of when editing digital negatives that are particularly helpful when fine-tuning colour balance, exposure and even reducing digital noise. These techniques are quick, basic and simple adjustments that will have you improving your images in minutes.

Histogram

The histogram will give you an instant visual graph of all the tonal information in your image. It will instantly tell you if you have clipped shadow detail or highlight detail. It will also give you a visual indication as to where the majority of the image data resides, such as the shadows, mid-tones or highlights. The histogram is something that many new photographers ignore; however, it can be a very useful tool when judging exposure or even to ascertain if you are clipping certain colours.

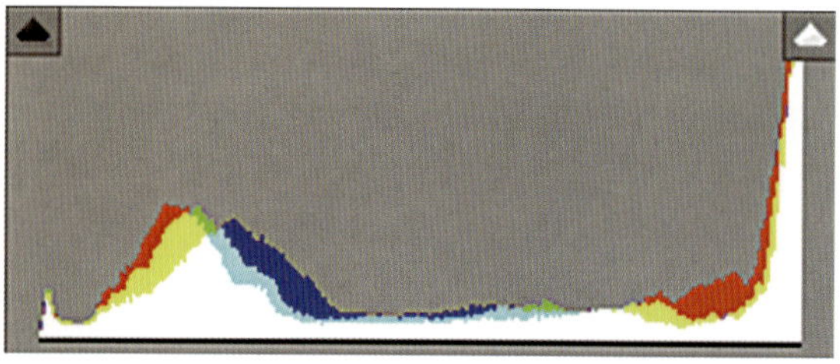

▲ Fig. 6.1
Adobe Camera RAW Histogram. Image © Christian Hough.

When looking at the histogram, you will see shadow detail to the left, mid-tones in the middle and highlights to the right. As a rule of thumb, if your histogram is more dominant to the right, then your image is possibly overexposed. On the other hand, if your histogram is more dominant to the left, then it is possible that your image is underexposed. It is important to remember that it is only a guide and you will find that shooting on dark and light backgrounds may push the histogram either way, yet your photograph will be properly exposed.

If you are seeing a large spike in the histogram it is usually a sign of clipping (where image data is being lost). It may be that the dynamic range of the scene is wider than your camera can capture; however, small adjustments to exposure will usually help.

BASICS TAB

White Balance Slider

Accurate white balance is of utmost importance in any genre of photography. For the most part, a camera's auto white balance (AWB) will do a reasonable job in the studio; however, over many frames its consistency can vary, leaving you the arduous task of colour-correcting many images.

There are a couple of simple things you can do to assist you in achieving a more accurate and consistent white balance, and they are to avoid AWB and to use a grey card.

Avoid AWB

Auto White Balance is very convenient, but not necessarily accurate. The most consistent and professional way of setting your white balance is to do it manually, either in-camera, via your capture software, or in batch processing using the White Balance tool and a grey card.

18% Grey Card

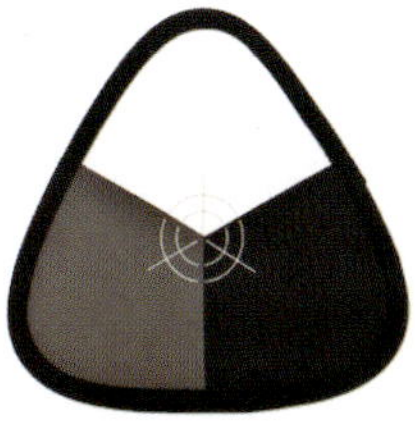

▲ Fig. 6.2
White balance: XpoBalance by Lastolite.

Grey cards are cheap. They are neutral (with no colour) and have 18% reflectance across the visible spectrum. At the start of each shoot or setup, it is advisable to take a single properly exposed frame of the 18% grey card, and this may be used as your white balance. You may find that different reflectors will reflect colours at slightly different temperatures, so when you change your lighting it is useful to shoot a frame with your grey card so that you may adjust your RAW settings later.

If you are processing your images using RAW processing software, such as ACR, then you can simply select the White Balance tool from the tool bar and click it onto the grey card. You will find that there is an instant colour shift as the software makes all the necessary adjustments. This setting can then be copied and applied to several RAW photographs without the need to open them. Of course, if you have shot without a grey card and are experiencing a strange colour shift in your image, then it is possible to use something that is a neutral black, grey or white within the frame. It may not necessarily be perfect, but may get you closer to a more neutral white balance. It will then be a case of using the Temperature and Tint sliders to fine-tune your image.

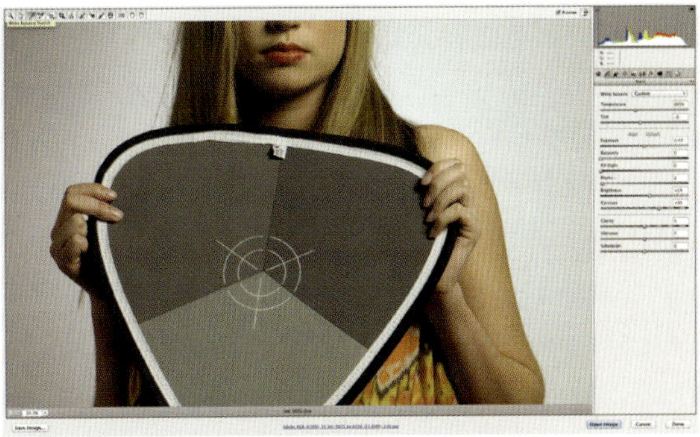

▲ Fig. 6.3
WB before.... Image © Christian Hough.

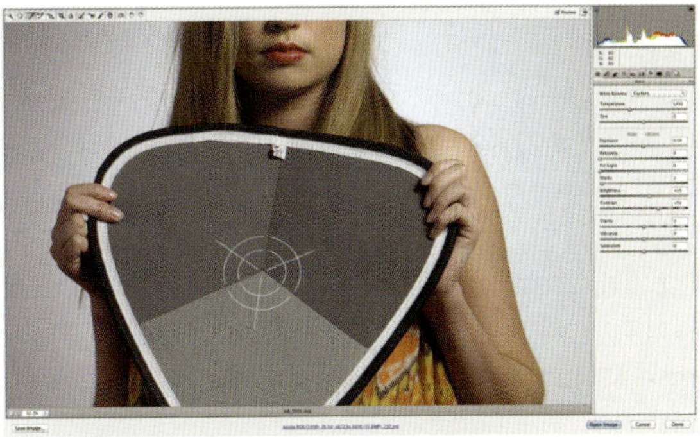

▲ Fig. 6.4
.... and WB after. Image © Christian Hough.

TEMPERATURE VS TINT

Remember: Adjusting the Temperature slider will make the photograph warmer or cooler, whereas the Tint slider compensates for the green or magenta tint.

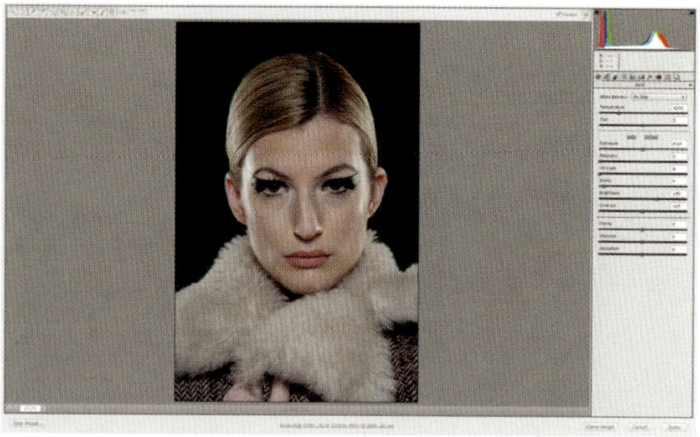

▲ Fig. 6.5
Exposure slider, underexposed. Image © Christian Hough. Model: Carmen Bellacassa.

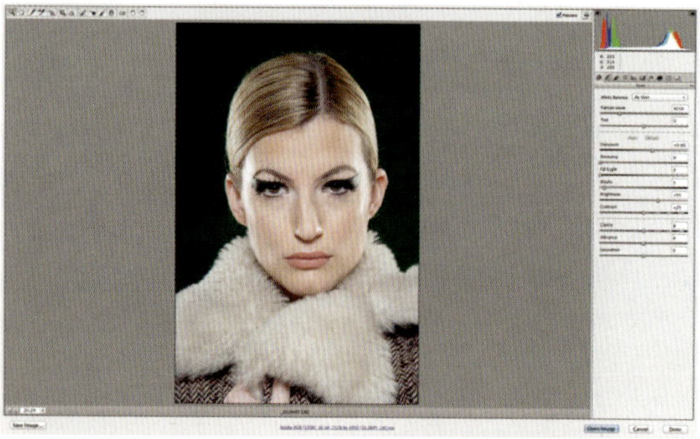

▲ Fig. 6.6
Exposure corrected. Image © Christian Hough. Model: Carmen Bellacassa.

Exposure Slider

It is always preferable to use a light meter and expose your images properly at the time of shooting. No amount of processing can beat a properly exposed photograph. However, there are of course times when exposure may not be as accurate as we had hoped for. It is common, even in studio photography and can be affected by subjects moving in and out of the light source or even by variances in power from cheaper flash heads. As you would expect, there are a few processing tweaks we can do when working with RAW files, but like everything, there is a caveat.

The Exposure slider essentially elongates the histogram and increases the clipping point of the highlights. Moving the slider to the right will lighten the image and moving it to the left will darken the image. The Exposure slider basically ascertains where the highlight data will clip, and then converts the clipped highlight value to 255. The remaining darker tones are lightened, and the histogram elongated and smoothed out.

All of this flexibility with exposure sounds great, but it is limited and its flexibility will depend entirely on the camera system you are using and the quality and bit depth of the image it produces. For the most part, increases above +1.00 can begin to introduce noise and artefacts into your photograph. You may also find that it causes shadow detail to break up and posterize. The higher the ISO used, the more noticeable these artefacts can become. Higher-end 35mm systems and medium-format digital can be pushed further without necessarily experiencing any degradation of image quality.

Recovery Slider

Traditionally, it is the highlight information in digital photography that is the most susceptible to being blown. This is in contrast to film, where there is less latitude within the shadows. The studio, for the most part, is a controlled environment, where lighting can be adjusted to ensure that photographers achieve a properly exposed photograph without blowing the highlights; yet there are occasions when highlights are clipped, due to reflective surfaces, lighting and positioning constraints or even movement. The Recovery slider can help you retrieve some or all of the lost highlight data, and this is one of the huge benefits of shooting RAW.

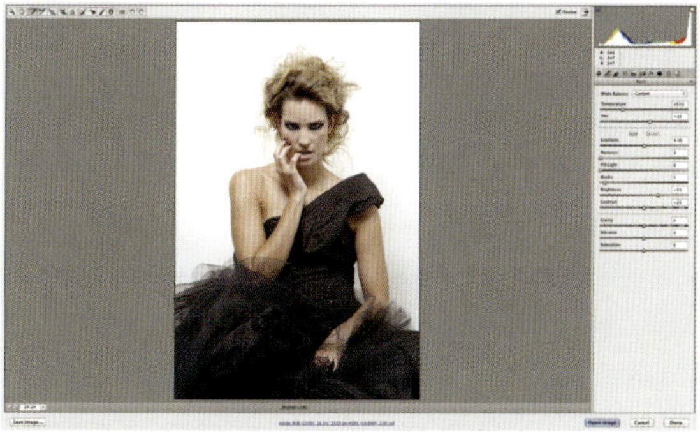

▲ Fig. 6.7
Normal exposure. Image © Christian Hough. Model: Carmen Bellacassa.

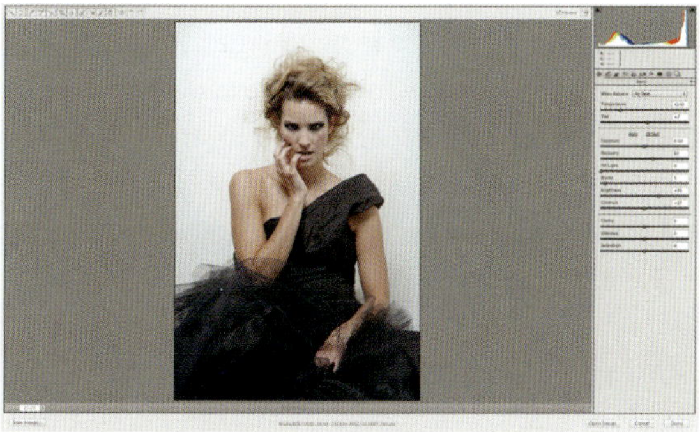

▲ Fig. 6.8
Effects of increasing highlight recovery slider. Image © Christian Hough. Model: Carmen Bellacassa.

You will find that moving the Recovery slider to the right will begin to slowly recover the highlights and as you move it, you will notice the highlight information on the histogram moving to the left and slowly bunching with the mid-tones. It is important to keep a close eye on the rest of the image, as pushing the slider too far will slowly begin to affect all of the lighter tones and can on some occasions make some highlights appear grey. Using the Recovery slider in conjunction with the Exposure slider will increase the rate of highlight recovery and retrieve most highlight data without the introduction of artefacts. It is an extremely useful and capable facility and it is possible to retrieve up to two *f* stops of information, but don't expect it to perform miracles!

Fill Slider

The Fill slider behaves like an artificial fill light. As you move the slider to the right you will see from the histogram how it will lift the shadow and mid-tone detail in the image, whilst the highlight detail remains stationary. It is particularly useful when you want to lift a small amount of shadow detail. Moving the slider too far to the right will begin to produce some unusual effects and will begin to make a photograph looks as if it is solarized. Despite being a useful tool, it is no replacement for a properly positioned and metered fill light and is best when used sparingly.

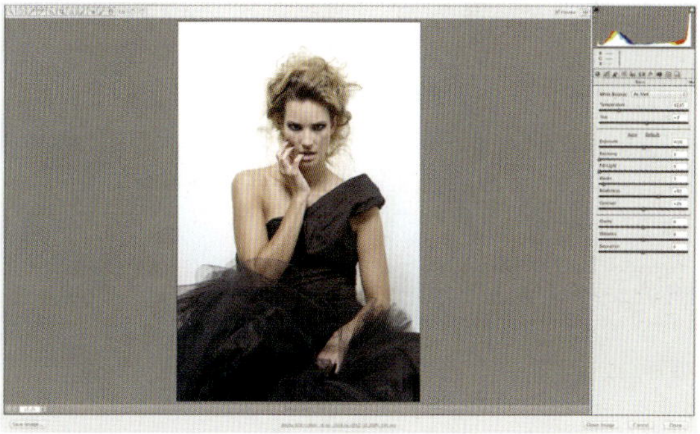

▲ Fig. 6.9
No adjustments. Image © Christian Hough. Model: Carmen Bellacassa.

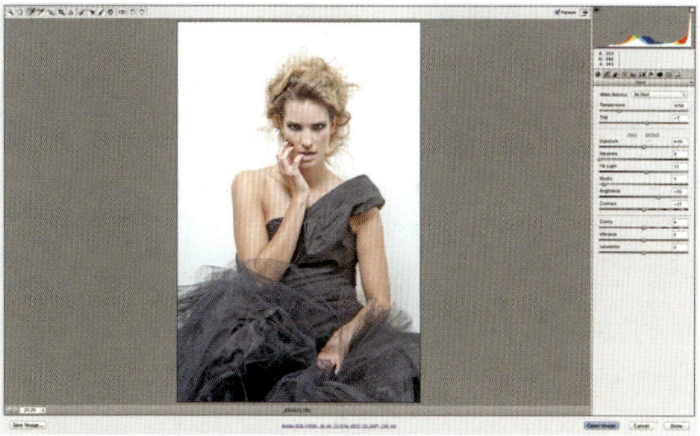

▲ Fig. 6.10
Effect of increasing the fill slider. Image © Christian Hough. Model: Carmen Bellacassa.

Blacks Slider

True to its name, this slider adjusts the darkest or blackest parts of the image, by setting a new clipping point for the shadows. It is a useful tool for tackling slight overexposure or mild haze as it elongates the histogram, pulling it down to the left whilst leaving the highlights intact and increasing the contrast within the shadows. The Blacks slider can be used to complement adjustments with the Fill slider if the image begins to look a little flat and lifeless.

It is worth remembering, though, that you are basically clipping the shadow detail out of the image before you export it into your editing software, so it is worth considering what further post-processing will be done and whether you could utilize some of that shadow detail later on.

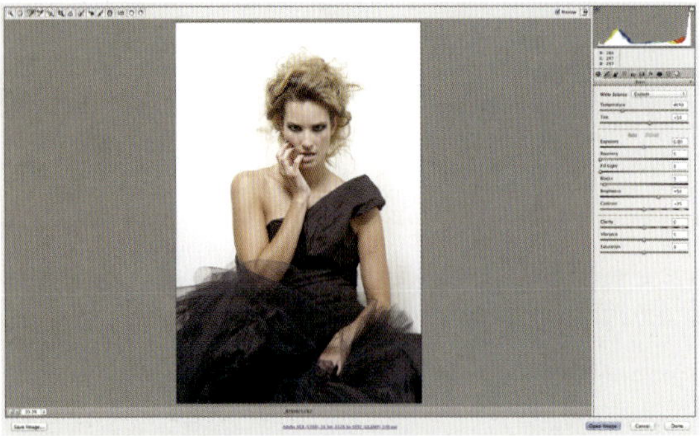

▲ Fig. 6.11
Blacks at normal level.
Image © Christian Hough. Model: Carmen Bellacassa.

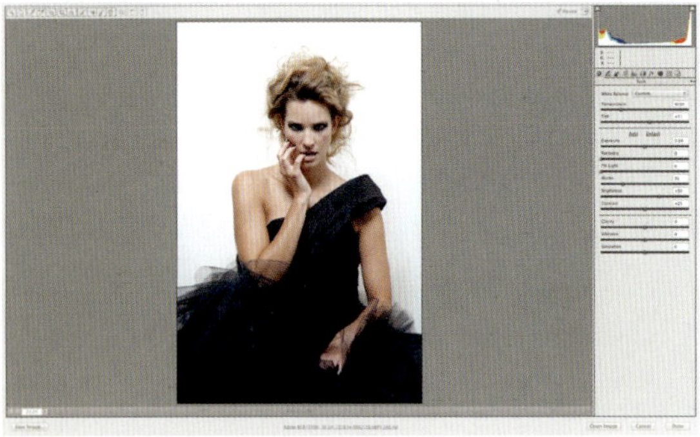

▲ Fig. 6.12
Effect of increasing the Blacks slider.
Image © Christian Hough. Model: Carmen Bellacassa.

Brightness Slider

Brightness should not be confused with the Exposure slider as they perform different tasks. Whereas the Exposure slider concentrates on the highlights, pushing the histogram to the right, the Brightness slider tends to concentrate on expanding the mid-tones whilst compressing the highlights. As you adjust the Brightness slider, the mid-tones push to the right, lightening the image.

Many photographers neglect the Brightness tool in favour of adding a tone curve during post-processing. Yet it remains very useful when used in conjunction with the Blacks and Exposure slider as a way of making those final adjustments to the equally important mid-tones. Like any adjustment, it needs to be done in moderation as too much can begin to make an image appear washed-out and lacking in contrast.

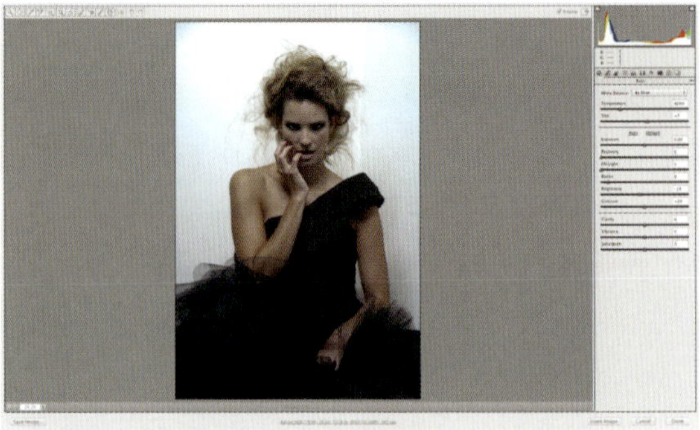

▲ Fig. 6.13
Effects of decreased brightness.
Image © Christian Hough. Model: Carmen Bellacassa.

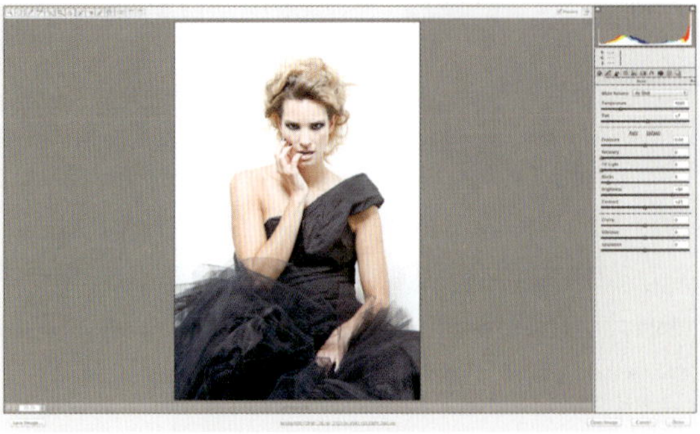

▲ Fig. 6.14
Effects of increased brightness.
Image © Christian Hough. Model: Carmen Bellacassa.

Contrast Slider

Every photograph needs contrast; otherwise it would look flat and lifeless. The task is to strike the right balance between the shadows and highlights, whilst keeping enough detail in the mid-tones. The Contrast slider is one of the tools I rarely use as there are many other more precise ways to add contrast. Even when processing RAW files, it is possible to increase contrast using a combination of the Blacks and Exposure sliders, before editing a parametric or point-based tone curve. The Contrast slider basically elongates the histogram, stretching the mid-tones whilst compressing both the shadows and the high-lights. It reality, it is the layperson's way of adding contrast and is best left for those quick fixes or batch processing contact sheets.

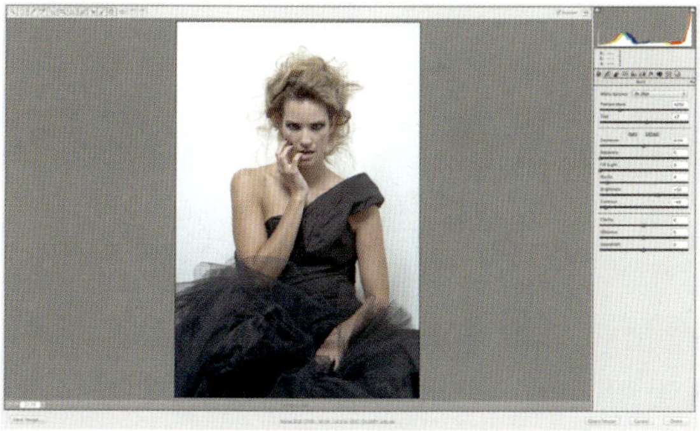

▲ Fig. 6.15
Effects of reduced contrast.
Image © Christian Hough. Model: Carmen Bellacassa.

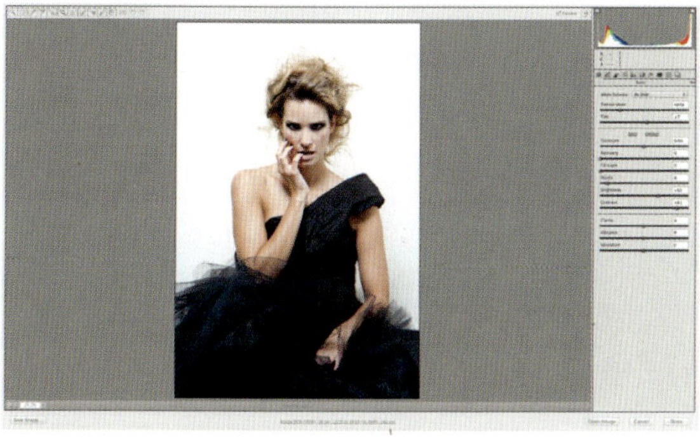

▲ Fig. 6.16
Effects of increased contrast.
Image © Christian Hough. Model: Carmen Bellacassa.

Clarity, Vibrance and Saturation

These three sliders are located under the Contrast slider in Adobe Camera Raw, and they are for the professional studio photographer, as more precise adjustments can be made later on during post-processing.

Clarity

The Clarity slider increases or decreases the contrast around the edges, which gives the impression that the image looks sharper. If you are processing high-contrast black and white street photography or environmental portraits with lots of texture, then the Clarity slider when pushed to the right may prove to be very useful. If you are working with models or even family portraits, however, then it is definitely one to avoid, as it has a tendency to pick out every imperfection – definitely not what most people want, and it will double the amount of healing and cloning during post-processing!

Vibrance

The Vibrance slider makes the image look more vibrant by way of increasing the saturation of the colours without clipping the already well-saturated areas. When pushed too far, it can make an image look rather false, as all the colours look too even, so less is definitely more. For studio work the use of the Vibrance control is limited, unless you are batch processing contact sheets, as more precise adjustments can be made during the later stages of post-processing.

Saturation

When increased, the Saturation slider increases the colour throughout an image, causing the colours that were already strong to be clipped. It can of course also decrease the colour, but tends to produce a rather flat and uninteresting black and white image. Unless you are batch processing, the Saturation slider is better left untouched, and instead an adjustment layer made in the latter stages of post-processing.

DETAIL TAB

By moving along the tabs located under the histogram, you will come across the Detail Tab. By selecting this tab, you open up the options to vary the sharpening and add an element of noise reduction if necessary. Both the Sharpening and Noise Reduction sliders are very useful tools, but care needs to be taken when using them as they can introduce unwanted artefacts into the image. It is important to remember that once the RAW image has been processed and exported into your editing software it has the ability to become more destructive the more you edit. Your use of the Sharpening and Noise Reduction sliders will of course depend entirely on your given market. So if you are photographing a hundred portraits a day and then batch processing the lot, the detail tab will be ideal for your workflow. However, if you are shooting commercially and will be editing a small number of photographs, you may wish to leave much of the sharpening to the later stages of post-production, where parts of the image can be masked and the layers peeled back if necessary or adjusted to the output size and medium.

Sharpening

Amount

As it suggests, moving the slider adjusts the strength of the sharpening. Moving the slider to the right increases the sharpening and moving it to the left decreases it. It is worth watching the image as you increase the sharpening, as too much has a tendency to produce halos and pixilation around contrasting edges. Default value is 25.

TOGGLE VIEW

When adjusting the Radius, Detail and Mask sliders, you can press and hold the <ALT> key to toggle between a greyscale mask to assist in visualizing the effects of the sharpening.

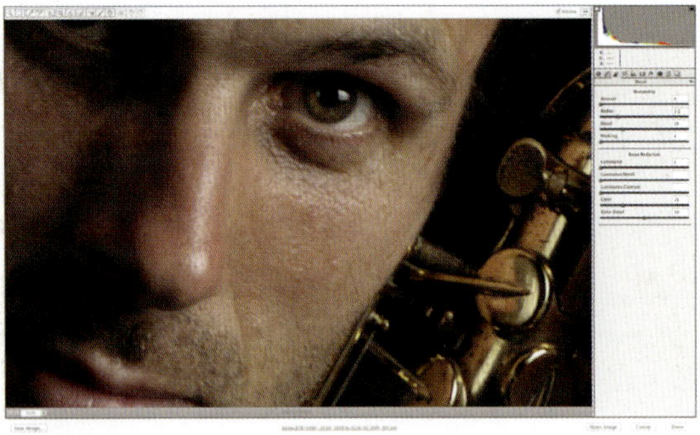

▲ Fig. 6.17
Close-up of unsharpened photograph.
Image © Christian Hough. Model: Gavin Randle.

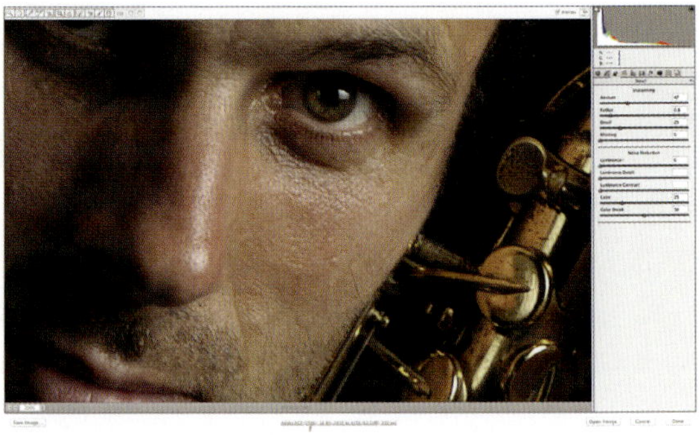

▲ Fig. 6.18
Close-up of sharpened photograph.
Image © Christian Hough. Model: Gavin Randle.

Radius

This is the area around or within a pixel where the sharpening will take effect i.e. the width of the halos. Increasing the radius basically increases the area that is sharpened, *or*, adjusts the size of the details that sharpening is applied to. Using a smaller radius will allow you to sharpen smaller and more subtle parts of the image, whereas a larger radius may assist you in correcting minor motion blur. A larger radius setting will also emphasize the finer edges and at the same time enhance the softer edges. Default value is 1.0.

Detail

The Detail slider suppresses the halo effects whilst allowing you to increase the Amount of sharpening without unwanted artefacts. When the Amount and Radius sliders are at their default values, the effect of the Detail slider is fairly subtle and is useful for bringing the fine edges of hair and fabric, even when pushed to the maximum value of 100. However, multiply this with a sharp increase with the Amount slider and the effect is immediate and unpleasant, producing unwanted noise and artefacts. For studio portraits, lower detail settings are recommended.

Masking

The Masking slider affords you some control over the overall sharpening effect. The more you increase the Masking slider, the more you begin to protect the flatter tones within the image from the effects of the sharpening. Utilizing the greyscale edge mask by holding down the <ALT> key will help you visualize your adjustments more clearly.

Noise Reduction

Noise is caused by several factors within the camera. This can be anything from the heat generated by the sensor, in-camera processing or even exposure times. Noise reduction (NR) is a very useful way of removing unwanted noise from images. As a rule, noise isn't a common issue with studio photography, given that most images will be taken between 100 and 200 ISO and be correctly exposed. However, there may be occasions when you find that you need to increase your ISO to compensate for depth of field or lack of power. It is occasions such as this when underexposure is a risk and where noise can begin to creep into the shadow areas. Applying noise reduction during RAW processing and post-processing is for the most part better than

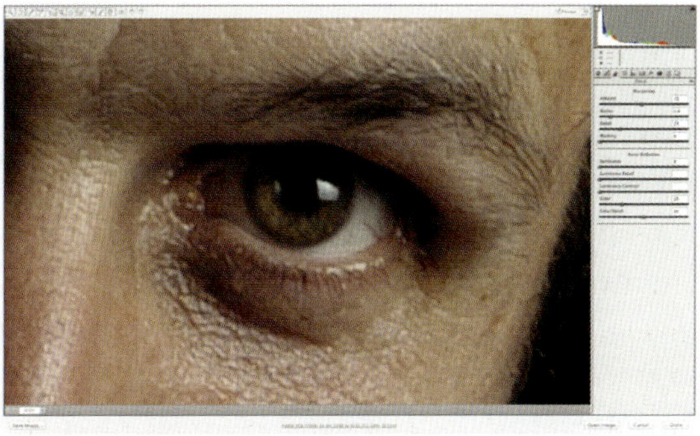

▲ Fig. 6.19
Image at 400 per cent without noise reduction.
Image © Christian Hough. Model: Gavin Randle.

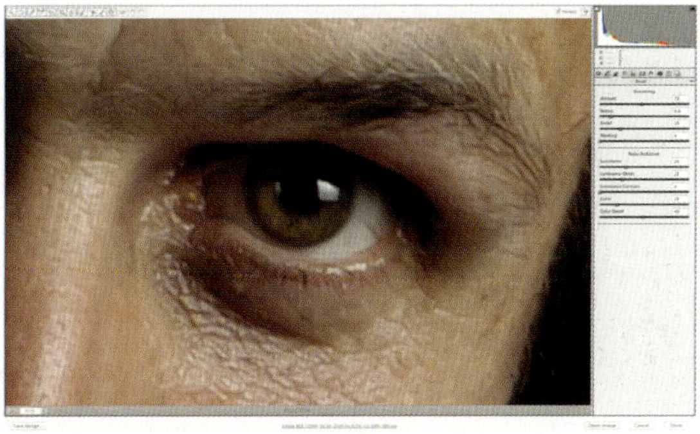

▲ Fig. 6.20
Image at 400 per cent. Increasing exposure can increase noise. Noise reduction can reduce 'grain', but will introduce artefacts.
Image © Christian Hough. Model: Gavin Randle.

doing it in-camera, simply because you have greater control over the whole process and will avoid introducing unwanted artefacts at the early stages. Noise reduction is destructive and if applied during RAW processing it becomes permanent. For this reason, it is advisable to leave noise reduction until the later stages of editing, so that it may be applied selectively and peeled back when necessary.

Luminance

The Luminance slider controls the type of noise we most commonly know as grain, also known as greyscale noise. The default value in ACR is '0', so moving the slider to the right will increase the noise reduction and decrease the film grain. It is important not to increase this too much as it will begin to remove the detail. Grain is rarely an issue, adds character to an image and is even less noticeable when printing.

Luminance Detail and Luminance Contrast

Unless you are shooting at very high ISO or pushing the exposure on a very underexposed image you are unlikely to benefit too much from using these sliders. The Luminance Detail slider controls the luminance noise threshold. On the face of it, the higher the value the more detail and noise it will return to the image, although the detail is more apparent on the edges, leaving the flatter tones looking smooth. The Luminance Contrast slider is useful for very noisy images. When used at higher values, it will assist in preserving the contrast, but will also introduce blotches of noise and mottling.

Colour

The Colour slider default is set at 25. It is not unusual in studio photography for the default setting to be zeroed in order to preserve the original colour. If you have noise in your image, moving this slider to the right will begin to remove the coloured speckles that you can see in noisy images, which are normally red, purple and green, know as chroma. Increase the Colour noise reduction too much and the image will become blotchy.

Colour Detail

The Colour Detail slider controls the colour noise threshold. It is there to assist in reclaiming some of the detail removed by Colour noise reduction. Pushing the slider to the right will protect finer, detailed colour edges, but increase colour speckling. Decreasing the amount of Colour Detail will remove coloured speckles at the risk of introducing colour bleed.

LENS CORRECTIONS TAB

The Lens Corrections tab offers a range of lens profiles to fit a range of common lenses from different lens manufacturers. The lens corrections compensate for the three most common lens aberrations, namely vignetting, geometric distortion and lateral chromatic aberration. By selecting the lens manufacturer and the lens used to take the photograph, ACR will then make a series of adjustments based on the lens calibration data available.

Correction Amount

Once your chosen lens has been selected, the three greyed-out adjustment sliders under the Correction Amount heading will become available.

Distortion and Chromatic Aberration

The Distortion slider will allow you to fine-tune bends in parallel and horizontal edges/lines, such as barrel or pincushion distortion. The Chromatic Aberration slider will help remove colour fringing along high-contrast edges. You will find that overuse of these sliders can frequently correct some areas of the photograph, whilst causing issues in others.

Vignetting

Vignetting is basically the gradual light fall-off that can be experienced towards the corners of a photograph. It is more prolific when using wide lenses, very long zooms and wide apertures. For studio work that is shot on standard lenses at apertures between *f*8.0 and *f*16 it is rarely a major issue. In fact it can actually prove to be fairly useful for portrait photographers as the gradual light fall-off assists in reducing the plainness of paper backgrounds, whilst making the viewer focus on the subject in the middle. Portrait and wedding photographers frequently add vignetting to their images.

Ultimately, how you use this RAW process will depend entirely on your workflow and intended results. It may be easier to remove a vignette globally that to add one. It should be applied in the same way as many other corrections and effects prior to post-processing. If it is possible to leave it until later on in post-processing, then this would afford you more flexibility over the finished image. On the other hand, if you are batch processing hundreds of images, it may be worth applying it globally to many images at the same time.

There are two common types of vignetting:

PHYSICAL VIGNETTING

This is usually apparent in the extreme corners of the lens and usually caused by a physical object intruding on the lens, such as a lens hood or lens filters. This will usually require cloning or cropping.

INTERNAL VIGNETTING

This is most often caused by the optical elements inside the lens and is easily correctable using software or by stopping down. If you are using a full-frame DSLR then you may suffer from the effects of vignetting more often than with a system utilizing a cropped sensor.

EFFECTS TAB

Post-Crop Vignetting

As opposed to a lens correction, the Post-Crop Vignetting tool under the Effects tab is intended to be used artistically, rather than as a lens correction.

Style

The Style has a drop down menu offering you three choices: Highlight Priority, Colour Priority and Paint Overlay. Highlight Priority will apply a vignette whilst protecting the contrast within the highlights, but may cause colour shifts within the shadow areas. Colour Priority preserves colour hues but can reduce the detail within the highlights. Paint Overlay will blend the colours within the image with a black or white vignette, with a possibility of reducing the contrast within the highlights.

Amount

Moving the slider to the right will lighten the corners of the image, whereas moving the slider to the left will darken them.

Midpoint

An increase in the Midpoint slider will restrict the area of adjustment near the corners, whereas a decrease will apply the adjustment to a larger area from the corners.

Roundness

Increasing the values by pushing the slider to the right will make the effect more circular, where moving the slider to the left will begin to make the effect more oval.

Feather

Higher values will begin to increase the feathering between effect and the surround pixels. Reducing the values will perform the opposite.

Highlights (Highlight Priority and Colour Priority)

This controls the punchiness of the highlights, such as the glow from various continuous light sources.

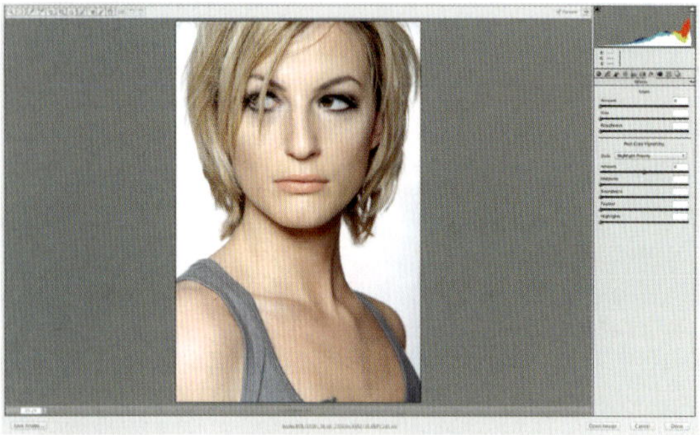

▲ Fig. 6.21
Standard image. Image © Christian Hough.

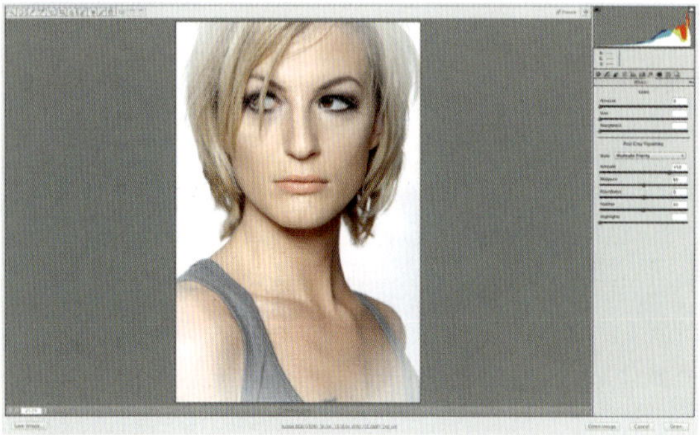

▲ Fig. 6.22
Image with white vignette applied. Image © Christian Hough.

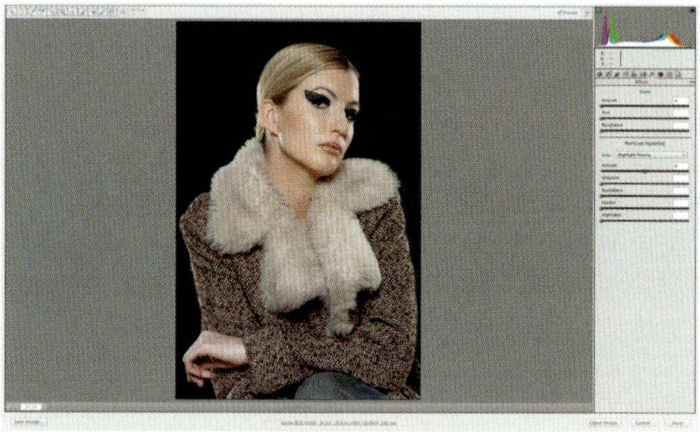

▲ Fig. 6.23
Standard image. Image © Christian Hough.

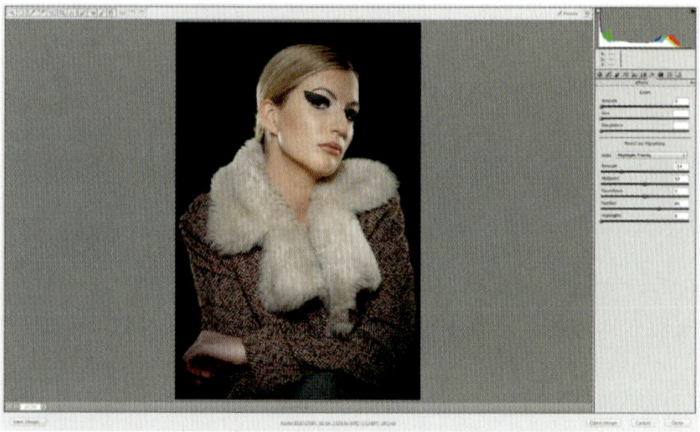

▲ Fig. 6.24
Image with dark vignette applied. Image © Christian Hough.

Glossary

APS-C (Advanced Photo System, type C) A smaller type of sensor than 35mm found in certain Digital Single Lens Reflex (DSLR) cameras. The size of the sensor affects the focal length of the lens, calculated using the multiplier (also known as a crop factor). Most common multipliers are x1.6 and x1.3 (sometimes known as APS-H).

ASA (American Standards Association) Film speed rating based on the chemical composition of the film, denoting its sensitivity to light as set out by the USA Standards Institute. The film equivalent to ISO.

aspherical lens Lens element that does not form part of a sphere.

asymmetrical power Allows the user to vary the power between multiple flash heads (see *symmetrical power*).

back light A light placed behind the subject.

ballast An electronic or magnetic device that controls and stabilizes the electrical current in a continuous light, usually an arc light.

barrel distortion An effect causing straight edges to bow outwards to give a barrel-like distortion.

battery generator A battery-powered (DC) lighting generator that powers and controls several generator flash heads. Some battery generators can be switched between AC and DC power supplies and also power monobloc heads.

beam light A light that produces a parallel beam of light. Also known as a parcan or parblazer.

beam spread The area that the beam covers. It is usually expressed in terms of angles. The smaller the angle, the narrower the beam. For example, a 16–30 profile spot will have a beam spread varying from 16° to 30°.

blonde Continuous HMI light source between 1000 and 2000w. Frequently used as a key floodlight for broad areas. Also frequently used in automotive and product photography.

blooming Streaks, halos and bright artefacts caused by overexposure to the camera's sensor. Also known as 'flare', a term more associated with film.

bokeh Derives from the Japanese word boke, meaning fuzziness or dizziness. It refers to out-of-focus areas of an image. The more 'creamy' or 'milky' the blur, the more pleasing the bokeh.

boom arm A pole attached to a lighting stand used to support a flash head. Frequently used with a counterbalance.

bounce head A feature of speedlites, allowing the head to be tilted and angled so that the flash can be bounced off different surfaces.

bounced light Flash light that is bounce (reflected) off a surface. Usually used to assist with the diffusion of light.

build Cinematic term for the gradual increasing of brightness.

cable release A cable that screws into the camera allowing the shutter to be fired remotely, reducing shake. Electronic cable releases are used with newer digital systems.

candela (cd) Unit of measurement for the luminous intensity of a light source in a given direction. Technically, the radiation intensity in a perpendicular direction of a surface of 1/600000 square metre of a black body at the temperature of solidification platinum under a pressure of 101,325 newtons per square metre. Also known as Candle.

CCD (charge coupled device) An integrated circuit with an array of coupled capacitors which are light sensitive. Also known as a 'sensor'.

centre-weighted metering A form of TTL metering, where the measurement is biased towards the lower centre of the frame.

chromatic aberration Commonly caused by a lens failing to accurately focus different wavelengths of colour/light onto the same point. Also known as colour fringing or purple fringing, achromatism or chromatic distortion.

clamp A tool that can be adjusted to clamp two or more items together. Frequently used to clamp stands and supports. Can be screw tightened or spring loaded.

CMOS sensor (complementary metal oxide semiconductor) A common alternative to the CCD (charge coupled device).

Colorama The term usually used for background paper, which is manufactured by the company Colorama. Usually available in a variety of different widths, most commonly 9ft and 4ft.

colour depth The amount of colours that can be captured by a digital device, usually ranging from 8bit to 16bit in cameras and up to 24bit in scanners.

Colour Rendering Index (CRI) A rating (0–100 scale) of the light's ability to reproduce colour accurately; the higher the CRI rating, the greater the colour fidelity.

colour temperature The temperature of light measured in kelvin (K). The higher the number, the 'warmer' the colour temperature, with daylight commonly set at 5600K.

compact flash A memory card used in digital cameras to store images. The larger the capacity, the more images it can hold. Read/Write speeds can vary between manufacturers.

compression A digital and mathematical process that reduces the file size of an image. By default, reducing the file size also reduces the image quality by varying degrees. Compression that is known as 'Lossy' will permanently lose data. Alternatively if known as 'Lossless' all the data can be returned. Higher compression results in smaller files but will reduce image quality.

console A system that controls a bank or group of stage lights. Operated by a lighting technician.

crop factor Measured against the 35mm standard. Describes how an APS-C, APS-H or Four Thirds sensor will crop an image. The crop factor will depend on the size of the sensor and how much smaller than the 35mm standard it is, leading to a crop factor, commonly between ×1.3 and ×1.6.

depth of field (DOF) The distance between the nearest and furthest area of a subject that remains in focus. The shallower the depth of field the smaller the focused area. Directly relates to aperture and focal length.

dynamic range (DR) Relates to the amount of tones between 0 and 255 (shadows to highlights) that a camera can capture. As a rule, the higher the number of bits the camera can capture, the more 'usable' tonal information it can produce. Most high-end medium-format systems can produce between 12–13 stops of 'noise free' tonal information.

ellipsoidal reflector spotlight (ERS) A form of stage lighting; the optics of an ERS instrument are roughly similar to those of a 35mm slide projector. The original ellipsoidal reflector was used to collect and direct the light through a barrel that contained a lens or lens train. Also known as profile spot, ellipsoidal, ellipse, Leko or Shakespeare light.

EV (exposure value) A combination of shutter and aperture value.

exposure The measurement of light reaching light-sensitive material or device. Exposure is determined by the sensitivity of the material/device, aperture or the lens and speed of the shutter.

exposure bracketing A method of taking several exposures of the same frame using different settings. Can be used to ensure correct exposure in difficult metering conditions or for HDR image composites.

exposure compensation Method of overriding the camera's automatic exposure metering. Usually measured in +/-EV.

exposure latitude Latitude of a film's tolerance to exposure. A film with a narrow exposure latitude, if under- or overexposed, cannot be pushed in processing as well as a film with a wide exposure latitude.

***f* stop** The lens focal length divided by effective diameter of the aperture gives the *f* stop that is used to indicate the aperture value. Also known as '*f* number'. Common *f* stops are 1.4, 2, 2.8, 4, 5.6, 8, 11, 16 and 22.

file format Most common digital file formats are PSD, DNG, TIFF, JPEG, PNG and BMP. Different formats have different qualities and are recognized by different systems and programs.

fill-in flash A method of using flash to lift shadow detail and reduce contrast by way of 'filling-in' the shadows. Usually a term associated with the use of speedlites/automatic flash.

fill light Light used on the subject to fill the shadows and reduce the overall contrast.

film format Type of film used by different film-based camera systems. 35mm film = 24×36mm; medium-format systems on 120 or 220 roll film = 6×4.5cm/6×17cm/6×6cm; or larger-format sheet film on 5×4in, 5×7in and 8×10in.

film speed A standard by which to measure the film's sensitivity to light. Most commonly known as ASA, but the current standard is ISO.

filter (optical) A piece of glass or plastic placed in front of a lens to change the properties of the light entering the lens. Most common optical filters are polarizing, gradated filters and coloured effects.

filter (digital) Software used to process an image and produce a digital effect. Digital filters frequently reproduce the effects of optical filters and film processing with varying degrees of success.

flagging A method of blocking light by placing a physical object (flag), of any shape, size or type of material, between the light and the subject in question. The flag often creates shadows which must then be controlled.

flash duration The time taken for a flash to reach 50 per cent of its peak value and then trough to the same value. The shorter the flash duration, the easier it is to freeze motion.

flash meter A form of light meter that is used to take an incidental measurement of flash via a white plastic diffusion dome.

flash output The amount of light/power produced by the flash.

flash range The average distance between the maximum and minimum range that a flash can illuminate.

flash sync A socket found on the camera to allow speedlites to be triggered remotely by cable.

flat A term to describe a photograph that lacks contrast.

flood/floodlight A wide-spreading light with an unfocused beam of light. These can be symmetric, casting light equally in all directions, or asymmetric, casting more light in one direction than others.

focal length The magnification and angle of view of a lens. Standard focal length for a lens is 50mm, with 35mm being wide and 85mm short telephoto.

focal plane The area behind a lens, where light is focused and converges to form a focused image.

fog Describes unexposed film which is unintentionally exposed to light, causing the photograph to have an unwanted haze or fog; this occasionally appears as streaks, where the camera is leaking light into the body.

follow-spot A stage light with an iris diaphragm and a handle so that it can be used to follow a performer around the stage in a beam of light of exactly the right size. Traditionally called a 'lime', hence the term 'being in the limelight' (produced from burning lime). These produce a very bright beam of light which is more powerful than that produced by any other lights. Modern limes almost always use CSI lamps.

footcandle (fc or ftc) Unit of measurement for light intensity, measured in lumens per square foot, and calculated as the brightness of one candle at a distance of one foot, which equates to approximately 10.7639 lux.

Fresnel A kind of spotlight in which the light is concentrated by a Fresnel lens (a lens with concentric ridged rings invented for use in lighthouses by Augustin-Jean Fresnel). It projects a variable angle soft-edged beam.

full frame Usually referred to as full 35mm, as opposed to APS-C, APS-H and four thirds sensors.

gels Coloured transparent filters that are placed over flash or camera lenses to change the colour of the light.

generator A single powered 'pack' that generates power to control several flash heads. Generators often offer faster recycle times and shorter flash durations than monoblocs/strobes. Power output is usually measured in watts/sec.

gradient A shade or colour that changes density across the frame.

18% grey card A grey-coloured card that reflects 18% of the light that falls upon it. Frequently used to obtain a neutral colour balance for digital camera systems and to calibrate light meters.

guide number A measurement of the power output of flash.

halogen Continuous light source, usually between 150 and 500w, in which a tungsten filament is sealed within a glass capsule filled with a halogen gas. Frequently used as a key floodlight for lighting large areas. This is a low-budget lighting solution often used in home movies and in some product photography where heat is not an issue (see also *incandescent light*).

hard light Light that causes well-defined shadows with hard edges, usually produced with bare reflectors without diffusion. Similar to direct sunlight.

high dynamic range (HDR) Software processing technique to make an image with a complete tonal range, produced from several exposures of the same frame/scene.

highkey An image that consists of mainly midtones and highlights to produce a light image.

high-key background A light or pure white background used in studio photography.

histogram A digital representation by way of a chart to represent the tonal information of a digital image.

HMI (hydrargyrum medium arc iodide) A flicker-free continuous light source most commonly associated with cinematic and theatrical lighting. In studio photography HMI is a professional high-end light which employs an arc lamp instead of filament bulb.

honeycomb grid A studio modifier that is used to directionally control light by way of a honeycombed grid.

hot shoe An attachment located on top of a camera used to attach flash gun and triggers and synchronize them with the shutter.

incandescent light Continuous lighting produced from standard household lighting, such as lamps, which produce light by heating a wire filament until it glows; the glow is caused by the filament's resistance to the current.

incident light The light falling on a subject as opposed to light reflected off a subject.

infrared slave cells Light sensors fitted to external flash units that allow several flashes to be operated simultaneously when a flash from one unit is detected; requires a visible flash to the sensor.

inverse square law A mathematical calculation, stating that light projected onto a surface is inversely proportional to the square of its distance from the source.

ISO (International Organization of Standardization) Used to standardize the light sensitivity of sensors and film, the standard being ISO 100. Formerly the standard was ASA.

joule Measurement of energy covering the storage of capacitors in an electronic flash. The joule is equivalent to the watt-second in units; therefore one joule (J) is the light output given by one watt burning for one second.

JPEG (Joint Photographic Experts Group) Method of lossy image compression to reduce image and file size.

key light The main light source on the subject, providing the most light and contrast.

kilowatt 1000 watts.

LAB Colour space A colour-opponent space for processing colour images, in which dimension *L* stands for lightness and *a* and *b* for the colour-opponent dimensions. *Lab* is now more often used as an informal abbreviation for the CIE 1976 (*L a b*) colour space (or CIELAB).

lantern Term used in the theatre for a light, derived from *luminaire*.

lens flare Unwelcome appearance of light on an image, usually manifest as starbursts, rings, or circles in a row. Generally caused by bright light sources within the scene that shine into the lens, producing a haze or a flare of light on the photograph. The distribution of the lens flare depends on the construction of the lens and the cause of the flare. The phenomenon is most common when shooting into the sun and can be reduced by the use of a lens hood, or by flagging the scene to prevent the sun or bright light entering the lens.

light meter An instrument used to measure light. Depending on the model, light meters can read incidental light, reflected light, flash light or all three.

luminance The light produced or reflected in a scene or the amount of light that passes through or is emitted from a particular area, measured in candela per square metre (cd/m^2).

lumen (lm) Unit of measurement for the flow of light or luminous flux. The output of artificial light sources such as continuous light is measured in lumens.

lux (lx) The metric equivalent of footcandle (one lux = 0.0929 footcandles). Lux is a unit of illumination equal to one lumen per square metre.

manual exposure An exposure where all the settings are manually input by the photographer.

mired (micro reciprocal degree) A unit of measurement used to express colour temperature in the process of colour correction. Wratten filters are a useful way to shift colour when placed onto a lens, especially with balanced film.

modelling light A continuous light built into a flash unit to facilitate modelling and shaping.

moiré pattern An often undesired artefact seen in images, especially when photographing certain fabrics, which can be overcome in texture mapping through the use of mipmapping and anisotropic filtering.

monobloc A self-contained flash head that does not require a generator to supply power as it contains its own power supply and controls. Power output is usually measured in watts/sec (also see *strobe*).

multiple flash A single flash fired several times within the same frame.

open white A stage light is said to be 'open white' when no filter or gel is applied to modify the light.

parabolic A reflector or umbrella in the shape of a circular paraboloid, which is used to project light forwards.

parcan A type of lantern that projects a near parallel beam of light, frequently used by rock bands. The lamp is a sealed-beam unit fitted inside the 'can'. Available, usually, in 300w or 1kw power. Sometimes known as parblazers or beamlights.

pinspot A small spotlight used for special effects, such as a mirror ball, or more usually in the theatre as a follow-spot. When its iris diaphragm is closed to its smallest diameter, it is frequently used to illuminate the face.

pebble/prism convex spotlight A spotlight having a convex lens with a pebbled rear surface, which produces a harder-edged beam of light than a Fresnel but softer than a profile. Also known as a prism convex light.

pepper light A small light source between 100w and 1000w, that is frequently used to produce a focused key or fill light.

polyboard/reflector board A studio-based polystyrene board mounted in a weighted floor-based support, with one side painted black and the other left white, allowing it to lift and darken shadows. Also frequently used to flag light.

RAW Refers to a RAW file in digital photography. If you are shooting in RAW your file is unprocessed – a digital negative (compare JPEG, TIFF).

rear curtain sync A camera mode that allows you to fire the flash just before the closing of the focal-plane shutter, enabling moving objects to leave a trail or streak behind them. Used to convey a sense of movement. Also known as second-curtain sync.

reciprocity failure A condition some films develop making them less responsive in low light and therefore requiring more time to expose than would be expected. It is a breakdown in the usual relationship between shutter speed and aperture. Some films are more susceptible to reciprocity failure than others.

recycle time The time it takes the capacitors within a flash unit to recharge and to be ready to flash again.

red eye The appearance of red eyes in a photograph is generally caused by low light, dilated pupils and direct or on-camera flash bouncing off the fundus at the back of the eye.

redhead Continuous HMI light source between 650 and 1000w. Often used as a key floodlight for broad areas. Also frequently used in automotive and product photography.

reflected light reading The measurement of lighted that is reflected from a scene or object. Method used by TTL metering systems.

reflector An item, usually white or reflective, used to bounce light back towards the subject. Some reflectors are painted black, thereby absorbing light and darkening shadow areas.

refraction Change in direction of light due to its velocity, causing light to 'bend'. Normally caused by passing through an optic or other transparent material, such as water. Basically, the phase velocity of the wave is changed but its frequency remains constant.

saturation The strength of colour within a photograph.

Scheimpflug principle A geometric rule describing the orientation of the plane of focus of an optical system (such as a camera) when the lens plane is not parallel to the image plane. Usually associated with large format and tilting camera systems.

soft light Light that is more diffused so it produces less defined shadows and softer edges. Similar to light produced on an overcast day.

spectral power distribution (SPD) A pictorial representation of the radiant power emitted by a light source at each wavelength or band of wavelengths in the visible region of the electromagnetic spectrum, namely 360 to 770 nanometres.

spectrometer An instrument which measures the spectrum of light.

spot meter A meter method that measures reflective light from a narrow point, usually between 1 and 5 degrees. Available in light meters and some TTL metering systems.

spotlight/spot A type of light whose beam is focused through a lens or series of lenses to make it more controllable to highlight a tight area.

stopping down/up Stopping down is decreasing the size of the aperture, whereas stopping up is increasing the size of the aperture.

strobe A self-contained flash that emits a regular, controllable series of high power flashes rather than continuous light. Strobes contain their own power supply and controls. Power output is usually measured in watts/sec (see *monobloc*). Also a US term for flash.

symmetrical power Splits power equally between multiple flash heads (see *asymmetrical power*).

sync lead A lead that physically connects a camera to a flash unit. Base voltage must be considered with all modern DSLR systems.

TIFF (Tagged Image File Format) A bitmapped file format what allows photographers to compress images using the more common LZW lossless compression, often used in image archives. Available in several formats, including greyscale, colour palette, RGB full colour. May include files with JPEG or CCITT Group 4 standard run-length image compression.

tone curve A graph used to illustrate tonal range. Moving the curve will affect contrast and the tonal qualities of the image. In its unchanged mode, the tone curve is a single 45-degree line, moving upwards from left to right.

trigger An electronic device used to trigger flash and cameras simultaneously. Most commonly used devices are radio triggers, although some systems still use infrared, which requires a visual path between the sender and receiver. Sound and movement may also operate triggers.

TTL (through-the-lens) metering Describes the metering method of a camera that takes an exposure reading of the light that passes through the lens.

tungsten Usually refers to light that is produced by an ordinary household bulb. Tungsten colour temperature is around 2800K to 3400K. Also known as incandescent light.

vignette A reduction of the brightness or saturation of an image towards the edges of the frame/periphery in comparison to that of the centre of the image.

X-sync The sync socket on a camera that triggers electronic flash at the precise moment when the shutter is fully open. More common in SLRs and older DSLRs. Cognizance of base trigger voltage of external flash is a prerequisite on most DSLRs.

Index

A
auto white balance (AWB) 154

B
babies, photographing 49–51, 84
background 25, 33, 41, 49, 52, 57, 58, 65, 69, 70, 73–80, 82–88, 90, 91, 92, 98, 100, 101, 105, 107, 110, 121, 123, 124, 125, 126, 131, 134, 136, 137, 138, 139, 140, 146, 149, 150, 163
  black 49, 68, 107, 112, 146
  highkey 66, 68
  light 56, 64, 66, 67, 68, 69, 70, 74, 78, 79, 80, 84, 85, 86, 87, 88, 91, 94, 95, 96, 112, 113, 114, 116, 117, 124, 128, 129, 132, 136, 137, 143, 144, 149, 150
  light falling into 51
  paper 52, 59, 64, 66, 68, 74, 76, 105, 107, 114, 125, 139, 149, 163
  support 49, 52, 59, 68, 76, 90, 91, 113, 116, 129, 136, 149
  white 66, 68, 70, 78, 79, 84, 86, 96, 121, 126, 128, 138, 146
  yellowing of 95
blacks slider 158
blown highlights 48, 60, 64
bokeh 24, 25
boom arm 32, 33, 43, 54, 59, 62, 64, 68, 73, 74, 90, 91, 96, 100, 129, 129, 131, 132, 136, 140, 143, 144, 149
broad lighting 35, 39, 42, 43, 96
brightness slider 158
butterfly lighting 39, 43, 64, 90, 91, 96, 110, 123

C
CDM lighting 10,
camera format 18–20
  bridge camera 18–19
  compact camera 13, 18, 19, 153
  interchangeable lens compact camera 19
  large format camera 20, 24, 26, 32, 124
  medium format camera 19–20, 22, 23, 24, 26, 28, 31, 34, 109, 124, 156
  SLR/DSR camera 19
clamps 33–34
clarity slider 159
colour bleeding 78
continuous light 9–12, 21, 31
contrast 13, , 27, 34, 35, 36, 48, 54, 56, 73, 82, 86, 87, 92, 98, 101, 109, 110, 113, 129, 132, 137, 146, 149, 158, 159, 162, 163
contrast slider 159
  luminance contrast slider 162
cool lights 11–12
contrast slider 159
cross lighting 58, 129

D
dynamic range (DR) 32, 46, 48, 105, 109, 154

E
exposure 9, 26, 28, 34, 48, 90, 103, 107, 109, 118, 153, 154, 156, 157, 159, 161, 162
  exposure slider 156–157, 159
extension bellows 28

F
fill slider 157, 158
five head lighting 88, 98–101
flash duration 14, 16, 17, 32, 70, 149
flash lighting 12–13, 16, 21
  flash gun 13
  pop-up flash 13
  speedlite 13
  studio flash 13
flash meter 31, 32
flat image 92, 101
four head lighting 88–97
fluorescent lighting 11

G
glass 27, 123, 128, 138, 141
gobo 37, 107, 109
gradient 37, 68, 69, 74, 76, 86, 87, 105, 136, 144, 150

H
hazy image 95
health and safety 11, 12, 110, 112, 146
HID lights 10–12, 37
highlights 46, 48, 54, 60, 62, 63, 64, 66, 67, 68, 80, 82, 84, 96, 109, 113, 123, 128, 138, 154, 156, 157, 158, 159, 163, 164

histogram 32, 80, 109, 154, 156, 157, 158, 159, 160
hot spots 53, 63, 64, 65, 68, 116, 117, 134

L

leaf shutter 30–31
LED light 11
lens filter 26, 163
  clear filter 27
  close-up filter 28
  colour correction filter 27
  diffusion filter 28
  ND filter 28
  polarizing filter 27
  skylight filter 27
  softening filter 28
  UV filter 27
lens 22–26
  flare 60, 73, 74, 92, 100, 101, 132, 150
  Fresnel lens 37
  macro lens 24, 26, 28
  prime lens 22, 23, 24, 25, 124
  telephoto lens 23, 24
  tilt and shift lens 20, 24, 26, 124, 126, 134, 143
  wide-angle lens 24, 25, 94
  zoom lens 18, 22, 23, 25, 113
light box 124
light meter 9, 29, 31, 59, 70, 88, 96, 107, 126, 132, 150, 165
light tent 124, 125, 126, 128, 138, 139
lighting stand 33–34, 43, 74, 116, 123, 141, 146, 150

M

matting spray 123
monobloc 12, 13, 14, 15, 118
movement 29, 66, 70–71, 79–80, 91, 122, 146

N

noise reduction 160, 161–162

O

one head lighting 46–54, 105–109

P

PC Sync 21, 22
perspective 20, 23, 24, 25, 26, 49, 54, 62, 68, 82, 94, 113, 124, 143, 144, 150
product table 124, 125, 129, 132, 136, 141, 143, 144, 146, 149

R

RAW 18, 48, 109, 153–164
recovery slider 156–157
red eye 118
reflection 27, 123, 124, 125, 126, 136, 138, 139, 140, 143, 144, 146
reflectors and shapers 34–37
  barndoor 35, 36, 37, 76, 88
  beauty dish 35, 36, 68, 78, 90, 91, 116, 117
  directional reflector 35, 48, 64, 79, 86, 87, 96, 113, 116
  egg crate 36
  Fresnel lens 37
  honeycomb grid 35, 36, 59, 64, 74, 76, 79, 82, 83, 86, 90, 91, 98, 100,107, 112, 117, 129, 131, 132, 136, 137, 143, 149, 150
  medium reflector 36
  softbox 15, 16, 33, 34–35, 36, 46, 48, 49, 52, 53, 54, 58, 59, 60, 62, 63, 64, 66, 68, 70, 71, 74, 78, 79, 83, 84, 91, 92, 94, 96, 97, 98, 100, 101, 114, 117, 124, 134, 136, 137, 138, 142, 143, 146, 149, 150
  snoots 35, 37, 46, 107, 137
  spotlight 37, 107
  standard reflector 95, 82, 91, 100, 107, 112, 126, 128, 140, 149, 150
  umbrella 34, 36, 48, 49, 54, 66, 70, 78, 79, 82, 83, 84, 85, 90, 91, 94, 100, 113, 114
  wide angle reflector 36, 96, 144
Rembrandt lighting 39, 41–42, 52, 56, 86
ringflash 15, 16, 118, 119

S

saturation slider 160
shadows 15, , 35, 37, 39, 40, 41, 42, 43, 46, 47, 48, 52, 54, 56, 58, 59, 62, 64, 68, 70, 74, 82, 83, 84, 85, 87, 90, 91, 92, 96, 97, 100, 101, 105, 109, 110, 112, 114, 116, 117, 118, 119, 123, 125, 126, 128, 129, 132, 140, 143, 144, 146, 150, 154, 156, 158, 159
short lighting 40, 41, 42, 49, 86, 105, 107

split lighting 39, 41, 48
studio generator 14, 138
  battery generator 15, 112
  battery pack 15
studio stand 32–33, 128, 143
tabletop studio 125, 129

T
tethered shooting 34
texture 59, 88, 91, 98, 103, 104, 110, 116, 129, 132, 134, 159
three head lighting 73–87
tone 46, 49, 104, 110, 113, 143, 154, 156, 157, 158, 159, 161, 162
  muscle tone 97
  skin 46, 49, 52, 57
triggers 29–30
  motion and sound triggers 30, 148
tripod 32–33, 118, 126, 131, 132, 136, 137, 141, 143, 149, 150
tungsten halogen lights 11–12, 27

V
vibrance slider 159

W
water 17, 30, 110–112, 122, 123, 141, 146, 148, 149